D0817228

REAL PROPERTY IN A NUTSHELL

SIXTH EDITION

By

ROGER BERNHARDT

Professor of Law
Golden Gate University, School of Law

ANN M. BURKHART

Curtis Bradbury Kellar Professor of Law
University of Minnesota Law School

WEST®

A Thomson Reuters business

Mat #40923594

Nutshell Series, In a Nutshell and the Nutshell Logo are trademarks registered in the U.S. Patent and Trademark Office.

COPYRIGHT © 1975, 1981, 1983 WEST PUBLISHING CO.
© West, a Thomson business. 2000, 2005
© 2010 Thomson Reuters
 610 Opperman Drive
 St. Paul, MN 55123
 1–800–313–9378

Printed in the United States of America

ISBN: 978–0–314–26187–8

For Christine
R.B.

For Nick and Brian Zorotovich
A.M.B.

INTRODUCTION

No other course in the first year of law school seems to involve as many rules as Property Law. Students suffer under the sheer number of rules thrown at them, and professors chafe at the amount of class time consumed in the brute articulation of all these rules. This book attempts to remedy that a little. For students, it offers a brief compilation of all or most of the rules that are covered in the standard Property Law casebooks and organizes them so as to minimize their seeming randomness and arbitrariness. For professors, it offers an opportunity to free up class time for an exploration of how the rules came to be, how they operate (or how to operate around them), and whether they work. Our goal is to make the mechanical statement of the rules the beginning, rather than the end, of the study of Property Law.

OUTLINE

OUTLINE

OUTLINE

Page

OUTLINE

OUTLINE

OUTLINE

OUTLINE

Page

PART TWO. CONVEYANCING

OUTLINE

PART THREE. MISCELLANEOUS PROPERTY DOCTRINES

OUTLINE

TABLE OF CASES

References are to Pages

LVIII

REAL PROPERTY
IN A NUTSHELL

SIXTH EDITION

PART ONE

INTERESTS IN LAND

CHAPTER ONE

POSSESSION AND OWNERSHIP

Real property (realty) consists of land and objects that are permanently affixed to land, such as trees and buildings. Real property generally is immovable, whereas personal property (personalty) consists of movable objects. Personal property can be tangible, such as a book or car, or intangible, such as an idea or the good will of a business. Property law largely consists of issues relating to real property, rather than to personal property. By and large, however, the rules are the same for both.

In this Chapter, we will examine three of the most commonly studied topics concerning the importance of possession: (1) possession of unowned and owned personal property, (2) gifts, and (3) adverse possession.

I. POSSESSION OF UNOWNED AND OWNED PERSONAL PROPERTY

A. UNOWNED PERSONAL PROPERTY

Possessors' claims depend on whether the property has a legal owner. If the property is unowned, such as wild animals and abandoned goods, the taking of possession may enable the possessor to claim ownership of the asset. At the very least, no other owner can assert rights against the possessor.

Illustration: Paul captures a whale on the high seas. While governments or conservation groups may challenge Paul's right to capture the whale, no other person can say "That whale is mine."

1. Possessor's Rights

Unless a person is legally prohibited from taking unowned assets, such as endangered species or rocks from a national preserve, the possessor of an unowned asset is its owner and is entitled to all the rights owners have over goods they purchased or inherited.

Illustration: Paul catches a fish in the ocean, and Sue purchases a fish in the grocery store. Paul's and Sue's rights with regard to their fish are the same.

2. Rival Possessors

The law gives priority to the person who first takes possession of an object. "First in time is first in right." However, this rule will not apply if the circumstances make it unfair.

Illustration: Paul spots a diamond lying on the ground. When he stoops to pick it up, Sue hits him from behind and takes the diamond. A court may not award the diamond to Sue as the first possessor.

3. What Constitutes Possession

Possession requires both physical control over the item and intent to control it or to exclude others from it. But these generalizations function more as guidelines than as direct determinants of possession issues. Possession is a blurred question of law and fact. The following Illustrations show some of the more common and troublesome situations.

Illustration – Killing: Paul was pursuing a fox on horseback when Sue took her gun and shot it. Pursuit of a wild animal alone does not constitute taking possession. However, if Paul had shot and killed the fox before Sue got to it, Paul would have been the prior possessor. If Sue's shot merely wounded the fox, rather than killed it, Paul might have prevailed if he got to it first. The result is the same whether the quarry being pursued is a wild animal (*in ferae naturae*) or previously had been captured by another and then escaped back into the wild (demonstrated an *animus revertendi*) and thereby had become unowned again.   State hunting statutes could alter these outcomes.

Illustration – Trapping: Paul threw a net around a school of fish, but Sue then caught some of them. If the net was closed so that the fish could not escape, Paul had possession. However, he did not have possession if the fish had a means of escape. Conservationists often criticize this result on the grounds that it encourages depletion of scarce resources.

Illustration – Spotting: Paul finds an ancient Greek treasure ship at the bottom of the ocean and leaves a marker on the ship. However, before he can return with the necessary equipment to raise it, Sue finds the ship and brings it to the surface. The outcome depends on whether leaving a marker on a sunken ship is a sufficient act of possession to qualify Paul as the first possessor.

Illustration – Unconscious Possession: Paul is standing on a $100 bill without realizing it. Sue asks him to lift his foot, picks up the money, and pockets it. Or Paul finds and removes a box lying in a trash can, but Sue opens it first and discovers a $100 bill in it. Arguably, Paul did not have possession in these cases because he was unaware of the money and, therefore, did not intend to appropriate or to exclude others. On the other hand, Paul had possession of the money, albeit unconsciously, in light of his undisputed physical control over it.

Illustration – Landowner's Possession: Paul finds money in Olga's house.   Courts often hold that a landowner has "constructive possession" of whatever is on her property, even if she does not know it is there. Therefore, Olga is the prior possessor. When this issue comes up in the case of previously owned goods, additional considerations apply.

B. OWNED GOODS

When someone takes possession of property that is owned by another, he has an obligation to return it to the owner. A borrower, renter, finder, and thief all are obligated to return the property to its owner on demand or according to the terms of their agreement. Each also has some duty of care in handling the property.

Illustration: Olga loses a camera, and Ann finds it. Ann loans it to Bob, and Cathy steals it from him. Cathy has a duty to return it to Bob, who has a duty to return it to Ann, who has a duty to return it to Olga. Any person's failure to do so creates liability for recovery of the camera or for damages. Additionally, each may be liable to the one with the prior claim for negligent handling of the camera. As the camera's owner, Olga can recover possession directly from Cathy.

1. Types of Possessors

A possessor's duties to an owner frequently depend on the nature of the possession. (1) Persons who take possession of goods with the owner's consent, such as borrowers, coat checkers, and auto mechanics, usually are referred to as bailees under a bailment transaction. The owner is the bailor.

(2) Persons who take possession of goods without the owner's consent, such as finders and thieves, sometimes are referred to as involuntary or constructive bailees. (3) Persons who do not take possession of goods that are stored in a space that they control, such as unattended parking lots and wet umbrella stands in store entrances, are not bailees. The space owner's duties are determined by rules other than those for bailments, such as by landlord-tenant law. (4) Courts sometimes distinguish between possessors and custodians who hold goods subject to the owner's direction and control, such as a friend or customer examining a book shown to him by the owner. The old criminal law distinctions between larceny and embezzlement depended on this characterization. (5) A person asked to take possession of a container does not necessarily possess its contents if they are unknown to him. For example, a person holding another's purse, briefcase, coat, or car may not have possession of its contents as a matter of law.

2. Duty to Return

A bailee has an absolute duty to return goods to their owner. He is liable if he fails to do so, even if the goods were stolen from him or were destroyed without his fault. An involuntary bailee may be liable for nonreturn only if it results from his negligence. A space owner has no duty to return goods that were never in his possession unless he agreed to do so or in special cases, such as when a parking lot ticket states that no bailment exists, but car owners believe that their cars are being watched by guards and by attendants who are visibly present.

3. Duty of Care

A possessor has some duty of care toward the item in his possession. Traditionally, the duty's extent depended on the nature of the possession. (1) When the bailment is solely for the bailor's benefit, such as when the bailee is doing the owner a favor by holding her goods, the bailee's duty of care is only slight. He is liable only for gross negligence. Finders generally have no duty of care for goods they see but do not pick up. But if a finder takes possession, he may come under the slight care standard. (2) When the bailment is for the bailee's benefit, such as when the owner is doing the bailee a favor by loaning him the item, the bailee's duty of care is extreme. However, he does not have an absolute duty of protection. For example, he is not liable for damage from an earthquake. (3) When the bailment is for the bailor's and bailee's mutual benefit, the bailee is liable for ordinary negligence. This standard applies when both parties benefit from the transaction, such as when an owner pays a shipper to transport goods. (4) If no bailment is created, the owner of the space may have no duty of care for the goods placed there by the owner. For example, a parking lot owner sometimes has no duty of care for cars parked in the lot. Today, many courts apply the ordinary negligence standard to every type of bailment relationship.

4. Exculpatory and Limitation of Liability Clauses

Many courts limit a possessor's ability to disclaim liability for nonreturn of goods. Such issues are not unique to property law. They apply in contract and tort law as well.

5. Possessors' Rights Against Others

A possessor's obligation to return goods to their owner is not a duty owed to anyone else, because the possessor has a better claim to the goods than they do. Therefore, the possessor does not have to give the goods to any third person (a "stranger to the title") who demands them from her, and the possessor may demand that any third person who takes the goods from her return them to her.

Illustration – Borrowing and Renting: Ann borrowed or rented a car for a week and then loaned or rented it to Bob for the day. At the end of the day, Bob must return the car to Ann, and Ann is entitled to demand the car from Bob.

Illustration – Finding and Stealing: Ann picked up a camera she found lying on the ground, but Bob stole it from her. Ann may recover the camera from Bob, even though she does not own it and will have to give it to the owner if he is ever identified. Just as the owner did not lose his rights to the camera when he lost it, Ann does not lose the rights she acquired on finding the camera just because Bob steals it. However, finding situations may be subject to statutory modifications.

A hierarchy of claims ("relativity of title") exists by virtue of the possessor's ability to demand that a third person return the goods on one hand, but the possessor's duty to return them to the owner on the other hand. In the last Illustration, the finder's rights are below the owner's but above the thief's. When more than one person claims the right to possess the same object, the conflict is resolved by determining who has the better claim to it. This standard may require a court to determine whether the first claimant's acts constituted possession, such as whether seeing or picking up a lost wallet constitutes possession. Considerations other than time of possession are irrelevant. Success does not depend on which claimant is needier, will make better use of the object, or has a morally superior claim.

One party need not have a perfect claim (i.e. be the owner), so long as her claim is better than the rival claimant's. Therefore, a person cannot take or withhold goods from another merely because they are owned by a third person. The person from whom they were taken still may have a better claim than the person who took them. In the previous Illustration, the thief cannot defend his wrongful retention by arguing that the finder does not own the goods.

Illustration – Finder v. Finder: Ann finds a camera but loses it. Bob then finds it. As between Ann and Bob, Ann has the better claim because she possessed it first. Except as against Olga, the owner, she has the same right to recover what she loses as an owner. She can recover "her" lost camera from the finder, Bob.

Illustration – Thief v. Thief: Ann steals a camera, and Bob steals it from her. Ann has a better claim to the camera than Bob, even though she acquired possession by theft. She is a wrongful possessor as far as Olga and the penal system are concerned, but she is the prior possessor against Bob and is higher in the hierarchy. Although Ann possibly should be sent to jail, strangers are not entitled to confiscate her goods.

Illustration – Thief v. Finder: Ann steals a camera but loses it, and Bob finds it. The outcome is the same as in the previous Illustration. The guilty possessor prevails over the innocent possessor because she possessed first. Commentators often attack this outcome, but property rules sometimes lack the reasonableness or fairness involved in torts analysis. For instance, Ann need not share possession of her property with Bob even though she has more than enough of everything and Bob has nothing. "Property rights" is not necessarily a "reasonable" concept, and the rules protecting possessors do not purport to eradicate the world's ills.

6. Landowner's Claims

Since goods often are found on land that belongs to or is possessed by someone else, conflicts often arise between the finder and the person on whose land it was found. This straightforward issue has not led to straightforward outcomes. Instead, courts employ a number of somewhat conflicting distinctions.

a. Finder's Status

The finder's claim to the found goods is weaker if he (1) is a trespasser on the property, (2) is on the property for a limited purpose, such as to repair the sink or to deliver the mail, (3) is on the property as an employee of the landowner, or (4) agreed to give any found goods to the landowner, as often occurs in agreements between hotels and their housekeeping crews.

b. Premises' Status

The finder's claim is weaker if the goods were found in a private, rather than public, place. For example, a person who finds a lost item in another's private home is less likely to prevail against the landowner than one who finds the item in a supermarket.

c.　*Status of Land Based Claim*

The strength of a land based claim may be affected by whether the claimant is a landowner who has not yet moved in, a landlord who has never resided on the premises, a long-term tenant, or a weekend guest.

d.　*Where Goods are Found*

Goods found under the soil, rather than lying on it, generally are awarded to the landowner, rather than to the finder. However, if the goods were buried intentionally, they may be characterized as treasure trove. In that case, the finder may be entitled to possession, or they may belong to the state.

e.　*How Goods Got There*

When goods are found in a public place, the finder is entitled to possession if the goods were lost or abandoned. However, the landowner is entitled to possession if they were mislaid—intentionally set down by the owner who forgot to pick them up later. The assumption is that the owner of mislaid goods will return to retrieve them, which will be facilitated if the landowner, rather than the finder, has the goods. Statutes regarding findings sometimes abolish these distinctions, but some courts have held that statutes that refer only to "lost" goods do not apply to mislaid goods.

7. Modern Status

Many issues in this area now are resolved by tort or contract concepts or by statutory rules, rather than by the earlier distinctions based on possession and bailment. Many states have estray statutes that regulate how individuals should deal with found goods. These statutes are helpful but are not essential knowledge in this part of the Property Law course, because finding is studied primarily as a method for acquiring possession.

II. GIFTS

A gift is a voluntary transfer of property by the owner for no consideration. The donor (the person making the gift) may make an inter vivos gift or a gift causa mortis to a donee (the gift recipient). A gift is inter vivos if it is between a living donor and donee and if the donor intends the gift to take effect immediately, irrevocably, and unconditionally. A gift is causa mortis if the donor makes it in anticipation of her imminent death. A third type of gift is a testamentary gift. A testamentary gift becomes effective only at the donor's death. It generally must be made by will, which is subject to statutory requirements. Because testamentary gifts are the subject of an upper-class course on Wills, we will not consider them further here.

A. INTER VIVOS GIFTS

The three necessary elements for an inter vivos gift are (1) intent, (2) delivery, and (3) acceptance.

1. Intent

The donor must intend to make a present, irrevocable transfer of a property interest. The gift can be of a presently possessory interest or of a future interest. However, if the donor intends the transfer of title to take effect in the future, rather than immediately, the transfer is a mere promise to make a gift in the future, which is unenforceable for lack of consideration.

a. *Effect of Conditions on the Transfer*

When a gift is subject to a condition, you must determine whether the condition is precedent or subsequent. If it is precedent, the condition must occur before the gift becomes effective. Therefore, the attempted gift is invalid because it is not a present transfer. If the condition is subsequent, a present transfer of the property occurs, but the gift will be revoked if the condition subsequently occurs. Because a gift subject to a condition subsequent is a present transfer, it is a valid gift. Determining whether a particular condition is precedent or subsequent requires an analysis of the donor's verbal and written statements.

Illustration: Daniel said to his friend: "If you get an A in Property Law, I will give you a new car." The language Daniel used indicates that he was promising to make a gift in the future if the condition of getting an A occurred. He said, "I *will* give," rather than "I give." Therefore, the gift was subject to a condition precedent and is unenforceable.

Illustration: Daniel said to a friend: "Here are the keys to my car. It is yours. But, if you don't get an A in Property, you must return the car to me." Daniel's language and actions reflect his intent to make a present gift, though the gift might be revoked in the future. Therefore, the gift is subject to a condition subsequent and is enforceable.

Illustration: Dora owns a painting. She writes a letter to her son that says: "In honor of your birthday today, I give you my painting. However, I am going to keep possession of it until my death." Dora's use of the present verb tense -"I give"- shows her intent to make a present transfer. Because her son is not entitled to immediate possession of the painting, it is a present transfer of a future interest in the painting.

b. Circumstances Surrounding Gift

To determine the donor's intent, courts may consider the surrounding circumstances, such as the parties' relationship, the gift's size in relation to previous gifts from the donor to the donee, and the donor's conduct after the transfer. For instance, in the preceding Illustration, the intent to make a present transfer is supported by the facts that the

transfer was made on the donee's birthday and that
the letter expressly referred to the birthday.

c.   *Effect of Donor's Retention of Rights*

Although a gift need not be of all rights in the
property, the donor's retention of certain rights may
invalidate the gift.   For example, if the alleged
donor retains control of the property, reserves a
right to revoke the gift, or continues to treat the
property as her own, the transfer probably is not a
gift.

A special issue arises when one person deposits
money into a joint bank account and retains the
right to make withdrawals. The issue is whether the
depositor intended to make a gift to the other party
named on the account or merely created the joint
account as a convenience for himself. A majority of
jurisdictions use gift theory in this situation and
apply the usual legal requirements of intent,
delivery, and acceptance.   The creation of the
account provides prima facie evidence of a gift, but
the evidence is rebutted if the alleged donor
maintained control over the account and did not
intend to give up control.

Illustration: Owen is preparing for a long overseas
trip. He transferred the entire balance of his bank
account to an account in the names of both himself and
his daughter so that she can write checks on the account
to pay Owen's bills while he is gone. He does not

intend that she can use the money for herself. Owen does not have the necessary intent to make a gift to his daughter.

A minority of courts apply contract theory and hold that the contract with the bank gives the donee a right to the money in the account.

2. Delivery

To satisfy the delivery requirement, the donor generally must transfer actual possession of the gift and must surrender all dominion and control over it. The delivery requirement serves three purposes. First, it impresses upon the donor the significance of her action. Second, it makes the donor's act unequivocal to witnesses. Finally, it gives the donee prima facie evidence that a gift was made.

a. Types of Delivery

The actions necessary for a valid delivery depend on the circumstances.

(1) Actual Delivery

Actual delivery consists of giving possession of the gift to the donee or to the donee's agent. It is a formal, immediate transfer of property, and it is always an accepted means for a legal delivery.

Illustration: Mother told Son that he could have two of her colts and that she would lend Son money to buy hay for the colts. Mother retained possession of the colts until her death one year later. Son did not give the colts hay until three days before Mother's death. Because there was no actual delivery of the colts, there was no gift.

(2) Constructive and Symbolic Delivery

If actual delivery has not occurred, a court may uphold the gift on the basis of constructive delivery. "Constructive delivery" refers to those situations in which a court determines that delivery has occurred even though it literally has not. "Symbolic delivery" is a type of constructive delivery in which a written instrument or some item is delivered that generally is accepted as a symbol of the gift or that provides access to it. Constructive and symbolic deliveries normally are sufficient only if the gift cannot reasonably be delivered manually or if other circumstances prevent actual delivery. Courts examine factors such as the property's proximity and size and the state of the donor's health.

Illustration: Father wanted to make a gift of stock to Son. The stock already was in Son's possession in a vault 3,000 miles from Father when he made the gift. Father directed his stockbroker to re-register the stock to Son's name. Because Son already had possession of the stock certificates, Father did not have to manually deliver them again, and the stockbroker's re-registration was sufficient to satisfy the delivery requirement.

Illustration: On Wife's birthday, Husband gave her a written instrument that said he was giving her stock for her birthday. At the time, the stock was in a safe deposit box in another state, which prevented Husband from manually delivering it. The instrument was a legally sufficient symbolic delivery.

Illustration: Mother manifested a present intent to give securities contained in a safe deposit box to Son. She gave him the key to the safe deposit box. This was sufficient delivery.

b.   Delivery to Third Parties

A gift is valid if the donor delivered it to someone other than the done, but only if the donor intended the gift to be irrevocable upon transfer to the third party and the third party is the donee's agent.

Illustration: Father wanted to make a gift of stock to Son and Daughter. The stock already was in Son's possession. Father directed Son to deliver Daughter's share to her. If Son is Daughter's agent for purposes of delivery, the gift is valid even before he physically delivers the stock to her.

In contrast, if the third party is the donor's agent, the delivery requirement probably has not been satisfied because the donor could revoke the gift by directing the agent to return it to him.

Illustration: When he was in failing health, Grandfather signed a document assigning twenty shares of stock to Granddaughter. Grandfather handed the document to Grandmother and told her to give it to Granddaughter when he died unless he changed his mind before then. Because Grandfather reserved the right to revoke the gift, Grandmother is not Granddaughter's agent, and a gift has not been made.

To uphold a gift that is otherwise invalid for lack of delivery, a court may hold that the donor held the property in trust for the donee. As beneficiary of the trust, the donee is entitled to the benefit of the property. To create a trust, there must be a settlor, a beneficiary, a trustee, and a res, and the settlor clearly must have intended to create a trust. The settlor is the person who creates the trust (the donor in this case). The beneficiary is the person who is entitled to the benefits of the property held in trust (the intended donee). The trustee is the person who holds the legal title to the trust property for the beneficiary's benefit. The trustee may be the settlor or a third party. The res is the property that is placed in trust. In this context, the res is the property that was the object of the gift.

Illustration: Aunt purchased bonds for Nephew and told Nephew's father that she had put the bonds aside for Nephew. After Aunt's death, the bonds were found in an envelope with a note that said Aunt was holding them for Nephew. This created a valid trust with Aunt acting as trustee for Nephew.

3. Acceptance

If an intended donee refuses to accept a gift, title to the property will not pass to the donee. When a gift is beneficial to the donee, acceptance is usually presumed. The presumption of acceptance is rebutted if the intended donee's actions indicate a refusal to accept or if other facts demonstrate that the gift would not be beneficial. Acceptance need not be contemporaneous with delivery of the gift.

B. GIFTS CAUSA MORTIS

A gift causa mortis is made in anticipation of the donor's imminent death. It is intended to give a person who is near death one last opportunity to dispose of her personal property. Land cannot be the object of a gift causa mortis. The substantial possibility for false claims to the decedent's property generally has caused courts strictly to apply the requirements for a gift causa mortis.

1. Elements

a. *Intent, Delivery, and Acceptance*

A gift causa mortis requires the same elements as an inter vivos gift—intent, delivery, and acceptance. In determining whether these elements have been satisfied, courts tend to be more exacting than for an inter vivos gift because of the greater potential for fraud inherent in a claim made against the estate of a deceased donor.

b. *Donor Anticipates Imminent Death*

For a gift causa mortis to be valid, it must be made when the donor is suffering from a life-threatening illness or injury. A generalized fear of death, such as a fear of flying or of nuclear war, is insufficient.

Illustration: Dan endorsed a check and laid it on a table with a note stating that it was for Elizabeth. Dan then committed suicide. Suicide can satisfy the requirement that the donor is stricken with a disorder that makes death imminent, though courts in some older cases have held otherwise.

c. Death as Anticipated

The donor must die from the illness or injury that prompted the gift, rather than from an intervening cause.

Illustration: A car accident victim is put in an ambulance after making a gift causa mortis. If the ambulance is struck by a train and the injured person dies from the injuries suffered in the train crash, the older view is that the gift is invalid because the injured person died from an intervening cause. The modern view is more liberal and treats the entire chain of events as one connected occurrence. Therefore, the gift would be valid despite the intervening train crash.

d. Donor Does not Recover

If the donor recovers from the illness or injury that prompted the gift, the gift is revoked by operation of law.

e. *Absence of Revocation by Donor*

Unlike an inter vivos gift, a donor can revoke a gift causa mortis.

f. *Donee Survives Donor*

Because a gift causa mortis is a gift to a particular individual, the gift is revoked by operation of law if the donee predeceases the donor. Otherwise, the donee's next of kin or legatees, rather than the donee, would receive the benefit of the gift.

g. *Condition Precedent or Subsequent*

Some courts will invalidate the gift if the donor uses language of condition precedent, indicating that the gift is to take effect only at the donor's death. These courts reason that the donor did not intend to make an immediately effective gift causa mortis, but only a testamentary transfer. Because the gift did not satisfy the legal requirements for a will, the attempted gift is invalid. However, the better opinions consider the donor's intent and the surrounding circumstances, because a donor who is about to die is unlikely to think about the legal requirements for a gift causa mortis or to articulate his wishes precisely. By definition, such gifts are emergency measures.

III. POSSESSION OF LAND APART FROM OWNERSHIP

A person who possesses land usually either owns it or has the owner's consent to possess, such as a tenant. However, a possessor may be neither the owner nor in possession with the owner's consent.

Illustration: Paul received a deed to Lot 1 but mistakenly moved onto Lot 2. Paul owns Lot 1 but possesses Lot 2 without owning it or having the owner's consent.

Illustration: Paul received a deed to Lot 1 and took possession of Lot 1, but the deed was defectively executed so that he does not own Lot 1.

Illustration: Paul received a valid deed to Lot 1 and took possession of Lot 1. However, by mistake, Paul built a fence that encroached five feet onto Lot 2 and then built his house up to the fence line. Paul possesses, but does not own, the five-foot strip.

Illustration: Paul is a squatter on Lot 1. He knows that he does not own Lot 1 but hopes that the real owner will not do anything about it. He intends to stay until evicted. Paul possesses, but does not own, Lot 1.

A. CONSEQUENCES OF POSSESSION UNCONNECTED TO OWNERSHIP

Possession always has been an important concept in our legal system. A possessor has a legal status in the common law even when she is not the owner. Rights and liabilities are associated with possession.

1. Possessor's Liabilities — Ejectment

If a possessor is not the owner and does not have the owner's permission to possess the property, the owner may bring an ejectment action to recover both possession and damages against the possessor. Ejectment is an action designed to restore possession to the person entitled to it. The plaintiff must prove his right to possession and the defendant's wrongful possession. If the defendant has not possessed the property but has trespassed on it occasionally, the proper cause of action is for trespass, rather than for ejectment.

2. Possessor's Rights

Even though a possessor does not own the property and is subject to ejectment by the owner, the possessor is entitled to maintain possession as against the rest of the world ("possession is nine points of the law"). If a stranger dispossesses him, he may bring an ejectment action against the stranger. It is no defense for the stranger to show that the former possessor is not the owner, unless the stranger owns the property or claims through the owner.

Illustration: Paul took possession of Lot 1 under a deed he believed to be valid. Rachel then ousted Paul from possession, and he brought an ejectment action against her. At the trial, Paul discovers that his deed is defective and did not convey title to Lot 1 to him.

Nevertheless, he may prevail against Rachel by virtue of having been in peaceable possession of the lot before her entry. Paul prevails because he is a prior possessor as against Rachel, though he is a wrongful possessor as against Olga, the owner.

3. Possession that is Rightful and Wrongful

Because a possessor who does not own the land may defend that possession against everyone except the owner, such possession is both "rightful" and "wrongful."

B. DURATION OF POSSESSION

A plaintiff in an ejectment action need not prove any particular duration of possession to claim as a prior possessor. Time is relevant only in that the plaintiff must have possessed first. It does not matter how long he was there, so long as he possessed when the defendant entered. But time is relevant with regard to the statute of limitations. The owner or a prior possessor has a cause of action the moment someone wrongfully takes possession of the property. And, like all causes of action, it expires after a certain lapse of time, except when the government owns the property. Thus, if a person has been in possession long enough, others who previously were entitled to eject him lose their rights to do so.

Illustration: Paul possessed Lot 1 but was dispossessed by Rachel eleven years ago. The statute of limitations for ejectment actions is ten years. Paul no longer can recover the property from Rachel, even if his prior possession had continued for fifteen years.

Illustration: Paul possessed Lot 1 for two years before Rachel dispossessed him five years ago. The statute of limitations for ejectment actions is ten years. Paul may bring an ejectment action against Rachel, though she possessed the property longer than he did.

Illustration: Paul wrongfully possessed Lot 1 for eleven years. The statute of limitations in ejectment is ten years. Olga, the owner, no longer can eject Paul.

C. ADVERSE POSSESSION

1. Duration and Adverse Possession

A possessor who does not own the property may protect that possession against everyone but the owner. The last Illustration shows that, if such possession lasts long enough, the possessor is protected even from the owner's claims. Because no one can eject him legally and because he can eject anyone who intrudes, he now owns the property. The possessor is a successful adverse possessor. Adverse possession does not transfer the former owner's title to the possessor. Rather, it creates a new and complete title in the possessor.

a. How Long Possession Must Continue

Statutes dealing with adverse possession vary from twenty years in some states to five years in others. More extreme time periods may apply to certain special cases. Different periods may exist within a single state, depending on whether the adverse possessor has "color of title" or has paid the property taxes.

b. Tacking

Even if the possessor has not personally possessed the property for the requisite time period, he may be able to "tack" (add) on the time that his predecessors possessed the property.

Illustration: Paul possessed property from 1990 to 1996 and then gave Rachel a deed to it. Rachel possessed it from 1996 to 2001. Under a ten-year statute of limitations, Rachel prevails against Olga, the owner, because Rachel can "tack" (add) Paul's six years to her five years to establish eleven years of possession.

(1) Privity

Tacking is not allowed unless privity of estate exists between the possessor and his or her predecessor. For privity to exist, the predecessor must have voluntarily conveyed her possessory interest to the next possessor.

Illustration: Paul possessed property for six years and then died. Rachel, his heir, then possessed the property for five years. The two periods may be tacked together because there is privity between ancestor and heir.

Illustration: Paul possessed property for six years and then sold it to Rachel, who possessed for five years. Because privity of estate exists between a grantor and grantee, the periods may be tacked together. Although Paul had no title to convey to Rachel, he had a transferable possessory interest, which Rachel acquired from him.

Illustration: Paul possessed property for six years and then was ousted by Rachel, who possessed for five years. Tacking is not permitted because Paul did not voluntarily transfer his possession to Rachel.

2. Acts of Possession Required—Standards

Under some state statutes, a person can qualify as an adverse possessor only by performing certain acts during the running of the statute of limitations, such as cultivating or fencing the property. However, in most states, no such requirement exists, and any acts of possession, if they have the correct quality, will support a finding of adverse possession. Any acts by the possessor during the statutory period that establish her possession for the requisite period of time will suffice.

No set rules exist concerning the types of activities that constitute possession. A standard sometimes applied is whether the possessor's activities would support an action for ejectment by the owner. For example, occasional trespasses would justify an action for trespass, but not for ejectment. Therefore, the occurrence of only those acts during the statutory period would not make the trespasser an adverse possessor. However, most courts prefer a less circular requirement and use standards such as "acts that publicly indicate control consistent with the character of the land" or "acts that an average owner of similar property would undertake."

a. Payment of Taxes

Under some state statutes, a person cannot become an adverse possessor without paying the taxes on the property being possessed. In other states, the time required for adverse possession may be shortened by the payment of taxes. One justification offered for this requirement is that, by checking the tax records, an owner can discover any potential adverse possession. Possibly, the requirement is based on the beliefs that squatters should be unable to acquire land by adverse possession and that possessors who believe they own the land will pay the taxes. In this light, payment of taxes is just another appropriate act of possession.

(1) When Both Parties Pay Taxes

When payment of taxes is required to acquire title by adverse possession, only the adverse possessor must satisfy this requirement. An owner who wants to eliminate threats of adverse possession need not pay the taxes to do so. As long as the adverse possessor is paying them, this test usually is satisfied, even if the owner also pays them. However, in some states, the issue turns on who paid the taxes first.

(2) Boundary Disputes

The tax requirement can cause particular trouble in boundary line cases when the disputed strip has not been separately taxed and both neighbors have been paying all the taxes billed to them. Probably no one involved, including the tax assessor, knows to which party the disputed strip has been assessed. Some courts strictly apply the tax payment requirement, but, in boundary line cases, the most sensible result may be to ignore that requirement.

3. Possession's Required Qualities

Although rarely provided in statutes, every court applies the common law requirements that the possession be "open and notorious, actual, continuous and uninterrupted, exclusive, hostile, and under claim of right." Some jurisdictions also require color of title. The adverse possessor has the burden of proving that the possession has satisfied these elements. From a strictly technical point of view, any possession that subjected the possessor to an action for ejectment should be sufficient.

a. Open

The requirement of open possession is just another way of saying that there has to be visible possession. A furtive possessor really is not a possessor at all. It is doubtful whether one could sustain a claim to have been a prior possessor by proof of nothing more than previous clandestine entries upon the land. An open possessor generally treats the property as a true owner would and leaves physical evidence of his possession. Thus, some cases state that the possession must be "appropriate" or that there must be permanent signs of possession, such as a building or a fence.

b. Notorious

"Notorious" is rarely mentioned separately from open, but it may serve a slightly different function. The owner need not know about the adverse possession, and her ignorance does not extend the limitations period. The absence of a knowledge requirement can be justified by notoriety as an element of adverse possession. If a possessor is using the property in a manner that all who investigate will know about it, the possessor has done everything that can be expected. Often, the possessor mistakenly believes that he owns the property he is possessing. In that case, he cannot be expected to notify an owner of whom he has never heard. Instead, the owner is obliged to check the property periodically.

Illustration: Paul lives in a house on Lot 1, which he believes he owns. However, Olga actually owns Lot 1. Everyone in the neighborhood knows that Paul lives on Lot 1, but Olga resides elsewhere and does not know. Paul will own the property after the statutory period has run, because Olga should have checked on her property. Paul had no duty to inform her of his possession.

Illustration: Paul's house encroaches onto Olga's property, but Olga does not realize it. Paul can acquire title to the encroachment area even though Olga does not have the property surveyed until the limitations period has expired.

(1) Subjacent Possession

A person may adversely possess property underneath another's land (the subsurface). However, for the adverse possession to be notorious, it must be visible in some way on the surface of the adversely possessed property. Only in this way will the owner and the community at large have notice that the adverse possession is occurring.

Illustration: Paul owns a coal mine. The entrance to the mine is on his property. He has extended the mine to take coal from beneath the land of his neighbor, Olga. Paul's mining activities under Olga's land are not open and notorious. Olga does not have a reasonable means of discovering the trespass.

c. Actual Possession

"Actual" possession means no more than real possession. Its main function is as a counterpoint to constructive possession. By itself, constructive possession never ripens into title by adverse possession. An ejectment action lies only against real possessors.

Illustration: For twenty years, Paul has claimed that he owns Olga's lot, but he has never set foot on it. No statute of limitations will run against Olga because she never had a cause of action against Paul for ejectment. She can sue Paul for ejectment only if he actually possesses her land. Although Olga might have a quiet title action against Paul's claim, that is not a possessory action.

(1) Constructive Possession and Color of Title

An adverse possessor can acquire title to an entire parcel of land even if she possessed only part of it if (1) she actually possessed part of the parcel, and (2) she entered onto that part based on a deed or a judgment that appeared to convey title to the entire parcel (i.e. gave her color of title to the entire parcel).

Illustration: Paul has a deed that appears to convey title to a five-acre parcel to him. However, the deed is defective and does not actually convey title to him. Paul lives on one acre but does not use the other four. At the end of the limitations period, Paul will acquire title by adverse possession to all five acres. The boundaries described in Paul's deed effectively serve as a substitute for a fence built by Paul, which probably would have made Paul an actual possessor of the five acres. Some states require that Paul have a good faith belief in his deed's validity for this doctrine to operate. Other states require that the deed be recorded in the public land records before it constitutes color of title.

(2) Constructive Possession and Prior Possession

The enlargement of area conferred by color of title protects a prior possessor from subsequent trespassers. Thus, a person who actually possesses only one acre under color of title to five acres should be able to eject subsequent intruders from any of the five acres.

(3) Limits on Constructive Possession

Constructive possession does not occur when (1) the property that is only constructively possessed is owned separately from the property that is actually possessed, (2) the part actually possessed is not being adversely possessed, or (3) the color of title does not describe the property in dispute.

Illustration: Paul has color of title to Lots 1 and 2, which are in fact owned by Olga and Owen respectively. Paul occupies only Lot 1. Paul will not acquire title to Lot 2 by adverse possession, because Owen never had a cause of action for ejectment against Paul.

Illustration: Paul has a deed to Lots 1 and 2. However, Paul's grantor owned only Lot 1, and Paul actually possessed only Lot 1. Paul cannot acquire title to Lot 2 by adverse possession because he has not adversely possessed it. His possession of Lot 1 was not adverse, because he really owned it.

Illustration: Paul has a deed to Lot 1 but mistakenly entered onto Lot 2 and possessed only part of it. Paul cannot claim constructive possession of any other part of Lot 2. Because his deed describes only Lot 1, it does not provide color of title to Lot 2. Paul can acquire title by adverse possession only to that part of Lot 2 that he actually occupied. The same result occurs when Paul claims strips of land outside the boundaries of the parcel described in his deed.

(4) Conflicting Constructive Possessions

Real title provides constructive possession without the need for actual possession. Thus, an absentee owner can eject wrongful possessors because his or her title provides constructive possession, which the trespassers have breached. The constructive possession claims of various parties may conflict. The following Illustrations demonstrate the resolutions of these conflicts.

Illustration: Olga is absent from her forty-acre parcel. Paul enters under color of title to all forty acres, but he actually possesses only one acre. Paul will acquire all forty acres by adverse possession because his constructive possession of thirty-nine acres, coupled with his actual possession of one acre, prevails over Olga's constructive possession.

Illustration: Olga is absent from her forty acres. Paul enters under color of title to all forty acres but actually possesses only one acre. Subsequently, Rachel enters the same forty acres under color of title to all forty acres but actually possesses only one different acre. Paul now can acquire title by adverse possession to only thirty-nine acres (the one acre he actually possesses and the thirty-eight acres no one else actually possesses). He cannot acquire title to the acre Rachel actually possesses, because her actual possession defeats his claim to constructive possession of it. If Rachel remains long enough, she can acquire title by adverse possession to the one acre she actually possesses, but she cannot claim constructive possession of the rest because Paul's claim of constructive possession, being prior in time, is superior to hers.

d. Continuous and Uninterrupted

"Continuous" does not mean constant. The adverse possessor need not possess the land every minute of the day. Many successful adverse possessors have made only seasonal use of the land, such as for grazing or hunting. In these situations, "continuous" means only that the activity is carried on regularly in a manner that is consistent with the property's normal use. For example, the grazer must graze animals every year during the grazing season. If the acts are too irregular, they will be viewed as a series of unconnected trespasses not amounting to a dispossession of the owner. Also, a possessor who abandons the property with no intent to return but then returns does not continuously possess the property, and the statute of limitations starts over from his re-entry.

The most common meaning of "uninterrupted" is that no one has possessed the property during the statutory period without the possessor's consent.

Illustration: Rachel intruded onto Paul's possession after he had been on the land for nine years, and she remained for a year. Paul cannot claim adverse possession under a ten-year statute because his possession was interrupted after nine years. This result also can be explained by saying that Paul's possession was not exclusive or actual for ten years.

Illustration: Paul possessed for five years and then was ousted by Rachel. As the prior possessor, Paul brought a successful ejectment action against Rachel and was restored to possession one year after his initial dispossession. He has been in possession the second time for three years. Most authorities agree that Paul should not have to start all over again, which would mean seven more years under a ten-year statute. However, they do not agree whether Paul can include the time Rachel was in possession. If Paul can include Rachel's year, he needs to possess for only one more year. If he cannot, he needs two more years. The result depends on whether the owner's cause of action against Paul is viewed as continuing to run during the year that Rachel had possession.

(1) Interruptions by Owner

A successful ejectment action, followed by an execution of the judgment, interrupts an adverse possession by revesting possession in the owner. A successful judgment relates back to the date the owner filed the complaint, so that the action only has to be filed in time. But a complaint that is not followed up in court will not interrupt an adverse possession.

Any act by the owner that constitutes a resumption of possession is an interruption. But a furtive entry, an accidental entry, or an entry based on the possessor's consent does not constitute an interruption because it is not a possessory act. To interrupt another's possession, the owner actually must become a possessor by committing acts that would entitle the possessor to bring ejectment if the acts were committed by someone other than the owner.

Illustration: A deed to Paul conveyed Lot 1, but he mistakenly possessed Lot 2. Olga, who owns Lot 2, possessed Lot 3 under a similar mistake. During the statutory time period, Olga frequently visited Paul on Lot 2. These visits did not interrupt Paul's possession, because they occurred with his permission.

e. Exclusive

"Exclusive" does not mean that no one other than the possessor is ever on the property. This term generally means that the possessor ousts anyone who is on the property without the possessor's consent. It derives from the notion that possession usually includes an intent to exclude others. Consequently, an adverse possession that fails for want of exclusivity is probably lacks other requirements as well.

Illustration: During Paul's ten years on the property, others frequently intruded and were not ousted by Paul. Paul will not acquire title by adverse possession because his possession was not exclusive. This result also can be explained by saying that Paul was not in actual possession, because a "real" possessor does not tolerate intruders.

Illustration: During the past ten years, Paul has sometimes possessed the property exclusively. However, at other times, he has brought friends with him or has leased the property to third persons. Paul is an adverse possessor, because the other activities occurred with Paul's permission.

f. Hostile

A great deal of disagreement exists concerning the meaning and significance of "hostility." All courts agree that a person who is possessing property with the owner's permission is not adversely possessing. Under an objective view of adverse possession, lack of permission is all that is required. Under a subjective view, however, more is required.

(1) Objective Standard

Most states hold that the possessor's state of mind is irrelevant. In these jurisdictions, the "hostility" element defeats a possessor's claim only if he disclaimed any intent to acquire title by adverse possession.

(2) Subjective Standard

Under the subjective view, an adverse possessor must have a certain state of mind throughout the time of his possession. However, the courts do not agree as to which state of mind is the "correct" one.

(a) Mentality of Thievery

If the possessor knows that he does not own the property, courts in some jurisdictions hold that he cannot become an adverse possessor. This rule is designed to keep squatters from acquiring title to land.

(b) Mentality of Mistake

On the other hand, if the possessor believes that she is the owner, courts in some other states hold she cannot become an adverse possessor. If the possessor testifies that she only intended to claim what she owned and would not have claimed the property if she had known the truth, her possession is not hostile to the true owner's title. In these states, only a "thief" can become an adverse possessor.

(3) Permissive Possession

A tenant's possession is not adverse to the landlord, because the lease transferred the landlord's possessory right to the tenant. Nor is a cotenant's possession adverse to the other cotenants, because each has a right to possess the entire property. In both these cases, the possession is permissive and does not give rise to a cause of action in ejectment. Consequently, such possession never ripens into title by adverse possession, no matter how long continued.

(a) Ouster

A permissive possession can become adverse if the possessor repudiates the owner's title, asserts an independent possessory right, and either notifies the owner of this claim or is otherwise appropriately notorious about it. These actions constitute an ouster of the owner and create a cause of action that will expire when the statute of limitations has run.

Illustration: Paul has been in possession for three years as a tenant under a lease from Olga. He now has told Olga that he no longer will pay rent to her, because he has learned that she is not the owner. Paul is wrong; Olga is the owner. If Paul stops paying rent, he will be an adverse possessor. However, in computing his period of adverse possession, he cannot include his first three years, because he permissively possessed during those years. However, many states have a special statute dealing with adverse possession by tenants.

Illustration: Paul and Olga are joint tenants, but Paul has been in sole possession for the past three years. Paul now has told Olga that he no longer will allow her to share in the ownership, profits, or possession of the property. Paul's possession will ripen into a full title after the limitations period expires. The first three years of his possession cannot be counted.

(b) What Constitutes Ouster

Any act that gives notice to the owner that the possessor no longer recognizes the owner's title to the property constitutes ouster. In the case of cotenants, a refusal to permit the other cotenant to enter, a refusal to account for profits, or sometimes merely a statement that the possessor regards himself as the sole owner can be sufficient. In the landlord-tenant context, a refusal to pay rent constitutes the clearest kind of ouster.

(4) Other Cases of Permissive Possession

A mortgagor's possession is not hostile to the mortgagee and does not become so until the mortgagor repudiates the mortgage or retains possession after his rights have been cut off by a foreclosure. A mortgagee in possession is not hostile to the mortgagor until the mortgagee refuses to account for the profits from the land.

A grantor of a valid deed who retains possession usually is not considered to be hostile to the grantee unless the grantor repudiates the deed. But a grantee's possession under a void deed can be considered to be hostile to the grantor.

In general, possession by a family member is not deemed to be hostile to the rest of the family.

g. *Claim of Right*

Jurisdictions vary widely concerning the meaning of "claim of right." In many, it means nothing more than the aggregate of the other elements of adverse possession or is treated as an aspect of hostility. In others, the adverse possessor must have claimed to be the owner during the limitations period.

h. *Color of Title*

In the context of adverse possession, "color of title" refers to a document that purports to convey actual title but fails to do so. A typical example is a void deed. Because the adverse possessor is always someone who does not own the property, any deed by which he or she claims title is by definition void. However, possession of a void deed may have important consequences, as discussed in the following sections.

(1) *Color of Title as Absolute Requirement of Adverse Possession*

In a few states, title cannot be acquired by adverse possession without color of title. An adverse possessor of property who has no document supporting the possession gets nothing.

(2) *Color of Title as Affecting Acts Required*

In a few states, color of title enables ordinary use of the property to qualify as adverse possession, whereas more significant possessory acts, such as fencing or cultivating, are necessary if color of title does not exist.

(3) *Color of Title as Affecting Time Period*

In a few states, a possessor with color of title needs fewer years of possession to adversely possess title than does a possessor without color of title.

(4) *Color of Title and Hostility*

In some states, a possessor with color of title is presumed to be hostile to the owner, whereas independent proof of hostility is otherwise needed.

4. **External Factors that Prolong Statute of Limitations**

a. *Disabilities*

Generally, a statute of limitations is tolled if a plaintiff is under a legal disability, such as infancy, mental impairment, imprisonment, or military service, when the cause of action arises. This is also true in adverse possession cases. Either the entire statutory period or some shorter period is allotted to the owner for suit after the disability ends. Further refinements of this principle are shown in the following Illustrations, all of which assume a ten-year statute of limitations.

Illustration: Paul wrongfully took possession in 1990, while Olga was mentally impaired. Olga recovered her mental health in 1993. Paul could not acquire title by adverse possession until 2003.

Illustration: Paul wrongfully took possession in 1990, when Olga was twelve years old and mentally impaired. The age of majority is eighteen. Olga recovered her mental health in 1993. However, Paul cannot acquire title by adverse possession until 2006, which is ten years after Olga reaches majority. If Olga remained mentally impaired until she was twenty years old (1998), Paul would have to wait until 2008. Whenever two disabilities exist when the adverse possession begins, both must be eliminated before the limitations period begins to run.

Illustration: Paul wrongfully took possession in 1990, and Olga was imprisoned in 1993. Paul acquired title in 2000, because subsequently occurring disabilities generally do not toll the statute of limitations.

Illustration: Paul wrongfully took possession in 1990, and Olga died in 1993, leaving a fifteen-year old daughter, Diana, as her heir. Paul acquired title in 2000. Diana's infancy was not a disability of the person who had the cause of action when it first accrued. However, some statutes refer to the time when "the adverse possession commences or the title first descends." These statutes can be interpreted as giving Diana up to ten years after she reaches majority. But even in states with this type of statute, courts often reach a contrary result by disregarding the daughter's disability.

b. Future Interests

Generally, the holder of a future interest is not entitled to bring an ejectment action against a wrongful possessor because the future interest gives no presently possessory right. Therefore, the statute of limitations does not begin to run against the future interest holder until that interest becomes possessory.

Illustration: In 1989, Olga died, leaving land to her husband for life and then to her daughter. In 1990, Paul wrongfully began possessing the land. In 2000, if Olga's husband is still alive, Paul gained only a life estate measured by the husband's life. Paul does not acquire the entire fee by adverse possession until he is there for at least ten years after the death of Olga's husband. Olga's daughter did not have the right to possess the property and to bring an ejectment action against Paul until her father died.

Illustration: Olga rented her property to Tom for a twenty-year term, ending in 2000. Paul wrongfully entered in 1985 and ousted Tom. In 1995, Paul adversely possessed Tom's tenancy. For Paul to adversely possess Olga's title, he must possess for ten years after her reversion becomes possessory at the lease's termination, including for nonpayment of rent.

Illustration: Paul wrongfully entered Olga's property in 1985. In 1990, Olga leased the property to Tom for fifteen years. In 1995, Paul gained the fee title by adverse possession. Because the adverse possession began before the lease, Olga leased adversely possessed land. The same would be true if Olga had conveyed the property to Tom after Paul had entered. The time for Paul's adverse possession is not thereby extended.

c. *Effect of Adverse Possession on Nonpossessory Interests*

Easements and restrictive covenants held by third parties are not automatically extinguished by adverse possession of the property. Those claims are not dependent on the owner's title and, therefore, do not fail merely because that title fails. They also are not necessarily affected by the acts of adverse possession on the property. But, if the adverse possessor has interfered with the rights of the easement and covenant holders, their interests also will be extinguished based on the running of the statute of limitations on their independent claims.

Illustration: Paul adversely possesses Olga's property and builds a fence around it. The fence blocks a right of way that Olga formerly had granted to Sam. If Sam fails to sue Paul to recover access, he will lose his easement. But if Paul's possessory acts do not interfere with Sam's easement, the title Paul acquires by adverse possession will be subject to Sam's easement.

Illustration: Olga owns property subject to a restrictive covenant that limits the height of any building to two stories. Paul adversely possesses the land but never constructs a building over two stories. At the end of the limitations period, Paul will have title by adverse possession, but it will be subject to the covenant because the covenant beneficiaries never had a cause of action against Paul for breach.

5. Consequences of Having Been an Adverse Possessor

When all the requirements for adverse possession have been met, two significant changes occur in the adverse possessor's status. First, she no longer is liable in ejectment or trespass for her former adverse possession.   Second, she acquires an original title to the property. From then on, she is freed not only from liability for her previous adverse possession, but also from the requirements of adverse possession, such as exclusive and continuous possession. The property is hers, and she may do with it as she pleases. A quiet title decree will be necessary for the former adverse possessor to have marketable title (i.e. one that he can force a contract purchaser to accept), but the decree itself only confirms the title she already has acquired. That title came into existence when the former owner lost the right to bring an ejectment action.

Illustration: Paul adversely possessed Olga's property for the requisite number of years. Thereafter, Paul failed to pay the property taxes. Even if payment of taxes is a requirement of adverse possession in the jurisdiction, Paul will prevail against Olga. Paul's failure to pay the taxes does not transfer title back to Olga.

Illustration: Paul adversely possessed Olga's property for the requisite number of years. During his period of adverse possession, Paul cut down a large number of trees. Paul is not liable to Olga for those trees. When he acquired title by adverse possession, his title related back to the day his adverse possession began.

CHAPTER TWO

COMMON LAW ESTATES

I. PRESENT (POSSESSORY) ESTATES IN LAND

A. KINDS OF ESTATES

The present estates are classified according to duration. The estates described in this Chapter are the only ones that our common law recognizes. They can be created for real and personal property.

1. Fee Simple

This estate provides the greatest ownership interest. The owner can dispose of the property as he or she pleases, and it will descend to the owner's heirs at death or according to the terms of the owner's will. The estate can be unconditional (fee simple absolute) or can be subject to a condition (defeasible).

2. Fee Tail

This estate passes from generation to generation of the family line and does not end until the family line ends. It passes to each holder's children at the holder's death and cannot be inherited by collateral heirs, such as the holder's siblings. This estate has been statutorily abolished or substantially modified in virtually every state.

3. Life Estate

This estate's duration is measured by the length of a specified person(s)'s life. It lasts as long as the measuring life continues.

4. Estate for Years (also known as Tenancy for a Term)

This estate lasts for a specified period, from 999 years or more down to a single day. Upon the death of the owner of the estate, it passes by will or by intestate succession.

5. Periodic Estate (also known as Tenancy from Period to Period)

This estate lasts for a certain term. Unless terminated before the end of the term, it repeats for another like term. The term may be for any length of time, such as a year, a month, or a week or less.

6. Tenancy at Will and Tenancy at Sufferance

The tenancy at will and the tenancy at sufferance are also sometimes called estates in land, but their significance is so slight that they will not be discussed here. They are covered, along with the other tenancies, in the Landlord and Tenant Chapter (Chapter 4).

B. FREEHOLD v. NONFREEHOLD ESTATES—SEISIN

The fee simple, fee tail, and life estate are called freehold estates. The tenancy for years and the periodic tenancy are nonfreehold estates. The time for termination of freehold estates cannot be precisely determined in advance because death (with or without heirs) is always the terminating event. In contrast, nonfreehold estates terminate on or before an ascertainable date.

The need for distinguishing between freehold and nonfreehold estates derives from the common law concept of seisin. The holder of a freehold estate had seisin (i.e. was seised of the land), whereas the holder of a nonfreehold estate had possession but not seisin. In England, all land titles came from the monarch, either directly to the possessor or by way of intermediate lords. The holder of a freehold estate owed certain services to the overlord, somewhat equivalent to modern rent or property taxes. Today, seisin equates most closely with title to property.

C. CREATION OF ESTATES (CREATING WORDS)

1. Fee Simple – "To Bob and His Heirs"

At common law, the only language that could create a fee simple was a grant to the transferee "and his (her) heirs." "And heirs" was the grantor's way of indicating that the estate was inheritable by the grantee's heirs. However, this language itself does not give anything to the heirs. They do not share the estate with the transferee and have no interest of their own from this conveyance. The words "and heirs" are "words of limitation," which designate the estate as being inheritable, rather than "words of purchase," which designate the taker ("to Bob"). Today, the need to use special words of limitation to create fee simple has been abolished in virtually every jurisdiction and has been replaced by a statutory presumption in favor of the fee simple estate.

2. Fee Tail – "To Bob and the Heirs of His Body"

Like the fee simple, the fee tail is inheritable because of the words of limitation "and the heirs of his (her) body." It is inheritable only by lineal descendants and not by collateral heirs. To create a fee tail, the conveyance must use words of indefinite succession, such as "heirs of the body" or "issue of the body." Any limitation on these technical terms of art causes them to become words of definite succession. Therefore, a conveyance "to Bob and the heirs of his body who are alive when he dies" cannot create a fee tail because the words "who are alive when he dies" limit the technical term "heirs of his body." Similarly, courts normally construe "and the heirs of his body share and share alike" as language of definite succession, because they seem to refer to those descendants who are living when Bob dies. Therefore, this language also does not create a fee tail.

a. Special Forms of Fee Tail

The fee tail may be a fee tail general, as described above, or it may be a fee tail special: "To Al and the heirs of his body and the body of his wife Jane." The fee tail special is limited to the lineal descendants of a specific man and woman. There may also be a fee tail male—"to Al and the male heirs of his body"—or a fee tail female—"to Al and the female heirs of his body." It is also possible to convey a fee tail special male or female.

b. Fee Simple Conditional

Before 1285, a conveyance to a person and the heirs of his body created a fee simple conditional. The fee simple conditional would become a fee simple as soon as the transferee had a child who was born alive. Because this result did not conform to the grantor's intent, the Statute De Donis Conditionalibus (1285) provided that a conveyance to a person and the heirs of his body created an estate that was descendible only to his issue and that the birth of a child did not enlarge the estate into a fee simple. This fee simple conditional thus became the fee tail. If the grantee conveyed his fee tail estate to another, either his issue (if there were issue) or the holder of the future interest following the fee tail (if there were no issue) could recover the estate upon the grantee's death. Today, three states still characterize a conveyance to a person and the heirs of his body as creating a fee simple conditional.

c. *Disentailing Conveyances – Common Recovery and Fine*

At early common law, certain collusive lawsuits, known as common recovery and fine, enabled a fee tail holder to enlarge it into a fee simple despite the Statute De Donis. Today, most states have abolished the fee tail estates, preserve it for one generation only, or provide a means by which its holder can convert it into fee simple.

3. Life Estate – "To Bob for His Life"

At early common law, a conveyance of a freehold estate that did not include the words "and heirs" or "and heirs of the body" was deemed to convey only a life estate. However, in virtually every jurisdiction today, intent to convey only a life estate must be clear to overcome the modern presumption in favor of fee simple. Therefore, words such as "to Bob for his life" must be used to create a life estate. A life estate also is created if the estate necessarily will terminate when the measuring life dies.

Therefore, "to Bob for so long as he farms the land" creates a life estate (a defeasible life estate), because the longest it can last is while Bob is alive.

A voluntarily created life estate is a "conventional" life estate (e.g. A conveys "to B for his life"). In contrast, a "legal" life estate is created by operation of law, such as the legally created marital property interests (e.g. dower and curtesy). When the life estate owner is the measuring life, it is an "ordinary" life estate. When someone other than the life estate owner is the measuring life, it is a life estate "pur autre vie."

a. Life Estate Pur Autre Vie – "To Bob for the Life of Cathy"

A life estate pur autre vie can be created by express terms ("to Bob for the life of Cathy") or when a life tenant who is the measuring life conveys the life estate to someone else ("to Bob for his life;" Bob then conveys the life estate to Cathy). At early common law, when the holder of a life estate pur autre vie died before the person who is the measuring life, no person was eligible to hold the estate; the holder's heirs could not inherit the estate, and the future interest holder had to wait until the measuring life died. Therefore, the land was open to the first person who occupied it, known as a general occupant. Today, a life estate pur autre vie can be conveyed at death by will or by intestate succession.

b.   *Legal Life Estate*

In contrast to a conventional life estate, a legal life estate is created by operation of law.

(1) *Fee Tail Special with Possibility of Issue Extinct*

The language "to Bob and the heirs of his body and the body of his wife Jane" gives Bob a life estate once Jane dies without issue, because no possibility exists that this estate will continue after Bob's death.   The fee tail becomes a life estate measured by Bob's life.

(2) *Marital Estates*

A landowner's spouse may have a life estate in the land when the owner dies. This common law right of dower (for a surviving wife) or curtesy (for a surviving husband) is created by operation of law.

4. Estate for Years – "To Bob for Ten Years"

There is no need to add "heirs" to the grant of an estate for years because it is a nonfreehold estate. It merely must specify the estate's beginning and ending dates. The estate for years is transferable inter vivos and passes at its owner's death by will or by intestate succession.

5. Estate from Period to Period – "To Bob from Month to Month" or "To Bob for $10 per Month"

To create an estate from period to period (also known as a periodic estate), the conveyance either can state that the term is periodic or can state a periodic rent without specifying a termination date. The length of the period is usually the period for which rent is stated. Therefore, the language "to Bob for $10 per month" will create a month-to-month tenancy. Other forms of periodic estates are covered in the Landlord and Tenant Chapter. See Chapter 4.

D. QUALITY OF ESTATES – ABSOLUTE OR UNQUALIFIED

All the estates described so far differ according to their duration and the events that cause their natural termination. A fee title can last indefinitely, a life estate ends when the measuring life expires, and a nonfreehold estate ends when the designated time interval passes. However, all these estates can terminate sooner if the grant specifies that they are subject to a condition (limitation). When and if that condition occurs, the estate terminates even though the condition occurs before the event that would cause the estate to terminate naturally. An estate that is subject to a condition is "defeasible," "qualified," or "base," while an estate that is not subject to a condition is "indefeasible," "absolute," or "unqualified."

A defeasible estate is either "determinable," "subject to a condition subsequent," or "subject to executory limitation." To distinguish among them, focus on two features: (1) When the qualified estate was created, did the grantor retain the future interest following it or convey it to someone else?; and (2) What words are used to connect the condition to the words conveying the estate?

1. Determinable Estate (also called Estate Subject to Special Limitation)

The determinable estate exists only when, in the document that creates the estate, the grantor retains the future interest. The conveyance must use words of time, such as "so long as," "until," or "during," to attach the condition to the words of grant. This estate lasts only as long as the condition described in it does not occur. Once the condition occurs, the estate automatically terminates.

Illustration: "To Bob and his heirs so long as the land is farmed." This creates a fee simple determinable. The moment the land is no longer farmed, the estate terminates.

Illustration: "To Barb and the heirs of her body so long as the land is farmed." This creates a fee tail determinable. The estate terminates when the land is no longer farmed or when there are no lineal heirs, whichever occurs first.

Illustration: "To Bob for life so long as the land is farmed." Bob has a determinable life estate, which will terminate when he dies or stops farming, whichever occurs first.

Illustration: "To Barb for ten years so long as the land is farmed." Barb's determinable term for years will terminate in ten years unless Barb stops farming before then.

2. Estate Subject to Condition Subsequent

The estate subject to condition subsequent exists only when, in the document that creates the estate, the grantor retains the future interest. The conveyance must use words of condition, such as "upon condition that," "provided that," or "but if," to attach the condition to the words of grant. Like determinable estates, these estates can end when the condition occurs. However, unlike the determinable estate, termination is at the election of the owner of the future interest, rather than automatic. Therefore, to decrease the possibility that an estate will be forfeited, ambiguous language is construed as an estate subject to condition subsequent, rather than as a determinable estate.

Illustration: "To Bob and his heirs, but if the land is used for a farm, the grantor may re-enter and repossess." Bob has a fee simple subject to condition subsequent.

Illustration: "To Barb and the heirs of her body, but if the land is used for a farm, the grantor may re-enter and repossess." Barb has a fee tail subject to a condition subsequent.

Illustration: "To Bob for life, but if the land is used for a farm, the grantor may re-enter and repossess." Bob has a life estate subject to condition subsequent.

Illustration: "To Barb for ten years, but if the land is used for a farm, the grantor may re-enter and repossess." Barb has a term for years subject to condition subsequent.

Illustration: "To Bob and his heirs, for so long as the land is used for a farm, but if he violates this condition, the grantor can re-enter and repossess." This grant uses both the language for a determinable fee simple ("for so long as") and for a fee simple subject to condition subsequent ("grantor can re-enter and repossess"). To reduce the possibility that Bob will lose the land, a court will construe it to be the latter.

3. Estate Subject to Executory Limitation

If, in the document that conveyed the defeasible estate, the grantor did not retain the future interest, the estate is subject to executory limitation. The words used to attach the condition to the words of grant are irrelevant. When the condition is breached, the estate automatically terminates.

Illustration: "To Ann for so long as the land is used as a farm, then to Barb." Ann has a fee simple subject to executory limitation.

Illustration: "To Ann provided that the land is used as a farm, then to Barb." Ann has a fee simple subject to executory limitation.

Illustration: "To Ann for so long as she farms the land, then to Barb." Ann has a life estate subject to executory limitation, because the estate will end when Ann dies or when the condition occurs, whichever happens first.

II. FUTURE INTERESTS

Every estate in land is either present (entitling its owner to immediate possession of the land) or future (potentially entitling its owner to possession in the future). There are five future interests: (1) reversion, (2) possibility of reverter, (3) power of termination (also known as right of re-entry), (4) remainder, and (5) executory interest. To begin the process of distinguishing among them, look to the document that created the future interest. If the grantor retained the future interest, it must be a possibility of reverter, power of termination, or reversion. If the document that created the future interest conveys it to a grantee, it must be a remainder or executory interest.

A. FUTURE INTERESTS RETAINED BY GRANTOR

1. Possibility of Reverter

If the grantor conveys a determinable estate, he retains a possibility of reverter. A possibility of reverter always follows a determinable estate, and a determinable estate is always followed by a possibility of reverter. The possibility of reverter automatically terminates the determinable estate when the condition is breached.

Illustration: Ann owned land in fee simple absolute. She conveyed it "to Bob and his heirs so long as the land is used as a farm." Bob has a fee simple determinable, and Ann has a possibility of reverter. Ann will get the land back automatically when it is no longer used as a farm. If Ann transfers her interest to Cathy, the interest is still a possibility of reverter though someone other than the grantor now owns it.

Illustration: Ann owned land in fee simple absolute. She conveyed it "to Bob for life so long as the land is used as a farm." Bob has a determinable life estate, and Ann has a possibility of reverter that will become possessory when the condition is breached. Ann also has a reversion that will become possessory at Bob's death if the condition was not breached.

Illustration: Ann owned land in fee simple absolute. She conveyed it "to Bob for ten years so long as the land is used as a farm." Bob has a determinable term for years, and Ann has a possibility of reverter and a reversion.

2. Power of Termination (also called Right of Re-entry)

If a grantor conveys an estate subject to condition subsequent, he retains a power of termination. The estate subject to condition subsequent and the power of termination always go together. The owner of a power of termination can recover the land if the condition subsequent is breached. However, the owner may elect not to exercise it and thereby waive it. Until the power of termination is exercised, the grantee retains his estate.

Illustration: Ann owned land in fee simple absolute. She conveyed it "to Bob for life, but if liquor is ever sold on the land, the grantor may re-enter and repossess." Bob has a life estate subject to condition subsequent. Ann has both a reversion (when Bob dies) and a power of termination (if liquor is sold on the land).

Illustration: Ann owned land in fee simple absolute. She conveyed it "to Bob for ten years, but if liquor is ever sold on the land, the grantor may re-enter and repossess." Bob has a term for years subject to a condition subsequent, and Ann has a reversion and a power of termination.

3. Reversion

If a grantor's future interest is neither a possibility of reverter nor a power of termination, it is a reversion. It exists when the grantor has not conveyed all her interest in the land. When determining whether a reversion exists, it is important to remember that a contingent remainder is not a property interest

For each of the following Illustrations, assume that Ann, the grantor, had fee simple absolute title before the conveyance.

Illustration: Ann conveys "to Bob for life." Ann has a reversion following Bob's life estate. If Ann conveys the reversion to Cathy, it is still called a reversion.

Illustration: Ann conveyed "to Bob for life, remainder to Cathy." Ann does not have a reversion because she has conveyed her entire title. After Bob's life estate terminates, Cathy will have fee simple absolute title.

Illustration: Ann conveyed "to Bob for life, then to Cathy if she survives Bob, otherwise to Dan." Ann has a reversion because Cathy and Dan have only contingent remainders, which are not property interests. When Bob dies, either Cathy or Dan will get fee simple absolute title, but Ann still has a reversion while the life estate continues.

B. FUTURE INTERESTS CREATED IN A GRANTEE

If the document that creates a future interest conveys it to a grantee, rather than retaining it for the grantor, the future interest is either a remainder or an executory interest (also known as an executory limitation).

1. Remainder v. Executory Interest

For a future interest to be a remainder, it must satisfy both elements of a two-part test: (1) The interest must be capable of becoming possessory as soon as the prior possessory estate terminates; and (2) It cannot divest a prior interest. If either element of the test is violated, the future interest is an executory interest.

a. Capable of Becoming Immediately Possessory

To satisfy this element, the future interest does not have to become actually possessory. The only requirement is that, if the future interest does become possessory, it will do so as soon as the prior possessory terminates.

Illustration: "To Ann for life, remainder to Bob." Bob's interest will become possessory as soon as Ann's life estate terminates. If Bob predeceases Ann, his remainder will pass to his heirs or devisees, and they can take possession as soon as the life estate terminates.

Illustration: "To Ann for life, then to Bob if he survives Ann, otherwise to Cathy." Bob and Cathy both have remainders, though only one of them will get possession. When Ann's life estate ends, either Bob's or Cathy's interest will become possessory immediately.

Illustration: "To Ann for life, then to Bob six months after her death." Bob's interest cannot become possessory as soon as Ann's life estate ends. Therefore, he has an executory interest.

b. Cannot Divest Prior Interest

A property interest is divested if it is terminated by the occurrence of a condition.

Illustration: "To Ann, but when the land is no longer used as a park, to Bob." Ann's interest in the land can continue potentially forever. However, when the land is no longer used as a park, Bob will get possession. Even if Bob played no part in terminating the land's use as a park, his interest is treated as divesting Ann's interest. Therefore, Bob has an executory interest.

Illustration: "To Ann for life, then to Bob, but if Bob marries, then to Cathy." While Ann is alive and Bob is unmarried, Bob has a future interest. Bob's interest is a vested remainder subject to condition subsequent. If Bob marries, the vested remainder is terminated. Because Cathy, rather than Bob, will get possession of the land at Ann's death, Cathy has divested Bob and, therefore, has an executory interest.

Illustration: "To Ann when she turns 21." If Ann is 19, the grantor's estate is a fee simple estate, because it can last forever if Ann dies before turning 21. However, the fee simple estate will be terminated if and when Ann turns 21, and Ann will get possession. In that case, Ann will divest the grantor and, therefore, has an executory interest.

2. Types of Remainders

After a future interest has been classified as a remainder, the next step is to determine the type of remainder that it is. Four types of remainders exist: (1) indefeasibly vested remainder, (2) vested remainder subject to open (also known as a vested remainder subject to partial divestiture), (3) vested remainder subject to condition subsequent (also known as vested remainder subject to total divestiture), and (4) contingent remainder (also known as remainder subject to condition precedent).

a. *Indefeasibly Vested Remainder*

To be indefeasibly vested, a remainder cannot be subject to a condition, and all its holders must be ascertainable.

Illustration: "To Ann for life, then to Bob." While Ann is alive, Bob's interest is an indefeasibly vested remainder. It is a remainder because it will become possessory as soon as Ann's life estate terminates and because it will not divest her. It is indefeasibly vested because it is not subject to a condition and because Bob is an ascertained person.

Illustration: "To Ann for life, then to Bob for life." Bob has an indefeasibly vested remainder. Although Bob's interest will become possessory only if he survives Ann, his remainder is not classified as being subject to a condition. Living long enough to get possession is an inherent feature of a life estate, rather than a condition.

b. *Vested Remainder Subject to Open (also known as Vested Remainder Subject to Partial Divestiture)*

When a remainder is conveyed to a class of people, such as "Bob's children," it is vested subject to open if at least one class member is ascertainable and if more members may be added to the class.

Illustration: "To Ann for life, then to Bob's children." If Bob has a child, Cathy, the remainder can vest in her because she is an ascertained person. Because Bob can have more children, Cathy's vested remainder is subject to open. When Bob has another child, Dan, Cathy and Dan each has a vested remainder subject to open. When Bob dies, no more class members can be born, so Cathy and Dan then will have indefeasibly vested remainders. On the other hand, if Bob does not have a child, the remainder cannot vest in anyone and, therefore, is a contingent remainder, which is the mere possibility of a vested property interest.

c. *Vested Remainder Subject to Condition Subsequent (also known as Vested Remainder Subject to Total Divestiture)*

If a remainder is subject to a condition, the condition must be classified as either a condition subsequent or a condition precedent. The distinction is important because the grant of a vested remainder subject to condition subsequent gives the grantee title to a future interest, though that title will be divested if the condition subsequently occurs. In contrast, the grantee of a remainder that is subject to a condition precedent (also known as a contingent remainder) does not have any title until the condition occurs. A condition is subsequent if it is in a separate clause that follows the words of conveyance to the grantee.

Illustration: "To Ann for life, then to Bob, but if Bob marries, to Cathy." Bob has a vested remainder subject to condition subsequent because the condition ("but if Bob marries") follows the words of conveyance ("to Bob") and is in a separate clause from the words of conveyance (i.e. is separated from the words of conveyance by a comma). Cathy has an executory interest because Bob's vested remainder will be divested if he marries.

d. *Contingent Remainder (also known as Remainder Subject to Condition Precedent)*

A contingent remainder occurs when (1) a remainder is subject to a condition precedent or (2) it is conveyed to an unborn or otherwise unascertainable person. A condition on a remainder is precedent if it is in the same clause as the words of conveyance or if it is in a separate clause that precedes the words of conveyance. If two contingent remainders are based on the same condition, they are "alternative contingent remainders."

Illustration: "To Ann for life, then to Bob if he survives Ann." Bob has a contingent remainder because the condition ("if he survives Ann") is in the same clause as the words of conveyance ("to Bob").

Illustration: "To Ann for life; if Bob survives Ann, then to Bob." Bob has a contingent remainder because the condition is in a clause that precedes the clause with the words of conveyance.

Illustration: "To Ann for life, then to Bob if he survives Ann, otherwise to Cathy." Bob and Cathy have alternative contingent remainders because they are based on the same condition—whether Bob survives Ann. Based on that condition, either Bob or Cathy will get possession when Ann dies. Unlike the Illustration for a vested remainder subject to condition subsequent, Cathy does not have an executory interest because Bob will not be divested if he dies before Ann. As the holder of a contingent remainder, Bob does not have a property interest. He has only the possibility of a property interest.

Illustration: "To Ann for life, then to her heirs." While Ann is alive, her heirs have a contingent remainder because they cannot be ascertained (the living have no heirs).

Illustration: "To Ann for life, then to Bob's children." If Bob does not have a child, the future interest following the life estate is a contingent remainder. A property interest can vest only in a living and identifiable person. When Bob has a child, the future interest will become a vested remainder subject to open.

3. Types of Executory Interests

Two types of executory interests exist—springing and shifting. If the grantor had possession of the property immediately before the executory interest became possessory, it is springing. If someone other than the grantor had possession immediately before the executory interest became possessory, it is shifting.

Illustration: "To Ann when she is 21." If Ann is 19, the grantor has a fee simple subject to executory limitation. Ann has a springing executory interest.

Illustration: "To Ann for so long as the land is used as a park, then to Bob." Ann has a fee simple subject to executory limitation, and Bob has a shifting executory interest.

C. TRANSFERABILITY OF INTERESTS

Vested interests generally were transferable at common law. The holder of a possessory estate, a vested remainder, or a reversion could convey it inter vivos and could devise it. When a future interest was conveyed at early common law, the consent of the holder of the present possessory estate often was required (attornment). Today, attornment generally is not required.

Partly because of their similarity to choses in action, nonvested future interests were initially not transferable or otherwise alienable at common law except to the owner of the possessory estate or to a vested remainder holder. Thus, a contingent remainder or power of termination could not be conveyed or devised. In the case of the power of termination, an attempted conveyance not only was ineffective, but also destroyed the power in many jurisdictions. Some states also prohibit an inter vivos conveyance of a possibility of reverter.

D. INHERITABILITY OF INTERESTS (INTESTATE SUCCESSION)

Any estate greater than a life estate was inheritable, unless the terms of a contingency made inheritability impossible, such as a contingency requiring a timely marriage by the remainder holder. In the following Illustrations, assume that Ann, the grantor, held in fee simple absolute.

Illustration: Ann conveyed "to Bob for life." Ann died intestate while Bob was still alive. Her reversion descended to her heirs. On Bob's death, Ann's heirs will have possession of the property.

Illustration: Ann conveyed "to Bob for life, remainder to Cathy and her heirs." Cathy died intestate while Bob was still alive. Cathy's vested remainder descended to her heirs at her death. When Bob dies, her heirs will have the fee simple absolute.

Illustration: Ann conveyed "to Bob and the heirs of his body, then to Cathy and her heirs." Cathy died before Bob's family line ended. Cathy's heirs will have the fee simple absolute whenever Bob's family line ends.

III. SPECIAL RULES CONCERNING FUTURE INTERESTS

A. RULE IN SHELLEY'S CASE

When a deed or will conveys an interest to a grantee and a future interest to that grantee's heirs, the Rule in Shelley's Case may apply. If it does, the heirs' interest instead will go to the grantee. If the grantee's interests are consecutive in time, they will merge to form one interest. The Rule is a rule of law and, therefore, applies regardless of the grantor's intent.

Although only a few states follow the Rule today, it still applies to conveyances that became effective before the Rule was repealed.

Illustration: Ann conveyed "to Bob for life, then to Bob's heirs." The Rule in Shelley's Case converts the remainder to Bob's heirs into a remainder in Bob. The Rule has changed the conveyance to "Bob for life, then to Bob." Because no interest separates Bob's two interests, they will merge together to form fee simple absolute.

Illustration: Ann conveyed to "to Bob for life, then to the heirs of Bob's body." The Rule in Shelley's Case converts the remainder to the heirs of Bob's body into a remainder in Bob. His two interests merge to give Bob a fee tail.

Illustration: Ann conveyed "to Bob for life, then to Cathy for life, then to Bob's heirs." The Rule in Shelley's Case converts the remainder to Bob's heirs into a remainder in Bob. In this situation, Bob's interests cannot merge because they are separated by Cathy's remainder. Therefore, Bob has a life estate and an indefeasibly vested remainder in fee simple absolute, and Cathy has an indefeasibly vested remainder in a life estate.

Illustration: Ann conveyed "to Bob for life, then to Cathy for life, then to Cathy's heirs." The Rule in Shelley's Case converts the remainder to Cathy's heirs into a remainder in Cathy. Cathy's two interests merge to give her an indefeasibly vested remainder in fee simple absolute.

Illustration: Ann conveyed "to Bob for life, remainder to his heirs. It is my intent that the Rule in Shelley's Case shall not apply so that I can provide for Bob's heirs." The Rule applies despite Ann's clear expression of intent, because it is a rule of law.

1. Rule's Elements

The Rule applies only if each of the following elements is satisfied. The Rule will not apply even if only one element is violated.

a. The Grantee's Interest must be a Freehold Estate

In the context of the Rule in Shelley's Case, this element requires the grantee to have a life estate or a fee tail.

Illustration: Ann conveyed "to Bob for life, then to Cathy for life, then to Cathy's heirs." While Bob is alive, Cathy has only a future interest. However, when Bob dies, Cathy will have a life estate, which is a freehold estate. Therefore, the Rule's requirement for a freehold is satisfied.

b. Grantee's Heirs must have a Remainder

If the grantee's heirs have an executory interest, the Rule does not apply.

Illustration: Ann conveyed "to Bob, but when the land is no longer used for a park, to Bob's heirs." Although Bob has a freehold estate—a defeasible fee— the Rule does not apply because Bob's heirs have an executory interest.

c. The Interests of the Grantee and of the Grantee's Heirs Must Have Been Conveyed in the Same Instrument

Illustration: Ann executed and delivered two deeds. In one deed, she conveyed land "to Bob for life." In the other deed, she conveyed the future interest following the life estate "to Bob's heirs." The Rule does not apply.

d. Remainder must use Words of Indefinite Succession

The Rule applies only if the grant of the remainder uses technical terms, such as "heirs" or "heirs of the body." Any limitation on those terms causes them to be words of definite succession.

Illustration: Ann conveyed "to Bob for life, remainder to his heirs if they have treated Bob, their father, kindly." The Rule does not apply because the reference to "their father" indicates that the grantor meant Bob's children, rather than all his lineal descendants.

e. Grantee's and Grantee's Heirs' Interests both must be Legal or both must be Equitable

For the Rule to apply, both interests must be conveyed outright (legal) or both must be conveyed in trust (equitable).

Illustration: Ann conveyed "to First National Bank in trust for Bob for life, then to Bob's heirs." Bob has an equitable life estate because it was conveyed in trust for him with First National Bank as the trustee. Bob's heirs have a legal remainder because it was conveyed to them directly, rather than in trust for them. Therefore, the Rule does not apply.

f. Real Property

The Rule applies only to conveyances of real property.

B. DOCTRINE OF WORTHIER TITLE

When a deed or will conveys an interest to a grantee and a future interest to the grantor's heirs, the Doctrine of Worthier Title may apply. If it does, the grantor's heirs will not acquire an interest. Instead, the grantor will retain that interest as a reversion.

The Doctrine still exists in about forty states. Unlike the Rule in Shelley's Case, it normally operates as a presumption, rather than as a rule of law. Therefore, the Doctrine does not apply if it would violate the grantor's intent.

Illustration: Ann conveyed "to Bob for life, then to Ann's heirs." Bob has a life estate. If the Doctrine of Worthier Title applies, Ann will have a reversion following the life estate, and her heirs will have no interest.

1. Doctrine's Elements

The Doctrine applies only if each of the following elements is satisfied.

a. Grantee's Interest must be a Freehold

The grantee can have a defeasible fee, fee tail, or life estate.

b. Grantor's Heirs can have a Remainder or an Executory Interest

Unlike the Rule in Shelley's Case, the Doctrine applies even if the heirs have an executory interest.

c. Grantee's and Grantor's Heir' Interests must be in same Instrument

Illustration: Ann conveyed "to Bob for life." Later, she conveyed her interest following Bob's life estate to her heirs. The Doctrine does not apply.

d. Grantor's Heirs' Interest must use Words of Indefinite Succession

The Doctrine applies only if the conveyance to the grantor's heirs uses technical terms, such as "heirs." Any limitation on those terms causes them to be words of definite succession, and the Doctrine will not apply. The Doctrine also does not apply to a conveyance to a named individual who turns out to be the grantor's heir.

e. The Doctrine Applies to Real and Personal Property

Unlike the Rule in Shelley's Case, the Doctrine applies to personal property, as well as to real property.

C. DOCTRINE OF DESTRUCTIBILITY OF CONTINGENT REMAINDERS

If a jurisdiction follows this doctrine, contingent remainders can be destroyed if (1) the contingent remainder cannot vest when the prior freehold estate terminates or (2) one person acquires the vested interests immediately preceding and succeeding the contingent remainder.

1. Contingent Remainder Unable to Vest

A contingent remainder is destroyed if it cannot vest when the prior freehold estate terminates. Whether the prior estate terminated by its terms or by renunciation is irrelevant.

Illustration: Ann conveyed "to Bob for life, then to Cathy if she is 21." If Bob dies when Cathy is 19, her contingent remainder is destroyed, and Ann will have the fee simple absolute title.

Illustration: Ann conveyed "to Bob for life, then to Cathy if she is 21 before Bob dies, otherwise to Dan." If Bob renounces his life estate before Cathy is 21, neither Cathy's nor Dan's contingent remainder can vest because it is unknown whether Cathy will turn 21 before Bob dies. Therefore, Ann will have the fee simple absolute title.

Illustration: Ann conveyed "to Bob for life, then to Cathy for life, then to Dan if he is 21." Bob dies before Dan is 21, but Cathy is still alive. Dan's contingent remainder is not destroyed, because his interest cannot become possessory until Cathy's life estate ends. However, his contingent remainder will be destroyed if he is not 21 before then.

2. Merger

Merger applies when one person owns two consecutive interests in land.

Illustration: Ann conveyed "to Bob for life." Bob later bought Ann's reversion from her. Because Bob now owns two consecutive interests in land—the life estate and the reversion in fee simple absolute that follows it—the two interests merge to form fee simple absolute.

Merger can destroy contingent remainders because they are only the possibility of a property interest. The holder of a contingent remainder has no ownership interest in the land. Therefore, if one person owns the property interest immediately preceding a contingent remainder and the interest immediately following it, those two interests will merge, thereby destroying the contingent remainder. However, merger will not destroy a contingent remainder if the interests immediately before and after it are conveyed to the same person in the same instrument, unless they later are conveyed to a third person.

Illustration: Ann conveyed "to Bob for life, then to Cathy if she is 21." Because Cathy's contingent remainder is not a property interest, Ann has a reversion following Bob's life estate. If Bob acquires Ann's reversion, he will be deemed to have two consecutive interests, as in the last Illustration. However, by merging Bob's interests in this Illustration, Cathy's contingent remainder is destroyed. The same result would occur if Ann had acquired Bob's life estate.

Illustration: Ann conveyed "to Bob for life, then to Bob's children who survive him for their lives, then to Bob and his heirs." While Bob is alive, his children have a contingent remainder. Merger does not destroy it because Bob acquired both his interests in the same document. However, if Bob conveys both his interests to Cathy, the contingent remainder will be destroyed.

D. RULE AGAINST PERPETUITIES

1. The Rule

"No interest is good unless it must vest, if at all, not later than 21 years after some life in being at the creation of the interest." This was common law version of the Rule. The Rule is concerned only with the remoteness of vesting and not with the duration of the interests once vested or with their alienability. Interests that may vest too remotely are void and are stricken from the conveyance.

2. Measuring the Time Period

An interest has to vest within 21 years, plus a period of gestation, after some life in being. If any possibility exists that the interest might vest at a later time, the interest is void.

Illustration: Ann conveyed "to Bob for life, then to Bob's children who reach 25." The gift to the children is void, because it could vest more than 21 years after the termination of all lives presently in being—the grantor, Bob, and Bob's children who are now living. However, if the doctrine of destructibility of contingent remainders applies in the jurisdiction where this gift occurs, the gift is valid, because Bob's children must be 25 by his death to take, and the possibility of taking long after his death no longer exists.

Illustration: Ann created an inter vivos trust "to my grandchildren when they reach 21." The gift is invalid. Ann may have additional children, and they cannot be used as measuring lives because they are not now lives in being. Those unborn children may have children of their own (Ann's grandchildren) who will not become 21 until more than 21 years after the settlor and all her presently existing children are dead.

3. Rule's Applicability to Different Interests

a. Contingent Remainders

Contingent remainders must be certain to vest within the perpetuities period, or they are void.

Illustration: Ann conveyed "to Bob for life, remainder to his children for their lives, and upon the death of the last of them, remainder to their children who are living at the time of Bob's death and their heirs." The gift to the grandchildren is a contingent remainder. However, the remainder will vest within the perpetuities period. The contingent remainder will become a vested remainder when Bob dies, because the gift is limited to those who are living when Bob dies. The gift is valid.

Illustration: Ann conveyed "to Bob for life, remainder to his children for their lives, and upon the death of the last of them, remainder to their children and their heirs." The gift to Bob's grandchildren is invalid. The contingent remainder will not vest in interest until the last of Bob's children dies, which may be more than 21 years after the death of all lives in being now since Bob may have more children. It does not matter that Bob may now be eighty years old. The law conclusively presumes him to be capable of having more children (the "fertile octogenarian").

b.   Executory Interests

Executory interests are not vested until they vest in possession. There is no such thing as a vested executory interest.

Illustration: Ann devised land "to Bob and his heirs, but if liquor is ever sold on the land, then to Cathy and her heirs." The gift to Cathy fails. This shifting executory interest may not become possessory until more than 21 years after the lives of Bob and Cathy.

Illustration: Ann conveyed "to Bob and his heirs once my will is probated." This springing executory interest to Bob fails, for it is possible (though unlikely) that it will take more than 21 years after the measuring lives to probate the will.

c. *Vested Remainders Generally are not Subject to the Rule*

Generally, the Rule does not apply to vested remainders because they already are vested. But a gift to a class of people is treated differently. Courts hold that the gift must vest in every member of the class in time.

Illustration: Ann conveyed "to Bob for life and then to all his children when they reach the age of 25." Bob has a son who is presently 25. The remainder is vested subject to open because that son is ready to take. But because Bob could have more children in the future who could reach 25 more than 21 years after the deaths of Bob and his living son, the gift fails as to all Bob's children.

d. *Reversions*

Reversions are always vested estates and, therefore, are not subject to the Rule. A reversion may not always become possessory, such as when it follows a contingent remainder and the contingency occurs in time. But it is a vested interest from the moment it is created.

e. *Powers of Termination and Possibilities of Reverter*

Powers of termination and possibilities of reverter are not subject to the Rule. Like a reversion, a power of termination is the portion of the estate remaining with the grantor after a conveyance of less than her entire interest in the land. Therefore, also like a reversion, it is vested from the moment of its creation.

In contrast, the power of termination is not a vested interest. However, because this interest was legally recognized for two centuries before the Rule was created, the Rule has not been extended to destroy powers of termination.

f. Other Interests

Options to purchase land and powers of appointment are subject to the Rule.

4. Consequences of Violating Rule

If a gift violates the Rule, it is stricken, and the rest of the limitation stands as written, unless the grantor's intent is better served by reserving a future interest to her.

Illustration: Ann conveyed "to Bob and his heirs, but if liquor is ever sold on the land, to Cathy and her heirs." The gift to Cathy fails, but the gift to Bob remains valid. It is now a fee simple absolute, unless the grantor's intent would be better served by keeping the condition on the title. In that case, Bob would have a fee simple subject to condition subsequent, and Ann would have a power of termination.

5. Modern Revisions to Rule

Approximately half the jurisdictions have abandoned the common law version of the Rule and have replaced it with a less demanding version, either by statute or by court decision.

a. *Wait-and-See*

In some jurisdictions, the validity of a future interest is tested against the facts as they actually occur, rather than against the worst possible set of facts when the grant is made. In all the previous Illustrations, the question in a wait-and-see jurisdiction is not whether the future interests described there *might* vest outside the measuring period, but whether they did under the actual facts of the case. Thus, the validity of an interest is determined later, rather than immediately.

Illustration: Ann conveyed "to Bob and his heirs, but if liquor is ever sold on the land, to Cathy and her heirs." If Bob sells liquor before he dies, Cathy's executory interest is valid. But if liquor is not sold until more than 21 years after both Bob and Cathy die, that executory interest (now held by Cathy's heirs or devisees) is invalidated.

b. *Cy Pres*

Another approach to modifying the Rule is to reform the grant to validate as much of it as possible to effectuate the grantor's intent to the greatest possible extent. This approach may be combined with the wait-and-see principle.

Illustration: Using the same wording as in the prior Illustration, a court may treat the grant as restricting liquor sales only during Bob's life, thereby saving much of the restriction.

IV. WASTE

A. PARTIES

When title to land has been divided into a presently possessory interest and a future interest, the law of waste prevents the present possessor from causing undue harm to the property. The law of waste is designed to protect future interest holders, as well as nonpossessing co-owners and, sometimes, mortgagees.

B. POLICY

The basic theory of waste law is that the future interest holder is entitled to receive the property in the same condition as when the future interest was created, ordinary wear and tear excepted. Thus, waste is often defined as the commission of any act that alters the character of the property. Waste law may even prohibit "ameliorating" waste—changes that increase the land's value but that change the land's character. More commonly today, however, waste is defined in terms of impairing the value of the future interest.

Illustration: Owen leaves his house to his wife for life and then to his children and their heirs. Unless he explicitly indicated to the contrary, Owen's wife will be limited in her use of the property to ensure that the children receive the full economic benefit of the house. This means that Owen's wife may be prohibited from activities such as cutting and selling timber and removing minerals.

C. TYPES

1. Active Waste

This type of waste consists of affirmative acts done by the possessor that harm the property. It is also known as affirmative, voluntary, or commissive waste.   *Per se* acts of waste at common law included cutting mature trees (except for cultivation, repairs, or fuel), changing the agricultural use of the land, opening new mines to remove minerals, and demolishing structures not erected by the occupant. These are all acts that destroy existing features of the property or that exploit limited resources. Today, these acts usually are characterized as waste only when they cause economic harm. Where the acts are done willfully, they may constitute malicious or wanton waste, and the damages for the waste may be trebled.

2. Passive Waste

This type of waste consists of the failure to make normal repairs to the property to prevent significant deterioration, such as keeping a building windtight and watertight. It is also known as permissive waste. It does not require a possessor to rebuild structures destroyed by an act of nature. The cases are divided concerning the possessor's liability to rebuild if a third party destroys the improvements. However, even when the possessor is not liable, a duty may exist to protect the premises from further harm, such as by boarding up a burned building. The failure to make hazard insurance, tax, or mortgage payments may be treated as a form of economic waste, because the consequences can be uncompensated damage to the property if it is uninsured or forfeiture of the title for nonpayment of taxes or the mortgage.

3. Ameliorating Waste

Ameliorating waste (also known as meliorating waste) consists of a change in the property's use that *increases* its economic value. For example, a life tenant commits ameliorating waste if she demolishes a house and replaces it with an apartment building. The underlying notion is that the future interest holder is entitled to receive the property in the same condition as the present interest holder received it. However, a court may refuse to find waste if the property no longer is usable in its existing condition.

D. REMEDIES

Damages for waste equal the cost of restoration if the action is brought when the future interest holder takes possession or the reduction in the present market value of the future interest if brought before then. Equity may enjoin the commission of active waste or appoint a receiver to stop passive waste

V. RESTRAINTS ON ALIENATION

Special rules deal with the validity of a provision that purports to limit the right of the holder of an estate to transfer it to other persons. The legal effectiveness of such a provision generally depends upon what type of restraint it is.

A. DISABLING RESTRAINTS

The terms of the grant may deny the grantee the power to transfer the estate to anyone else or may declare that any attempted transfer is void. With the exception of spendthrift trusts (not covered in this book), such disabling provisions are void.

B. FORFEITURE RESTRAINTS

By its terms, a qualified grant may provide that any attempt to transfer title will terminate ownership. Courts often uphold this type of restraint if it is restricted as to duration or persons.

Provisions giving the grantor the right to repurchase the property or to match a third person's offer before selling it (preemptive rights) are usually upheld.

Where an estate smaller than a fee simple is involved, a forfeiture restraint is more likely to be upheld. For example, a lease provision prohibiting the tenant from assigning or subletting the property without the landlord's consent is usually valid, as are similar restrictions on life estates, installment land contracts, and options.

C. PROMISSORY RESTRAINTS

The grant may include a covenant by the grantee not to alienate the property. Courts generally decide the validity of such promissory restraints according to the same principles as govern forfeiture restraints. Co-owners of property who covenant not to partition it often do so by way of mutual promises and may be entitled to have the covenants specifically enforced. However, restrictive covenants that prohibit conveyances to a person based on race, religion, sex, national origin, color, familial status, handicap, and other factors violate federal, state, and local fair housing laws.

VI. MARITAL ESTATES

The spouses in a legally recognized marriage may acquire a life estate in the lands of the other if certain conditions are met. These are "legal" life estates, because they are created by operation of law, rather than by a voluntary conveyance.

A. WIFE'S ESTATE—DOWER

Upon the death of her husband, a wife receives a life estate in one-third of certain lands owned by her husband during their marriage.

1. Conditions for Dower

a. Freehold Estate

The husband must have owned a freehold estate (seisin) in the land during the marriage.

Illustration: Hubert owned the fee simple absolute title to Blackacre. He conveyed it to Xerxes before marrying Wilma. Wilma has no dower rights in Blackacre because Hubert did no own it during their marriage.

Illustration: Hubert owned the fee simple absolute title to Blackacre when he married Wilma. If Hubert conveys Blackacre to Xerxes, Wilma still has dower rights in it because Hubert owned it during their marriage. Hubert need not own the land throughout the entire marriage or even at his death so long as he owned it sometime during the marriage.

Illustration: Hubert had a term for years in Blackacre when he married Wilma. He subsequently conveyed the land to Xerxes. Wilma does not have dower rights in

Blackacre because Hubert did not have a freehold estate. A term for years is a nonfreehold estate.

Illustration: Hubert had a remainder in fee simple in Blackacre but died before it became possessory. Wilma has no dower rights, because Hubert never possessed a freehold estate. Whether the remainder was vested or contingent is irrelevant.

Illustration: Hubert is trustee of a fee simple for the benefit of a beneficiary. Wilma has no dower rights, because Hubert has only bare legal title.

b. *Inheritability*

The estate must be inheritable by the wife's issue for her to claim dower at her husband's death. The wife need not have issue in fact, so long as any such issue would qualify as heirs of the husband. Thus, an estate held in fee simple by the husband is subject to dower because any issue of the marriage would qualify as heirs of the husband, even if in fact the marriage produces no offspring.

A fee tail is subject to dower even though death without issue otherwise would terminate the estate. In that case, the fee tail will not terminate until the widow dies, because her dower is viewed as an extension of the fee tail. If there are issue of the marriage, they do not take the wife's share until she dies, thereby terminating her dower interest. If the estate is fee tail special, excluding issue of the present wife, she cannot claim dower even though her husband died with other issue capable of inheriting the estate.

There is no dower in a life estate measured by the husband's life, because this estate is not inheritable by her issue.

2. Extent of Dower

a. *Before Husband's Death*

Before her husband's death, a wife has no estate in his lands. At this point, her dower interest is called dower inchoate. This interest is protected by the courts against fraudulent transfers by her husband.

b. *After Husband's Death*

After her husband's death, dower gives the wife a life estate in one-third of the lands subject to her dower interest. Usually, the husband's heir sets aside an appropriate share for her. If the wife is dissatisfied, she may go to court for judicial allocation.

B. HUSBAND'S ESTATE

The nature of the husband's interest in his wife's estate depends on their stage of life.

1. Upon Marriage and Before the Birth of Issue – *Jure Uxoris*

In this situation, the common law gave the husband a right by *jure uxoris* (right of marriage). In effect, *jure uxoris* was a life estate measured by the husband's and wife's joint lives. It terminated upon the death of either unless it had been replaced by curtesy.

2. Upon Birth of Live Issue – Curtesy Initiate

If a child was born alive and if the wife did not die in childbirth, the husband's shared freehold (*jure uxoris*) was converted into a life estate in his own right in all his wife's freeholds. This life estate was measured only by his life. His previous smaller life estate (measured by the husband's and the wife's joint lives) merged into it. Curtesy initiate existed in all the wife's freeholds that were inheritable by issue of the marriage. Unlike dower, curtesy initiate included the wife's equitable estates. Because a husband had a present life estate in his wife's lands, all that she could claim was a reversion, which would become possessory if she survived her husband.

3. After the Wife's Death – Curtesy Consummate

Once his wife died, the husband's curtesy initiate became curtesy consummate. His right was not limited to one-third of her property, as is true of dower. Instead, it applied to all property in which she had a freehold interest. Since he already was entitled to possession, there was no change in that regard. The issue born alive need not still be living at the wife's death.

C. MODERN STATUTORY FORCED SHARE

Dower and curtesy have been replaced in virtually every jurisdiction by statutes that provide a share of the decedent's estate to the surviving spouse. The surviving spouse typically is given a specified share of the decedent's estate even if the decedent intended to leave nothing to the survivor.

D. COMMUNITY PROPERTY

Some jurisdictions have community property ownership, which is a form of marital co-ownership derived from the civil law system. It is based on the principle that both spouses contribute equally to a marriage and, therefore, should own equal shares in all property acquired during the marriage even if the title is in just one spouse's name. In general, property may be held as community property only between parties who are legally married, although certain similar property rights may be held to exist between persons who believe they are married, hold themselves out as married, or, sometimes, merely live together.

Community property rights vary widely among the states that recognize them. Generally, however, "community property" includes everything the spouses acquire during their marriage. Wages earned by either spouse during the marriage are usually the most significant form of community income, together with income closely related to wages, such as pensions (saved wages) and personal injury awards (wage substitutes). Any asset acquired with such income also becomes a community asset.

"Separate property," which includes property either spouse owned before the marriage, is not converted into community property by marriage. The income earned from separate assets, such as dividends from separately owned stock, is commonly treated as separate property, though not always. Generally, gifts received by one spouse also are treated as his or her separate property. Property that the spouses acquire during the marriage but to which they take title as tenants in common or joint tenants is also separate property. However, some states have a presumption that family residences are community property even if the title appears otherwise.

Separate property may be transmuted into community property, and vice versa, by agreement or by gift between the spouses. Where spouses have "commingled" separate and community funds, a court either will trace currently-held assets to their separate original sources or, if untraceable, will treat such assets as being entirely community property.

The Uniform Marital Property Act, which has been adopted in Wisconsin, employs the same principles as community property, though the terminology is different. "Marital property" is equivalent to "community property," and "individual property" is equivalent to "separate property" in community property jurisdictions.

Illustration: When Bob and Ann married, he moved into the house she owned. The house was originally Ann's separate property and did not become community property because she married or because Bob moved in (unless it can be shown that she elected to make it a gift to Bob or to the community). After the marriage, community income (wages) was used to pay for the balance of mortgage on the house. Whose wages were used is irrelevant, because Bob's and Ann's incomes both are community property. Therefore, the house is now either partly Ann's separate property (the share she owned before the marriage) and partly community property or entirely community property if tracing cannot allocate the respective interests. Ann would have to show that Bob made a gift of all his interest in the community earnings to her to make the entire house her separate property. Bob would have to show that Ann made a gift of her separate interest in the house to him or to the community to claim a larger share of it.

Illustration: Before marrying Bob, Ann owned and managed an apartment building. After their marriage, she continued managing the building and used the rents from it to buy a car. The apartment building was and is Ann's separate property, and much of the rent it produced is therefore also her separate property. However, to the extent that the rental income is attributable to her management efforts, it is community income because it is earnings for her services. It also makes some part of the car community property, rather than her separate property.

Illustration: As a wedding present, Ann's parents purchased a house for Ann and Bob. If her parents conveyed the title only to Ann, it is probably her separate property because it was a gift. This also would be true if Bob paid for the house with money he inherited before the wedding and put title in Ann's name. However, if her parents put the title in both names, it would be community property unless the deed said "to Ann and Bob as joint tenants." In that case, both spouses would have separate property interests as joint tenants, unless residential joint tenancies are presumed by state law to be community property or unless Ann and Bob agreed it was community property notwithstanding the form of the title.

1. Community Ownership's Characteristics

a. *Management and Control*

In earlier years, the husband had the sole power to manage and control the community property and could convey it without his wife's signature or consent. Today, spouses generally are given equal rights to management and control, and both may be required to join in the execution of any document affecting title.

Illustration: Ann and Bob, spouses, hold title to their house in joint tenancy. If this truly is a joint tenancy, either may convey his or her half interest without the knowledge or consent of the other. The grantee would be a tenant in common with the other spouse, because the joint tenancy is severed by the conveyance. But if the house is deemed to be community property, a deed executed by just one spouse cannot transfer any part of the title. The same may be true for mortgages executed by only one spouse.

b. Severance

Unlike property owned in joint tenancy, community property cannot be severed, because neither spouse alone can convey any fractional interest in the property. Also unlike property owned in joint tenancy or tenancy in common, community property cannot be partitioned by a court in an ordinary judicial proceeding. Instead, it is divided between the spouses in a marital dissolution proceeding.

c. Death Transfers

Each spouse has testamentary control over one-half the community property. If this power is not exercised, that half will pass to the surviving spouse.   In this respect, community property resembles the right of survivorship in joint tenancy and tenancy by the entirety.   But it resembles tenancy in common if a spouse dies testate, because the property will be distributed according to the terms of the will, rather than automatically going to the surviving spouse.

d. Liabilities

Community property cannot be seized to satisfy the separate debts of either spouse, such as debts incurred before marriage.   For those claims, a creditor must look solely to the debtor spouse's separate property. Debts incurred by either spouse during the marriage may or may not entitle the creditor to reach community assets for satisfaction. The answer depends on whether the debt was a community debt, was acknowledged by both spouses, was for common necessities, was based in contract or tort, and other factors relevant under local law.

VII. RULES REGULATING EARLY COMMON LAW ESTATES

Note that the rules described in this section of the book are primarily of historical interest. As you will see, many of them use the word "seisin." The meaning of "seisin" evolved during the earliest centuries of the common law.   Very generally speaking, however, it is equivalent to our modern conception of ownership.

A. LEGAL INTERESTS IN LAND

1. Seisin can never be in Abeyance

Someone always must be seised of the land.

2. Seisin Passes out of the Grantor Only by Livery

Livery was necessary for a grantor to transfer seisin. To perform a livery of seisin, the grantor and grantee would go to the land to be transferred, and the grantor (feoffor) would hand a clod of dirt or other part of the land to the grantee (feoffee). This ceremony was called a feoffment. It immediately transferred seisin to the feoffee without the necessity for a writing.

Seisin sometimes could go from one grantee to another without livery. When seisin was not involved, as in the case of an estate for years or other nonfreehold estate, feoffment was not required. Similarly, the transfer of a nonpossessory future interest did not require a feoffment.

3. No Springing Interests (No Freehold to Commence in Future)

Because seisin can pass from a grantor to a grantee only by livery, a grantor cannot give a grantee a freehold estate to begin in the future unless it is supported by some present estate in a third person. Either the grantee gets the seisin by livery now, in which event he has a present estate, or he must get seisin from the grantor at a later time, in which case the livery of seisin will have to be made then.

Illustration: Ann conveys "to Bob and his heirs one year from now." Bob has nothing. Ann must have the seisin for this year, or it would be in abeyance. Bob can get seisin only if Ann makes a livery next year. If Bob did have an interest now, it would require that an estate "spring" out of Ann's estate next year. The rule against springing interests prevented this from happening.

a. Remainder Cannot Spring

Illustration: Ann conveys "to myself for life, and then to Bob and his heirs." The gift to Bob is invalid. As a remainder, it would have to spring, which is not allowed. For Bob to take, Ann must make livery of seisin to Bob, which cannot be done now because Ann wants a presently possessory life estate. Ann cannot make livery when her life estate terminates because she will be dead.

Illustration: Ann conveyed "to Bob for life, and one year later to Cathy and her heirs." The gift to Cathy fails. Bob received seisin, but it will revert to Ann upon his death because Cathy is not to be seised until a year later and seisin cannot be in abeyance. Seisin in Ann, the grantor, can be transferred to Cathy only by livery, which clearly cannot be done now. If Cathy's remainder became possessory, it would have to spring out of Ann's reversion without a livery. But a remainder cannot spring, and so Cathy gets nothing.

b. Remainder must be Created in same Document as Estate Supporting it

The holder of a possessory estate is deemed to accept seisin for both herself and for any remainder holder. Therefore, when the first estate terminates, seisin goes directly to the remainder holder without reverting back to the grantor. However, for this theory to work, the remainder must be given in the same instrument as the prior possessory estate.

Illustration: Ann conveyed "to Bob for life and then to Cathy and her heirs." Cathy's vested remainder in fee simple is valid. Seisin passed immediately from Ann to Bob, who holds it both for himself and for Cathy. When Bob dies, seisin will pass to Cathy from him. Because the grantor is no longer involved, seisin may pass at a later time without livery. The rule barring transfers of seisin without livery refers only to transfers from the grantor. Bob is not a grantor in relation to Cathy.

Illustration: Ann conveyed "to Bob for life" in one document and "to Cathy and her heirs when Bob dies" in another document. Cathy's interest is invalid, because it would be a springing remainder. Bob cannot be said to hold seisin for Cathy, because she was not a grantee in the conveyance to Bob. So Cathy must get seisin from Ann, if from anyone. But that would involve a transfer of seisin from the grantor in the future without livery, which is impossible. To avoid this problem, Ann could have transferred her reversion to Cathy by deed of grant, which would make Cathy a reversioner, rather than a remainder holder.

(1) Application to Nonfreeholds

The rule that remainders must be created in the same document applies whether the supporting estate is a freehold or a nonfreehold.

Illustration: Ann conveys "to Bob for ten years, and then to Cathy and her heirs." Cathy has a valid estate. Livery of seisin can be made presently either directly to Cathy, because Bob's nonfreehold estate does not give him seisin, or to Bob as Cathy's agent. In this case, characterizing Cathy's estate as a remainder in fee simple after Bob's term is permissible, but it was more descriptive and accurate at common law to say that Cathy had fee simple subject to Bob's term, thereby indicating that Cathy has seisin.

c. No Contingent Remainder after Term of Years

Illustration: Ann conveys "to Bob for ten years, and then to Cathy's heirs." If Cathy is alive when the conveyance is made, the gift to her heirs fails because it is a gift of a contingent remainder (unascertained takers). An unascertained taker cannot be seised, and, therefore, Bob cannot hold seisin for them as their agent. Bob does not have seisin for himself because he has a nonfreehold estate. Therefore, seisin remains in Ann. For Cathy's heirs to take, they would have to receive seisin from Ann even if they can be ascertained before Bob's death. The heirs would take by a springing remainder if they took. Therefore, "no contingent remainder can be supported by a term of years" is another way of saying "no springing remainders."

4. No Shifting Interests—No Condition in a Stranger

Illustration: Ann conveyed "to Bob and his heirs, but if Bob ever sells liquor on the land, then to Cathy and her heirs." At early common law, Cathy's estate would fail, because she cannot get seisin. Bob cannot hold seisin for Cathy, because Cathy does not have a remainder. The holder of a present estate can accept seisin for himself and for his remainder holders because a remainder does not become possessory until the prior estate naturally terminates. But in this case, Cathy's interest will divest Bob's interest. Therefore, seisin cannot pass from Bob to Cathy. When Bob's estate ends, seisin must revert to Ann. If it then automatically transferred to Cathy, it would be an impermissible springing interest. Thus, there can be "no condition in a stranger."

B. EQUITABLE INTERESTS IN LAND—USES

Because seisin passed only by livery at common law, the grantee would have no legally recognized interest in the land unless livery was made directly to him or to his agent. However, the court of equity recognized certain situations in which a person acquired the land though seisin had not been transferred to him by livery.

1. Equitable Conveyances

Certain conveyancing methods enabled the court of equity to treat a person as having a *use* (an equity) of the land, even though seisin was in someone else.

a. Conveyance for Use

Illustration: Ann conveyed by livery "to Bob and his heirs for the use of Cathy and her heirs." Although Bob is seised, equity would regard Cathy as having the use of the land in fee simple, even though she does not have legal title. Equity would compel Bob to put the land to Cathy's use. Today, this document would be construed as a conveyance to Bob in trust for Cathy.

b. Covenant to Stand Seised

Illustration: Ann covenanted "to stand seised to the use of my brother, Bob, and his heirs." Without livery, Bob does not have seisin. However, equity would give Bob the use in fee simple because a covenant was made and because Bob, the cestui que use (i.e. the beneficiary), is a relative.

c. Bargain and Sale Deed

Illustration: Ann gave a bargain and sale deed to Bob and his heirs. The deed recited a valuable consideration, which creates a conclusive presumption. Without livery, Bob does not have seisin. But because consideration was given, Bob is the equitable owner and has a use in fee simple.

d. Resulting Use

Illustration: Ann conveyed by livery to Bob, but Bob gave no consideration. Although Bob has seisin, equity creates a resulting use for Ann because of the absence of consideration.

2. Uses Compared to Common Law Estates

Uses can be possessory or nonpossessory (future interests). They can be a life estate, fee tail, fee simple, reversion, or vested or contingent remainder. All the legal rules relating to remainders apply to equitable remainders.

Illustration: Ann conveyed "to Bob and his heirs for the use of Cathy for life, and then for the use of Don and his heirs if Don survives Cathy, or if Don does not survive Cathy, then to the use of Eve and her heirs." Bob has the legal fee simple. Cathy has an equitable life estate. Don and Eve have alternative equitable contingent remainders in fee simple absolute. Because no vested remainder in fee simple absolute has been given, Ann has an equitable reversion in fee simple absolute and may take possession if both contingent remainders are destroyed. This is the way the estate would look at common law without the uses.

3. New Equitable Estates (Executory Interests)

Considerations of seisin prevented remainders from springing or shifting as a matter of law. But because seisin is in someone else when a use is involved, no reason exists in equity to bar springing and shifting uses.   Therefore, equity recognized these interests, which were called executory limitations (executory interests).

a. *Springing Use*

A springing use springs out of the grantor's estate in the future.

Illustration: Ann bargains and sells "to Bob for life and, one year after Bob's death, to Cathy and her heirs." Cathy's interest cannot be a remainder, because it will not become possessory immediately upon termination of Bob's life estate.   The interest springs out of the grantor's interest one year after Bob's life estate ends. Therefore, Bob has a life estate, Ann has a reversion in fee simple subject to executory limitation, and Cathy has a springing executory limitation. All these estates are equitable, because Ann has legal title.

Illustration: Ann bargains and sells "to Bob for ten years and then to Cathy's heirs." Cathy is alive. The gift to her heirs is an executory limitation. It cannot be a remainder, because it would be a contingent remainder, which cannot be supported by a term of years. Therefore, Bob has a term for years, and Ann has fee simple subject to Bob's term and subject to a springing executory limitation in fee simple absolute in Cathy's heirs. All these estates are equitable. Ann has legal title.

b. *Shifting Use*

A shifting use shifts possession from one grantee to another grantee.   The second grantee has an executory interest, because it divests the first grantee's interest when the shift occurs.

Illustration: Ann bargains and sells "to Bob and his heirs, but if liquor is ever sold on the land, then to Cathy and her heirs." Cathy has a shifting executory limitation because, if liquor is sold on the land, possession shifts from Bob to Cathy. Cathy's interest cannot be a remainder because it divests Bob's prior fee estate by cutting it short. Cathy's interest is characterized as "divesting" Bob's interest even though she had nothing to do with liquor being sold on the land. Therefore, Bob has fee simple subject to executory limitation (also called a fee simple subject to an executory interest), and Cathy has a shifting executory limitation in fee simple. Both estates are equitable. Ann has legal title.

Illustration: Ann bargains and sells "to Bob for life and then to Cathy and her heirs." Cathy has a remainder and not an executory interest. A remainder can become possessory immediately upon the natural termination of the prior estate and not sooner or later. In contrast, an executory interest always takes either before the prior estate naturally would terminate (shifting interest) or remotely after it terminates (springing interest). In this Illustration, Cathy's interest becomes possessory immediately upon the natural termination of Bob's life estate, so it is a remainder, just as it would be if there had been a common law livery to Bob. However, because there was no livery, it is an equitable remainder.

4. Indestructibility of Executory Interests

The doctrine of destructibility of contingent remainders was a corollary of the rule against springing remainders. But because uses can spring, executory interests are indestructible.

Illustration: Ann bargains and sells "to Bob for ten years and then to Cathy's heirs." The executory interest in Cathy's heirs is indestructible. Therefore, it will continue in existence even if Bob predeceases Cathy. Therefore, Bob has a term for years, Ann has a reversion in fee simple subject to executory interest, and Cathy's heirs have a springing executory interest in fee simple absolute. All these interests are equitable. Whenever Cathy dies, her heirs will get the equitable fee simple. If Cathy predeceases Bob, her heirs will have fee simple subject to Bob's term. If Bob predeceases Cathy, Ann's reversion becomes possessory until Cathy dies.

Illustration: Ann bargains and sells "to Bob for life, and then to Cathy and her heirs if Cathy is 21." Bob dies before Cathy is 21. Cathy has nothing because her interest was an equitable contingent remainder and not an executory interest. Contingent remainders are destructible even in equity. This remainder was destroyed by its failure to vest when the life estate terminated. NOTE: The great majority of jurisdictions have abolished the doctrine of destructibility of contingent remainders.

5. Statute of Uses (1536)

The Statute of Uses provided in part: "Where any person be seised of lands to the use or trust of any other person, such person that shall have the use or trust in fee simple, fee-tail, for term of life or for years, shall from henceforth be deemed in lawful seisin and possession in such like estates as [he] had in use [or] trust." In other words, the Statute "executed" uses by transferring seisin from the trustee to the cestui (beneficiary).

Illustration: Ann made livery "to Bob and his heirs for the use of Cathy and her heirs." By its terms, this conveyance gave seisin to Bob for the use of Cathy. Despite this language, the Statute executes the use and gives seisin to Cathy. Instead of Bob having legal fee simple and Cathy having equitable fee simple, Cathy has legal fee simple.

Illustration: Ann bargains and sells "to Bob and his heirs." Before the Statute, Ann retained the legal fee simple, and Bob had the equitable fee simple. Now, Bob has legal fee simple.

Illustration: Ann made livery "to Bob and his heirs for the use of Cathy for ten years." Cathy's equitable use for a term becomes a legal term for years. The Statute does not require that the cestui have a freehold. Ann has a resulting use for the "reversion" following the term unless Bob gave consideration. If Ann had a resulting use, the Statute would execute it and give her the legal fee simple subject to Cathy's term.

Illustration: Ann conveys "to Bob for ten years for the use of Cathy for ten years." The Statute does not apply because Bob is not seised to the use of Cathy. The trustee must have a freehold estate, even though the cestui need not.

a. Statute's Effect on Future Interests

(1) Executory Interests

After the Statute of Uses, springing and shifting uses became valid legal interests. However, the springing and shifting executory interests became legally valid only when they would have been a valid equitable use before the Statute.

Illustration: Ann bargains and sells "to Bob for life and, one year after his death, to Cathy and her heirs." As a result of the Statute, Bob has a legal life estate, Ann has a legal reversion subject to a springing executory interest, and Cathy has a springing executory interest in fee simple absolute.

Illustration: Ann bargains and sells "to Bob and his heirs but if liquor is ever sold on the land, then to Cathy and her heirs." After the Statute, Bob has legal fee simple subject to shifting executory interest, and Cathy has a shifting executory interest in fee simple absolute. Ann has nothing.

Illustration: Ann made livery "to Bob for life and, one year after his death, to Cathy and her heirs." Cathy's interest fails even after the Statute of Uses because it would have been a springing remainder at common law. This arrangement would work if done by a bargain and sale deed because the deed would create a valid equitable use, which the Statute then could execute into a valid legal executory interest. But here the livery created no equitable use, so there is nothing to execute, and the Statute has no effect. If an equitable conveyance created a valid use before the Statute, the same conveyance will create a valid legal interest after the Statute. But if a legal conveyance could not create a valid future interest before the Statute, the same legal conveyance is still ineffective after the Statute.

(2) Contingent Remainders

Contingent remainders are unaffected by the Statute. Therefore, they are still destructible in jurisdictions that apply the doctrine of destructibility.

Illustration: Ann bargains and sells "to Bob for life, and then to Cathy and her heirs if Cathy is 21." Bob dies before Cathy is 21. Cathy has nothing. Her equitable contingent remainder is executed by the Statute into a legal contingent remainder. But the Statute does not make it indestructible, because it is still a remainder and is governed by the rules for remainders.

(3) Remainder or Executory Interest?

An executory interest exists only where a remainder is impossible. Therefore, whenever an interest is limited so that it can take effect as a remainder, it is a remainder, even though it also could take effect as an executory interest. This is the rule of *Purefoy v. Rogers*, 2 Wms. Saund. 380, 85 Eng. Rep. 1181 (1670).

Illustration: Ann bargains and sells "to Bob for life, and then to Cathy and her heirs if Cathy reaches 21." If Cathy becomes 21 after Bob dies, Cathy would take by way of springing executory interest from Ann. But if Cathy becomes 21 before Bob dies, she would take by way of remainder when his estate terminates. Because the interest can operate as a remainder or as an executory interest, it will be treated as a remainder and not as an executory interest. Thus, it is destructible. If Cathy is not 21 before Bob dies, her interest fails under the doctrine of destructibility.

Illustration: Ann bargains and sells "to Bob for life, and then to his first daughter who becomes 21." This future interest can take effect either as a remainder (for the first daughter who is over 21 when Bob dies) or as an executory interest (where no daughter becomes 21 until after Bob dies). Therefore, the interest will be treated as a remainder. Unless Bob has a daughter over 21 when he dies, the remainder will fail.

Illustration: Ann bargains and sells "to Bob for life, remainder to his first son over 21 at Bob's death, or if there is no son over 21 at Bob's death, then to the first son who becomes 21 after Bob's death." Rather than making a gift of one interest that can take effect either as a remainder or as an executory interest, the grantor has separated it into two different interests. There is a gift of a remainder to any adult son and a gift of an executory interest to any minor son. Because the executory interest in this case cannot possibly take by way of remainder (a gift to a minor that will become possessory only when he reaches majority must be a springing interest), it is indestructible.

6. Unexecuted Uses

The Statute of Uses does not transform every use into a legal estate. Some uses remain uses.

a. *Active Trust*

Whenever the person seised to the use of some beneficiary (cestui que use) has any active duties regarding the land, the use is not executed. The grantee retains the legal title, just as the modern trustee does.

b. *Use on a Use*

Before the Statute of Uses, a use on a use (e.g., a conveyance "to Bob for the use of Cathy for the use of Don") was void. The use to Don was void because it was repugnant to Cathy's use. However, shortly after the Statute, the use on a use was declared to be valid and was treated as an unexecuted use. The first use was executed, so that the first cestui got the legal title. But the second cestui kept the equitable title because a second execution did not occur.

Illustration: Ann made livery "to Bob for the use of Cathy for the use of Don." The Statute executes the use to Cathy and gives her legal title. But it does not execute the use to Don. Therefore, Don has equitable title, and Cathy has legal title.

Illustration: Ann bargains and sells "to Bob for the use of Cathy." The bargain and sale gives Bob only a use. But the Statute executes it and gives Bob legal title. No second execution occurs. Therefore, Bob has legal title for the use of Cathy.

Illustration: Ann made livery "to Bob to his own use to the use of Cathy." The first use to Bob is executed but not the second use to Cathy. This is the use in *Doe v. Passingham*, 6 B. & C. 305 (1827).

Illustration: Ann made livery "to Bob and his heirs, for the use of Cathy for life, and then for the use of Don and his heirs." Both Cathy's and Don's uses are executed, and both have legal estates. Don has a use after a use, but not a use on a use, because Cathy's use is not for the use of Don.

c. Uses and Seisin

Whether a use is executed is important when ascertaining whether a holder has seisin, as in the case of dower. A widow has dower only in estates of which her husband was seised.

Illustration: Ann made livery "to Bob for the use of Carl and his heirs." Because the Statute gives Carl a legal estate and, therefore, seisin, Carl's widow will have dower.

Illustration: Ann made livery "to Bob for the use of Carl for the use of Don." Because Don's use is not executed, Don does not have seisin, and Don's widow will not have dower.

CHAPTER THREE

CONCURRENT OWNERSHIP

I. FORMS OF CONCURRENT OWNERSHIP

Although a life tenant and the future interest holder may be viewed as sharing ownership of the same property, their ownership is divided in time. At no time do they share the same rights in the property. In contrast, concurrent owners own the same interest at the same time. There is no chronological separation in their ownership. Their ownership is "undivided" because each owner has the right to possess the entire property that is owned concurrently. Both real and personal property can be owned concurrently. A joint bank account is an example of the latter.

Our legal system recognizes only a limited number of types of concurrent ownership—joint tenancy, tenancy in common, and tenancy by the entirety. Be aware that the word "cotenant" can refer generically to all three forms of concurrent ownership or just to a tenancy in common, so pay careful attention to the context when you see that term.

Coparcenary was an earlier form of concurrent ownership that applied when female heirs took together by descent, but it is generally nonexistent today. Tenancy in partnership is a form of concurrent ownership recognized by statute in some states, but it is generally covered in a Business Associations course, rather than in Property.

A. CHARACTERISTICS OF THE VARIOUS TYPES OF CONCURRENT OWNERSHIP

At common law, certain preconditions, called unities, had to be satisfied to create concurrent ownership. Today, many jurisdictions have substantially limited the necessity for the unities.

1. Unity of Time

For two or more owners to be joint tenants or tenants by the entirety, each must have received its interest in the property at the same time. Tenancy in common does not require the unity of time.

Illustration: Owen conveyed "to Ann and Bob." Depending on whether the other unities are satisfied, Ann and Bob may be joint tenants, tenants by the entirety, or tenants in common. The unity of time is satisfied, because Ann and Bob were grantees at the same time. This is not a requirement of a tenancy in common, but its presence does not prevent that form of ownership.

Illustration: Owen conveyed an undivided half interest in Blackacre to Ann in 2008. In 2009, Owen conveyed the other undivided half interest to Bob. Ann and Bob can only be tenants in common. Because they acquired their interests at different times, the unity of time is not satisfied.

Illustration: Ann owns Blackacre and conveys an undivided half interest in it to Bob. At common law, Ann and Bob cannot be joint tenants or tenants by the entirety because the unity of time is not satisfied. Ann acquired her interest in Blackacre before Bob acquired his interest. To create a joint tenancy or tenancy by the entirety with Bob, Ann could convey her entire title to a third person (a "dummy" or "straw person") who then would convey it back to Bob and her as joint tenants or as tenants by the entirety. In this way, the unity of time would be satisfied. Today, many jurisdictions permit an owner of property to convey directly to another person and to herself as joint tenants or as tenants by the entirety without first conveying title to a third person.

2. Unity of Title

No joint tenancy or tenancy by the entirety can exist unless both owners receive title from the same source. Tenancy in common does not have this requirement.

Illustration: Ann owns Blackacre and conveys an undivided half interest in it to Bob. At common law, they could only be tenants in common. Neither the unity of time nor the unity of title is satisfied, because Bob's title came from Ann, and Ann's title came from her grantor at an earlier time. As described above, Ann could create a joint tenancy or tenancy by the entirety by using a straw person, or the jurisdiction where the land is located may no longer require the unity of title.

Illustration: Owen conveyed undivided half interests to Ann and Bob in the same instrument. Bob conveyed his undivided half interest to Cathy. As between Ann and Cathy, only a tenancy in common is possible. Cathy's title came from Bob, while Ann's title came from Owen.

3. Unity of Interest

Joint tenancy and tenancy by the entirety require that each owner has an equal interest in the land. If one has a greater interest, only a tenancy in common exists.

Illustration: Owen conveyed an undivided one-third interest to Ann and an undivided two-thirds interest to Bob. Ann and Bob can only be tenants in common because the unity of interest is not satisfied.

4. Unity of Possession

Joint tenancy, tenancy by the entirety, and tenancy in common all require that each tenant has an equal right to possess the whole of the property. This is the significance of the term "undivided ownership." If separate (divided) rights to geographic segments are given, there is separate ownership of different parts, rather than concurrent ownership. The parties are neighbors, not co-owners. If possession is given to one but postponed for the others, there is a division of estates into possessory and future interests, rather than concurrent ownership, and again the rights are "divided."

Illustration: Owen conveyed to Xerxes for life and then in equal undivided shares to Ann and Bob. Ann and Bob may be tenants by the entirety, joint tenants, or tenants in common. Although neither has a present right to possess, their right to possess in the future is equal between them. Xerxes is not a cotenant of any sort with Ann and Bob.

5. Unity of Person

A tenancy by the entirety can be created only for a couple in a legally recognized marriage. At common law, unity of person exists between husband and wife. Neither joint tenancy nor tenancy in common has this requirement.

B. PREFERENCE FOR ONE ESTATE OVER ANOTHER

At common law, a presumption existed in favor of the joint tenancy over the tenancy in common. Therefore, if a gift to two or more persons could be construed as a joint tenancy, rather than as a tenancy in common, it would be. Today, the constructional preference is for tenancy in common over joint tenancy. To create a joint tenancy, the deed must overcome this preference by including language such as "to Ann and Bob as joint tenants, and not as tenants in common, with right of survivorship." (See the next section for the right of survivorship).

Similarly, at common law, an ambiguous gift to spouses was construed as a tenancy by the entirety. Today, only thirteen states still recognize this form of cotenancy. Where it still exists, some states have a constructional preference for it, whereas other states require a clear expression of intent to overcome the usual preference for a tenancy in common.

II. CONSEQUENCES OF DIFFERENT TYPES OF OWNERSHIP

A. SURVIVORSHIP

A defining characteristic of a joint tenancy and of a tenancy by the entirety is the right of survivorship. When one cotenant dies, the surviving tenants keep the decedent's share as a matter of law. It is not a question of inheritance or descent because the surviving cotenants take the decedent's share even if they are not the decedent's heirs or devisees. During the lives of the joint tenants or of the tenants by the entirety, each cotenant is viewed as owning the entire estate, subject only to the others' equal claims. When one cotenant dies, ownership is merely freed from the decedent's previously existing equal claim. Thus, the survivors do not "inherit" the decedent's share but merely continue their full ownership.

Tenants in common have separate, though undivided, interests in the property. Therefore, the interest of each is inheritable by his or her heirs or passes by will. A surviving tenant in common takes the entire estate only when he or she is the heir or devisee of the deceased.

Illustration: Ann and Bob, a married couple, were tenants by the entirety of Blackacre. Ann died before Bob. Her will left all her property to the Red Cross. The Red Cross will acquire no interest in Blackacre. Bob is now its sole owner based on the right of survivorship.

Illustration: Ann and Bob were joint tenants. Bob died. Wilma, his widow, was his only heir. However, Wilma takes no interest in the jointly owned property by descent or by devise. Ann has the entire title by right of survivorship. Any claim to dower by Wilma will be defeated, because Bob did not have an inheritable estate. (See Chapter 2.) Ann is now the sole owner.

Illustration: Ann and Bob were joint tenants. Bob died. Wilma, his widow, was his only heir. Then Ann died without a will. Her son, Harry, was her only heir. Harry now owns the entire estate. Ann acquired the entire title by survivorship. Upon Ann's death, Harry inherited her entire interest.

Illustration: Ann and Bob were tenants in common. Bob died. Wilma, his widow, was his only heir. On Bob's death, Wilma inherited his tenancy in common interest in the property and became a tenant in common with Ann. Ann's interest is unaffected by Bob's death. Because this is not a tenancy by the entirety or joint tenancy, she does not take any part of Bob's interest by survivorship.

Illustration: Ann, Bob, and Cathy were joint tenants. Cathy died, leaving a son, Jay, as her only heir. Jay takes nothing, because the right of survivorship prevails over the rules of descent. Ann and Bob acquire Cathy's interest. Thus, the property becomes the joint tenancy property of Ann and Bob alone. They each hold an undivided one-half interest, rather than an undivided one-third interest in it. If Ann dies before Bob, he will be the sole owner.

B. SEVERANCE

1. Severance of Joint Tenancy

A joint tenancy interest is severed when a joint tenant conveys his or her interest to another, thereby destroying the unities of time and title as to that interest. The cotenants become tenants in common with respect to the share that was severed, but the other shares continue in joint tenancy.

Illustration: Ann and Bob were joint tenants. Bob conveyed his interest in the property to Cathy. Ann and Cathy are now tenants in common. There is no unity of time or title between them, because Cathy acquired her interest at a different time and from a different instrument than Ann. The joint tenancy has been severed, and a tenancy in common relationship now exists.

Illustration: Ann, Bob, and Cathy were joint tenants. Cathy conveyed her interest to Dora. Dora owns a one-third interest in the property as a tenant in common with Ann and Bob. Ann and Bob continue as joint tenants with regard to the two-thirds interest they still hold. If Ann dies first, Bob will take her one-third interest by survivorship, and Dora's interest will be unchanged. Bob and Dora will then be tenants in common, with Bob owning an undivided two-thirds interest and Dora owning an undivided one-third interest. If Dora dies before Ann and Bob, her heir will inherit her one-third, and Ann and Bob will still own their two-thirds interest as joint tenants. When Ann or Bob dies, the survivor will then hold the undivided two-thirds interest in tenancy in common with the undivided one-third interest owned by Dora's heir.

Illustration: Ann, Bob, and Cathy were joint tenants. Cathy conveyed her interest to Bob. Ann and Bob still own a two-thirds interest in the property as joint tenants. However, Bob now also holds the one-third interest that he received from Cathy as a tenant in common, because he acquired it at a different time and by a different instrument than the two-thirds interest held in joint tenancy with Ann. If Ann dies before Bob, he will acquire her interest by right of survivorship and will be the sole owner. If Bob dies before Ann, she will acquire his interest in the joint tenancy. If Bob's will left all his property to the Red Cross, Ann and the Red Cross will be tenants in common, with Ann owning an undivided two-thirds interest and the Red Cross owning an undivided one-third interest.

Any voluntary or involuntary conveyance by one joint tenant severs that tenant's interest from the joint tenancy. Generally, a contract to convey the property also severs by virtue of the doctrine of equitable conversion. (See Chapter 8.) In some states, a lease severs a joint tenancy. In states where a mortgage is viewed as conveying title to the mortgaged land to the mortgagee, the mortgage causes a severance. A mortgage also can cause a severance in some states that treat a mortgage as transferring only a lien on the property.

2. Severance of Tenancy by the Entirety

A tenancy by the entirety cannot be severed by one tenant. No conveyance of such an estate is valid unless both spouses sign. A tenancy by the entirety ends when the cotenants divorce. Normally, the estate is converted into a tenancy in common to avoid the right of survivorship.

Illustration: Ann and Bob, a married couple, are tenants by the entirety. Ann gives Cathy a deed for Ann's interest. Cathy acquires no interest. Ann and Bob are still tenants by the entirety.

C. PARTITION

Any joint tenant or tenant in common can force a partition of the property, but a tenant by the entirety cannot. Partition can be in kind or by sale.

1. Partition in Kind

Partition in kind is a physical division of the property. In the case of land, the former cotenants become neighbors. Instead of undivided ownership of the entire property, each cotenant now owns a separate parcel. Thus, it differs from severance in that severance does not alter undivided ownership but merely eliminates the element of survivorship. The parties remain cotenants after a severance, whereas there is no cotenancy after a partition. Partition in kind can occur by court action for partition or by voluntary cross-conveyance among the cotenants.

2. Partition by Sale

When physical partition will harm the property or cannot be done equally, a court will order that the property be sold and that the sale proceeds be divided among the former cotenants.

III. POSSESSION, PROFITS, AND EXPENDITURES

The one unity shared by all forms of cotenancy is the unity of possession. Each tenant has an equal right to possess the whole property, and none is entitled to exclude the others or to claim sole possession of any part. When one cotenant does "oust" the others, the excluded tenants may bring an action in ejectment to recover possession. If they do not assert their possessory rights, they risk losing title by adverse possession.

A. RENTS

1. Rents from Possessing Cotenant

Because each cotenant is entitled to possess the entire property, the majority rule is that a tenant in sole possession is not liable to the nonpossessing cotenants for rent. The other cotenants' failure to possess cannot render the possessor liable for what he or she has a right to do. The nonpossessing cotenants' right is to share the possession and not to charge the possessing cotenant. However, if the possessor makes expenditures on the property and seeks contribution from the nonpossessors, the value of his possession may be allowed as an offset against the duty to contribute. Also, a cotenant who ousts the others is liable for rent in an ejectment action brought by the excluded cotenants to recover possession.

2. Rents and Profits from Third Parties

In many jurisdictions, a cotenant can lease his or her possessory interest to strangers. In those jurisdictions, a lease signed by one cotenant conveys to the lessee whatever possessory rights that cotenant has. The other cotenants need not join in the execution of the lease. The lease entitles the lessee to take possession of the property, subject to the restriction that the other cotenants cannot be excluded from possession. For this reason, the common law originally provided that the leasing cotenant was entitled to retain all rent paid by the lessee. However, the Statute of Anne (1704) compels the leasing cotenant to share rents and profits received from a third person with the other cotenants. Most states follow this statute.

Illustration: Ann and Bob are tenants in common or joint tenants. Ann was in exclusive possession, but recently she rented the property to Cathy for a rent of $1,000 per year. Under the majority rule, Bob may not recover from Ann for the rental value of the property while she was in possession. However, Bob is entitled to $500 per year if the Statute of Anne is in force in the state. If it is not, Ann is entitled to keep all the rent.

B. EXPENDITURES

1. Payment of Purchase Price

When the cotenants made unequal contributions toward the purchase price, they may own correspondingly unequal shares of the property.

Illustration: Ann and Bob purchased property as tenants in common. Ann paid $20,000 of the price, and Bob paid $10,000. A court may determine that Ann owns an undivided two-thirds interest and that Bob owns an undivided one-third interest.

Illustration: The same facts as above except that Ann and Bob took title as joint tenants. A court may now conclude that the taking of title in joint tenancy, with its attendant unity of interest, requires that the parties be treated as equal one-half owners. The excess contribution made by Ann would then be treated as a gift or loan to Bob.

2. Necessary Payments

A cotenant who pays expenses that are necessary to preserve the title, such as for property taxes and mortgage payments, generally can recover the other cotenant's share of the expenses in an action for an accounting or in a partition suit. However, an action for contribution is available only if the nonpaying cotenant was personally liable for these expenses.

Illustration: Ann and Bob are cotenants and both are in possession of the property. Ann makes the entire payment of $500 for the annual property taxes. If the jurisdiction makes owners personally liable for property taxes, Ann can recover $250 from Bob by bringing an action for contribution. However, if the jurisdiction provides that the taxes are only a charge against the land and not against its owners, Ann does not have an action for contribution against Bob. But, in an action for an accounting for rents collected from the property or in a partition action, the court can offset the $250 from the amount that otherwise would be due to Bob. A court also may give Ann a lien on Bob's interest in the property if the action for contribution is unavailable to her.

Illustration: Ann and Bob are cotenants, but Ann is in sole possession. Ann makes the same property tax payment. In an action against Bob to recover half the payment, Bob may be permitted to offset the value of Ann's sole possession.

3. Improvements

A cotenant who improves the property has an action for contribution against the other cotenants only if they either agreed to be liable before the improvement was made or ratified the expense afterwards. The improver cannot force the cost of improvements onto an unwilling cotenant. The improver can claim the costs of improvement in an accounting for rents and profits collected from a third party only to the extent that the improvement caused an increase in the rents. Unless the other cotenants pay their share of the cost: (1) In a partition in kind, the improved part of the property may be awarded to the improver; and (2) In a partition by sale, an increased share of the proceeds will be awarded to the improver to reflect the increase in the property's value that resulted from the improvement.

Illustration: Ann and Bob own a two-acre parcel as cotenants. Ann built a house on the property at her sole expense. In a partition by kind, Ann should be awarded the acre containing the house, and Bob should get the unimproved acre.

Illustration: Ann built a house at her sole expense, which added $20,000 to the value of the property. If the value of the land alone is $10,000, and there is a partition sale for $30,000, Ann should receive $25,000 of the proceeds, and Bob should receive $5,000.

4. Repairs

Generally, no right of contribution for repairs exists unless the nonrepairing cotenant agreed to be personally liable. However, adjustments may be made in a partition or in an accounting action. Moreover, some jurisdictions provide an action for contribution if the repairs were necessary and the repairing cotenant gave reasonable advance notice to the others.

IV. CONDOMINIUMS, TIME SHARING, AND COOPERATIVES

A. CONDOMINIUMS

In a typical condominium project, each owner has fee simple absolute title to his or her individual "unit" and also has undivided title to the "common areas" of the project as a tenant in common with the other condominium owners. In a typical residential condominium, a unit is the equivalent of the apartment that its owner would occupy under a lease.   The unit owned is generally the area encompassed by the interior walls.   The walls themselves, the halls, plumbing, and other structural components of the building are common areas or elements owned by all unit owners as tenants in common.   Condominium ownership gives exclusive right of possession over the unit owned and shared possessory rights to the common areas.

Illustration: Ann and Bob own different units in a condominium project. As the sole owner of Unit #101, Ann is entitled to exclusive possession of it, and she may exclude Bob from it and may rent it to Tina. As co-owner of the hallway and the project swimming pool, Ann is entitled to use these facilities along with the other unit owners. She cannot exclude Bob from these areas. If the project includes a garage, both Ann and Bob may have exclusive easements or fee title for designated parking spaces.

State condominium enabling statutes specify the legal requirements to create a condominium. Generally, the developer must record (1) a condominium declaration, which describes the units and the intended condominium arrangement, (2) a map of the entire project that includes vertical and horizontal dimensions, and (3) various supplementary documents regulating the operation of the condominium, such as the articles of incorporation and by-laws of the owners' association and the covenants, conditions, and restrictions applicable to the project. Thereafter, deeds are executed and delivered to purchasers who become owners of individual units, co-owners of the common areas, and members of the owners' association. The owners' titles are subject to the association rules and to the covenants and restrictions running with the land.

In most condominiums, management of the common areas is vested in a community or homeowners' association that is composed of all unit owners in the project. The condominium documents generally address questions of membership and voting rights in the association, its rights and duties with respect to the common elements, and its power to levy assessments on individual units to pay for maintenance of the common elements. These documents also often include restrictions on partition and provisions concerning partial and total destruction of the buildings.

B. TIME SHARING ARRANGEMENTS

Condominiums and other forms of co-ownership may be divided on a time-sharing basis, so that different parties have exclusive rights of possession at different times of the year. One method is to convey ownership to each purchaser during an annual recurring period for a term of years, together with an undivided fee in the remainder ("interval ownership"). Another method is to convey a tenancy in common interest to each purchaser, together with an exclusive right to possess the unit during a certain period of time each year ("time-span ownership").

Illustration: An interval ownership time-sharing deed provides that the grantor conveys a designated unit and an interest in the common elements from January 1 to January 31of each year until the year 2030, together with a remainder in fee simple absolute to the unit as a tenant in common with the other owners of the unit. A time-span deed provides that the grantee takes an undivided interest in the entire project, together with the exclusive right to occupy a designated unit and the common areas during the specified use periods, and excepts from the grant the right to use at any other time of the year.

C. COOPERATIVES

In a cooperative, a corporation usually holds title to the property. An individual then purchases stock in the corporation and receives, along with the stock, a lease to an individual unit within the project, rather than fee title. In both a condominium and a cooperative, the members share the common expenses. Failure to make such payments may be treated as a form of financial waste, because the consequences can be uncompensated damage to the property (if uninsured) or forfeiture of the title (for nonpayment of taxes or the mortgage). Unlike condominium units, cooperatively held units often cannot be separately mortgaged and taxed because they are merely leased, rather than owned outright.

CHAPTER FOUR

LANDLORD AND TENANT

I. TYPES AND CREATION OF TENANCIES

The parties to a lease are the landlord and the tenant, also known as the lessor and lessee. The tenant usually pays for his right to possess the property in the form of rent. In this section, "Lil" will be the landlord in the Illustrations and will be referred to by feminine pronouns in the text. "Tom" will be the tenant and will be referred to with masculine pronouns in the text.

Illustration: Lil, who owns a building in fee simple absolute, leases it to Tom for a period of five years. During the lease term, Tom has the exclusive right to possess the building and many of the other normal incidents of ownership. Unless the lease provides otherwise, he may decide what to do on the premises, such as whether to permit others to enter and whether to repair or improve it. At the end of the lease, possession and control of the building revert back to Lil. During the five-year period, Lil has a reversion, or she may be regarded as having the fee title, subject to a five-year leasehold. In this case, Tom and Lil are not neighbors, as would result from a physical division of the building, nor cotenants, as would result from a division of the present interests, nor dominant and servient tenants relating to an easement, as would result from a division of permitted uses on the property. The landlord-tenant relationship divides ownership differently than those other relationships.

Our legal system recognizes four different types of tenancies: (1) tenancy for a term, (2) periodic tenancy, (3) tenancy at will, and (4) tenancy at sufferance. The distinctions among them relate primarily to the methods of their creation and termination.

A. TENANCY FOR A TERM

A tenancy for a term (also known as a tenancy for years) is created when the landlord and tenant agree that the tenant will hold the property for a fixed period of time and for no longer. Despite its name, a tenancy for years can have a term of less than one year, such as one month. Whatever time period is specified, at the expiration of the lease term, the tenancy automatically terminates unless a new lease is executed. Depending on the jurisdiction, the Statute of Frauds may require any tenancy for a term to be in writing or only any tenancy for a term that is longer than a specified period, such as one year or three years.

B. PERIODIC TENANCY

The tenancy from period to period or periodic tenancy is created when the landlord and tenant agree that the tenant will pay a periodic rent, such as weekly, monthly, or annually, but do not specify a termination date for the tenancy. The tenancy automatically renews for an additional period unless either party gives timely notice of intent to terminate it. State law specifies how far in advance notice must be given. A periodic tenancy can be created expressly ("Lil and Tom hereby enter into a month to month tenancy") or impliedly by the regular payment of rent.

1. Implied Periodic Tenancies

Since a periodic tenancy requires only the payment of a regular rent without an agreement as to a termination date, this tenancy can be created by the parties' actions without an express agreement.

Illustration: Lil and Tom drafted a five-year lease that required annual rent payments. However, they did not sign the lease. Because the Statute of Frauds requires that a lease for this term be signed, it is invalid, and Tom does not have a fixed five-year term. But if Tom takes possession and pays Lil the annual rent, Tom has a periodic tenancy (from year to year).

Illustration: Lil and Tom executed a one-year lease that specified an annual rent. Tom took possession and paid the rent. He held over after the year ended and made another annual rent payment to Lil, which she accepted. Tom now may be a periodic tenant (from year to year) because there is a regular rent and no agreement as to a termination date.

2. Length of the Period

In most jurisdictions, the period is measured according to the specified rent interval. A weekly rent creates a tenancy from week to week, a monthly rent creates a tenancy from month to month, and an annual rent creates a tenancy from year to year. The period can be based on how the rent is calculated, rather than on how it is paid. Thus, a stated rent of $1,200 per year, payable $100 per month, generally is held to create a tenancy from year to year, rather than month to month.

C. TENANCY AT WILL

This tenancy is created whenever a landowner permits another person to possess the property without any agreement between them as to a termination date or as to the payment of rent. In most states, as soon as the tenant begins to pay rent on a regular basis, the tenancy at will becomes a periodic tenancy. However, a tenancy at will can be created expressly ("Lil grants Tom the right to possess at will").

1. Implied Tenancies at Will

Because the essence of this estate is simply that the landlord has not objected to the tenant's possession, this estate may arise in a number of ways.

Illustration: Lil and Tom prepared a five-year lease but did not sign it, as required by the Statute of Frauds. If Tom takes possession, he is a tenant at will. As soon as he begins paying rent on a regular basis, the tenancy at will becomes a periodic tenancy.

Illustration: Owen conveyed property to Ann by a void deed, and Ann took possession. Because the deed failed to transfer title, Owen still owns the property. Ann's possession under the void deed makes her a tenant at will.

Illustration: Lil and Tom entered into a valid tenancy for a term. At the end of the term, Tom asks Lil's permission to hold over for two additional days. If Lil consents, Tom is a tenant at will for those two days.

D. TENANCY AT SUFFERANCE

A person becomes a tenant at sufferance by holding over after the expiration of his tenancy without the landlord's consent. The tenancy at sufferance can arise after the termination of any of the other types of tenancy. Because the tenant does not have the legal right to remain in possession, he could be characterized as a trespasser. However, if he is a trespasser, the statute of limitations begins to run on the owner's action to recover possession. Her failure to bring suit within the limitations period could cause her to lose title to the property by the former tenant's adverse possession. To avoid this result, the former tenant is characterized as a tenant at sufferance, rather than as a trespasser.

Illustration: Tom's lease expired on January 1. On January 2, Tom is still in possession without Lil's consent. He is a tenant at sufferance.

Illustration: Tom was a month to month tenant. Lil gave proper notice to terminate his tenancy at the end of the month. If Tom is still in possession when the next month begins, he is a tenant at sufferance.

Illustration: Tom was a tenant at will, but Lil terminated the tenancy. If Tom does not leave, he is a tenant at sufferance.

II. TENANT'S POSSESSORY INTEREST

The essence of a lease is the landlord's transfer of a temporary right of exclusive possession. The tenant has a nonfreehold possessory estate. The right to exclusive possession distinguishes a tenancy from an easement, because an easement merely gives its holder the right to use property for some limited purpose.

As the person with the exclusive right to possess, the tenant is entitled to exclude all others from the property. Even the landlord may be excluded unless the lease permits entry without the tenant's consent. The common law also recognized a limited right in the landlord to enter to "view waste."

A. TENANT'S REMEDIES FOR DISTURBANCE OF POSSESSION

1. Remedies Against Strangers

A tenant is entitled to protect his right to possession against all others. If trespassers intrude, the tenant, rather than the landlord, has standing to sue. The tenant may recover damages for trespass and may recover possession from the intruders in an ejectment action. Because the tenant, rather than the landlord, has the action for ejectment, the tenant is not excused from paying rent when he is dispossessed by strangers.

2. Remedies for Landlord's Interferences

Every lease includes a covenant of quiet enjoyment, which is the landlord's covenant that she will not interfere with the tenant's possession. Based on this covenant, the tenant may exclude the landlord from the premises, just as he may exclude everyone else. If the landlord wrongfully dispossesses the tenant, the tenant may be allowed to terminate the tenancy.

Illustration: Lil entered and dispossessed Tom when he had one year remaining on his lease. Tom may sue to recover possession or may treat Lil's eviction as a breach of the covenant of quiet enjoyment and declare the leasehold to be terminated.

Illustration: Lil brought a summary dispossession proceeding against Tom for his failure to pay rent, and she recovered possession. Tom is probably excused from further rent liability. Although Lil was entitled to enter and is not liable in ejectment or tort or for breach of covenant, Lil eliminated the condition on which Tom owed rent—possession. Therefore, Tom's rent liability should cease.

3. Eviction by Paramount Title

If the owner of a paramount title dispossesses a tenant, the tenant cannot recover possession. Instead, he can recover damages for the landlord's breach of the covenant of quiet enjoyment.

Illustration: Lil failed to pay the debt secured by a mortgage on property rented by Tom, and the mortgagee foreclosed. If the mortgage is superior to the lease, Tom's lease is terminated, and he is excused from further rent liability to Lil.

B. REMEDIES WHEN NEW TENANT IS PREVENTED FROM TAKING POSSESSION

1. When Landlord is at Fault

If the landlord is in possession of the leased premises and fails to leave when the tenancy begins, the tenant has the same remedies as if the landlord subsequently interfered with his possession. The tenant can sue to recover possession or can terminate the lease and can recover damages. Similarly, when a third person is in possession with the landlord's consent, the tenant can terminate the lease and can recover damages from the landlord for breach of covenant. Whether the tenant can sue to recover possession from the third person depends on which of them has the superior right. If the tenant's lease is superior, his right of possession is superior. But if the third person is in possession under a lease executed before the tenant's lease, the tenant probably cannot eject him.

Illustration: Tom signed a lease on January 1 that granted possession on February 1. On January 15, Lil signed another lease for the same property that gave Ann the immediate right to possess. On February 1, when Tom is unable to enter, he may terminate his lease and sue Lil for damages, or he may bring an ejectment action against Ann.

Illustration: Tom signed a lease on January 15 that granted possession on February 15. On January 1, Lil had executed a lease for the same property with Ann, and Ann took possession on February 1. On February 15, when Tom is unable to enter, he may terminate his lease and sue Lil for damages, but he probably cannot eject Ann.

Illustration: Tom's tenancy is to begin on February 1. The lease of the former tenant, Ann, terminated on January 15, but she held over. On January 20, Lil elected to make Ann stay as a periodic tenant. Thus, Tom cannot enter on February 1. Tom may terminate the lease or may be able to recover possession from Ann.

2. When Third Party is at Fault

The states are divided concerning a tenant's right to terminate his tenancy if he cannot take possession at the beginning of his lease term because a third party is possessing the property without the landlord's consent.

a. English Rule

In several states, the tenant may terminate the tenancy. This rule imposes an obligation on the landlord to provide the tenant with actual possession at the beginning of the tenancy.

b. American Rule

Under this rule, the landlord is obligated to deliver only the right of possession and not actual possession. This rule does not permit the tenant to terminate the lease. It limits him to a cause of action against the wrongful possessor.

Illustration: Tom cannot take possession when his lease begins because Ann, the former tenant, failed to leave despite Lil's request for her to do so. Under the American rule, Tom still owes rent and has an ejectment action against Ann. Under the English rule, Tom may terminate his lease.

C. RIGHTS INCIDENTAL TO POSSESSION

In a multi-unit building, the tenant has the right to possess only that part of the building actually leased to him. However, the tenant also shares with the other tenants certain additional rights, such as the right to pass through the hallways, ride the elevators, and use the laundry room. In these "common areas," the tenant's right is for shared use, rather than for exclusive possession. These rights may be regarded as easements in the common areas that are incidental to the possessory right to the space actually leased.

D. LIABILITIES AS A POSSESSOR

As the person in possession of the leased premises, the tenant, rather than the landlord, usually is subject to the normal tort duties owed by occupiers of land to invitees, licensees, trespassers, and others. For example, the tenant may be liable to a guest who is injured as a result of the premises' physical condition.

III. RENT

"Rent" refers to the periodic charge the tenant must pay for his use of the landlord's property. Usually, the lease specifies the amount of "rent reserved." However, if the lease does not specify an amount, a rent equal to the fair rental value of the property is implied unless a gift was intended.

A. PAYMENT

For common law agricultural tenancies, rent was a share of the crops harvested by the tenant. This practice was the origin of the term "rent," because it was something torn or "reserved" from the land. Today, the rent may include a share of the tenant's profits from the business he conducts on the premises ("percentage rent"). For other types of cash rent, payments usually are due at the beginning of each rental period.

The rent amount frequently stays the same over the lease term, but it may be increased periodically either by a fixed amount provided in the lease or by a cost of living ("escalator") clause in the lease. For periodic tenancies, a unilateral demand by the landlord for an increase often must be given at least one period in advance because, in essence, the landlord is terminating the tenancy at the former rent and is offering to enter into a new tenancy at the increased rent. The tenant need not agree to accept the new tenancy.

B. RENT CONTROL

By ordinance, some cities limit the amount by which residential landlords can increase their tenants' rents. Courts generally uphold rent control against attacks that it is preempted by state law, constitutes a "taking" of the landlord's property, denies landlords due process or equal protection, and violates the antitrust laws. Common features of such ordinances are described below.

1. Premises and Persons Covered

Rent control rarely includes commercial premises. The rent control ordinance also may exclude certain forms of housing or tenants, such as boarders in single family homes, single family or two family dwellings, and luxury housing. The tenant may be required to show that the premises are his "primary residence" or that he is related to the originally protected tenant. The tenant also may be limited in the amount he can charge if he sublets the premises.

When the premises become vacant, some ordinances permit the landlord to increase rents without restriction ("vacancy decontrol"), while others continue the rent control. Ordinances that permit vacancy decontrol generally prohibit landlords from evicting tenants merely to increase rents. Such "good cause eviction" restrictions limit tenancy termination to cases of tenant default or misbehavior or the landlord's personal need to occupy the premises.

2. Rates

To eliminate the incentive for landlords to raise rents when a rent control ordinance is about to be enacted, most ordinances "roll back" the allowable rent to the rent charged at some earlier date, such as one year before the ordinance was enacted or was first considered. Increases then may be made only pursuant to a formula applicable to all units, such as an annual increase equal to 50% of the consumer price index increase for that period. The rent control board may be given authority to permit an increase in an individual case after the landlord has demonstrated a special hardship, such as an increase in the cost of necessary services or an inability to make a fair return on investment.

3. Ancillary Restrictions

Landlords subject to rent controls may seek to convert their buildings to more profitable, unrestricted uses. To prevent depletions in the rental housing stock, rent control ordinances often are accompanied by restrictions on condominium conversions, conversions to nonresidential use, and demolition. Such restrictions may completely prohibit conversions and demolition or may provide a rationing system that permits, for example, 1,000 conversions a year. Landlords also may be required to pay compensation to existing tenants in the form of mandatory relocation services, reduced "insider" prices, or lifetime tenancies in newly converted condominiums.

IV. PROBLEMS ARISING FROM DISREPAIR OF THE PREMISES

A. PARTIES' BASIC DUTIES

At early common law, the landlord had no legal responsibility for the condition of the premises. The doctrine of caveat emptor applied for defects that existed when the lease began, and leases were viewed as including no implied warranties. The landlord also had no duty to repair or correct defects that arose after the tenancy began. The landlord's only obligation was the same as for everyone else in the world—not to harm the premises after the tenant had taken possession.

The tenant's only duty to the landlord for the condition of the premises was not to commit waste. The tenant was prohibited from committing both active waste (harm caused by his acts) and passive waste (harm caused by a failure to make repairs). The landlord was entitled to receive the premises at the end of the lease term in the same condition as at the start, with the exception of reasonable wear and tear.

Illustration: Lil broke a fence on the premises before she rented them to Tom. Lil has no duty to repair the fence if she made no warranties to Tom concerning the condition of the premises. Tom also does not have a duty to repair the fence because he did not damage it, and its continued disrepair will not cause material harm to the reversion.

Illustration: Lil broke a fence on the premises during Tom's term. Tom may sue Lil for the damage, just as he could sue anyone else who broke the fence during his tenancy.

Illustration: Tom broke a fence on the premises during his term, which constitutes active waste. Tom owes Lil a duty to repair the fence.

Illustration: An unknown person broke into Tom's apartment and damaged it. Lil is not liable to repair the damage. Tom is liable only if he did not exercise reasonable diligence to prevent the damage. For example, Tom would be liable if he left the apartment door unlocked when he went on vacation. In either event, the third party is liable for the damage, and any damage award should be used either to repair the damage or to compensate Lil and Tom for their respective losses. The damage diminished the values of Tom's tenancy and of Lil's reversion.

Illustration: An unknown person broke a window during Tom's term. If the window is not repaired, rain may get inside and cause the floors to warp. In this case, Tom has a duty to repair the window to avoid waste.

1. Duties Owed to Third Persons

Even though neither party may have a duty to the other to make a certain repair, either or both of them may owe duties to the public generally and may be held liable in tort for injuries to others due to the disrepair.

2. Modern Changes in Basic Duties

Modern building and housing codes frequently change the common law rule by imposing a duty to repair. Some codes impose a duty to repair that is owed to the municipality. This duty indirectly may affect the duties owed to the other party to the lease. Other codes impose the duty of repair with a direct right of enforcement vested in the landlord or the tenant.

3. Duties Regarding Common Areas

The tenant's duties with respect to waste apply only to those premises over which he receives exclusive possession. The landlord is regarded as the possessor of the common areas. Consequently, instead of a landlord-tenant relationship in the hallways and other common areas, there is a possessor-invitee relationship. Although the tenant has no duty regarding waste, both the landlord and tenant may have duties arising out of their possessor-invitee relationship.

Illustration: Tom damaged a step in the common stairway. Tom is as liable for the damage as any third person would be.

Illustration: Lil cared for the common steps so negligently that Tom was injured. Tom may recover for his injuries from Lil in the same manner that an outsider could recover from her for negligent care of the land.

B. ALTERING THE BASIC DUTIES BY COVENANT

Unless prohibited by statute, either the landlord or the tenant can agree to undertake duties of repair that do not otherwise exist. Either can agree to make general or special repairs.

1. Enlarging Scope of Tenant's Duties by Covenant to Repair

Absent a covenant, the tenant's duty to avoid waste does not obligate him to perform extensive structural work or to rebuild unless he caused the injury. However, in many states, a tenant's general covenant to repair includes the obligation to rebuild regardless of the cause of the destruction.

2. Diminishing Scope of Tenant's Duties by Landlord's Covenant to Repair

When the landlord gives a covenant to repair, the tenant may be relieved of the repair obligations that the doctrine of waste imposes. However, the landlord's covenant to repair generally does not require her to repair damage caused by the tenant or to rebuild the premises if they are substantially destroyed.

C. RIGHT TO RECOVER COST OF REPAIRS

The availability of a particular remedy is not always determined simply by demonstrating that the other party defaulted on a duty to repair. This section describes when a party to a lease can sue for repair costs after the other party has refused to make a repair.

1. No Right to Recover when no Duty to Repair Exists

If the nonrepairing party was not obligated to make the repair, the other party cannot recover the repair cost.

Illustration: Lil refuses to repair a fence that was broken by an unknown third party. Because a landlord has no general duty to make repairs, Tom cannot sue Lil for the cost if he makes the repair.

Illustration: Tom refuses to repair a fence that was broken when he took possession. Failure to repair a pre-existing defect that will not cause greater loss later does not constitute waste. Therefore, Lil cannot sue Tom for costs if she repairs the fence.

2. Tenant's Right to Recover when Landlord has Duty to Repair

a. *Duty Arising from Building Code*

Building codes generally impose duties on owners, including landlords. But, unless the code expressly provides that a tenant can enforce it, he cannot recover repair costs from the landlord.

Illustration: The local building code requires property owners to keep fences in good repair. If the fence is in disrepair and Tom fixes it, he cannot recover the cost from Lil. Lil's obligation under the code is to the local government and not to Tom. The local government can compel her to fix the fence, but Tom cannot.

b. *Duty Arising from Habitability Law*

More than forty states require landlords of residential premises to keep them in habitable condition throughout the term. In some jurisdictions, a tenant can make necessary repairs and deduct the cost from the rent (repair-and-deduct law). A statute or ordinance may provide how often this right can be exercised, a maximum amount, and whether the tenant can make the repair personally or must hire outside contractors. It is unsettled whether several tenants can combine their rights to make a single large repair.

c. *Duty Arising from Covenant*

If the landlord violates her covenant to repair, the tenant generally is entitled to make the repair and to recover the cost from the landlord. In fact, to mitigate damages, the tenant may be required to make the repair promptly to prevent further deterioration. The resolution of most questions concerning rights and duties under a covenant to repair depends on the covenant's precise wording.

d. Duty Arising in Common Areas

If the landlord fails to keep the common areas in good repair, the tenant probably cannot make the repairs and recover the cost. Although the landlord may be liable in tort to the tenant for injuries suffered as a result of the disrepair, the tenant normally cannot recover repair costs in this situation.

3. Landlord's Right to Recover When Tenant has Duty to Repair

If the tenant has a duty to repair under the doctrine of waste or under a covenant to repair, the landlord generally can recover repair costs from him. The cost of repairs is the usual measure of damages when the landlord does not sue until the end of the term. If the landlord sues before then, the measure of damages may be the diminution in the reversion's value.

Illustration: Tom broke the fence with one year remaining on the lease term, and Lil sued immediately. It will cost $500 to repair the fence, but the value of Lil's reversion (i.e. the price for which she could sell her interest) is reduced by only $400. If Lil sues now, her recovery will be limited to $400. To recover $500, she must wait to sue until the lease term expires.

a. Recovery When Building Code Applies to Tenant

Building and housing codes normally impose duties only on the landlord as owner, rather than on the tenant. However, when a tenant's use of the property subjects it to special code requirements, the tenant may have this increased burden. But, just as a tenant generally cannot enforce the code against the landlord, the landlord probably cannot enforce it against the tenant.

b. Recovery under Modern Statutes

Some recent residential statutes impose certain repair duties on the tenant. These statutes also provide that, if the tenant fails to perform his duties, the landlord can make the repair and add the cost to the rent.

c. Effect of Insurance

Both the landlord and tenant have insurable property interests. Each party who purchases insurance against disrepair or destruction is entitled to any proceeds that are paid. This right to recover under the policy may be independent of any rights given under the lease.

Illustration: A fire destroyed the premises. Although Tom covenanted to repair, Lil had purchased her own casualty insurance policy. Tom's duty to repair is not eliminated because Lil receives an insurance award, and

Lil's insurance company may be subrogated to her rights against Tom.

Illustration: A fire destroyed the premises. Tom has his own insurance policy and did not covenant to rebuild. The majority rule is that Lil is not entitled to share in Tom's insurance proceeds, and Tom may keep the proceeds even though he is not obligated to rebuild. Under the minority rule, Lil can compel Tom to use the proceeds to restore the premises.

D. RIGHT TO TERMINATE TENANCY

This section discusses whether a party can terminate the tenancy if the other fails to repair.

1. Landlord's Right to Terminate

Because the early common law treated lease covenants as independent, a landlord could not terminate the lease even if the tenant was liable for waste or for breach of a covenant to repair. The landlord could only obtain damages or an injunction. Today, this doctrine generally has been modified by statute or by lease provision so that the landlord can terminate the tenancy.

a.   *No Right to Terminate if Tenant has no Duty*

If the tenant did not cause the disrepair and does not have a duty to repair, the landlord cannot terminate the tenancy for the tenant's failure to repair.

b. Right to Terminate After Destruction

Many modern statutes and lease covenants permit either party to terminate if a substantial part of the premises is destroyed.

2. Tenant's Right to Terminate

A statute or lease provision often permits a tenant to terminate the tenancy if the premises are substantially destroyed. Absent such a statute or provision, the common law rule applies, and destruction of the premises does not terminate the tenancy.

Illustration: The leased premises were destroyed by a fire of unknown origin, and neither a statute nor a lease provision addresses this situation. Neither party can terminate the tenancy. However, neither party can compel the other to rebuild. Tom is obligated to pay the rent but is not obligated to pay the cost of a new building. Lil also is not obligated to rebuild.

Illustration: The premises were destroyed by fire, and a statute or a lease provision permits termination in this situation. Tom or Lil now may terminate, and neither party is obligated to rebuild.

Illustration: The premises were destroyed by fire. No statute or lease provision permits termination, but Tom gave a covenant to repair. In this situation, Tom cannot terminate, and Lil can compel him to rebuild. If Tom fails to rebuild, Lil probably can terminate the lease for breach of covenant and can recover the cost of rebuilding.

Illustration: Tom caused the premises to be destroyed by fire. Although a statute permits termination after destruction, it probably is inapplicable to destruction caused by the party desiring to terminate. Thus, Tom cannot terminate. Based on the statute, Lil can terminate, and she can sue Tom for the cost of repairs because the destruction constitutes active waste.

Illustration: Lil caused the premises to be destroyed by fire. Tom had covenanted to rebuild, and a statute permits termination after destruction. Lil cannot terminate, because she caused the fire. Tom can terminate, even without the statute, because Lil breached the covenant of quiet enjoyment. Alternatively, Tom may be able to stay and to compel Lil to rebuild, or Tom may receive monetary compensation for the loss of the building. However, Tom cannot compel Lil to rebuild if Tom elects to terminate the tenancy.

If the building falls into disrepair, rather than being destroyed, the tenant may terminate only if the landlord has a duty to repair and fails to do so.

a. *When Building Code Applies to Landlord*

If a building code expressly prohibits landlords from renting premises that violate the code, courts often hold that a lease is unenforceable if substantial code violations exist when the landlord and tenant enter into the lease. However, if the violations are insubstantial or arise after the tenant has taken possession, the landlord's failure to comply with the building code usually does not entitle the tenant to terminate the lease. Similarly, if the code does not expressly prohibit landlords from leasing defective premises, the tenant normally cannot terminate the lease for violations. In that case, courts hold that the landlord owes the duty of code compliance to the government, rather than to the tenant.

b. When Special Statutory Duty Applies to Landlord

In most jurisdictions, a statute requires landlords to maintain residential premises in habitable condition. The same statute often authorizes a tenant to terminate the tenancy if the landlord fails to do so. This termination remedy often is provided as an alternative to the tenant's remedy of making the repair and deducting its cost from the rent.

c. Failure to Repair Common Areas

The landlord's failure to maintain the common areas in good repair does not entitle the tenant to terminate the tenancy unless the condition seriously impairs the tenant's enjoyment of the demised premises.

d. Failure to Honor Covenant to Repair— Constructive Eviction

If the landlord covenanted to make repairs but fails to do so, the tenant may be entitled to terminate the tenancy. Although the jurisdiction generally may treat lease covenants as being independent, the tenant's covenant to pay rent is dependent on the landlord's covenant of quiet enjoyment. The covenant of quiet enjoyment clearly is breached when a landlord evicts the tenant. It also is breached when the landlord's failure to perform lease obligations substantially impairs the tenant's enjoyment of the premises.

Illustration: Lil covenanted to make repairs. A fence on the demised property is broken, but Lil refuses to repair it. Tom cannot terminate the tenancy merely because Lil has breached her covenant to repair. But if nonrepair of the fence substantially impairs Tom's enjoyment of the premises, he may be entitled to terminate the tenancy.

For a plea of constructive eviction to succeed, the tenant must show that (1) the landlord had an obligation imposed in the lease or by law, (2) the landlord failed to perform the obligation, (3) the failure substantially impaired the tenant's enjoyment of the premises, and (4) the tenant promptly quit the premises as a result.

Illustration: Tom's lease does not expressly provide that the landlord must provide heat to the leased premises. During the winter, Lil fails to provide heat. At common law, Tom may not claim a constructive eviction, because Lil had no duty to furnish heat. She has breached no lease covenant and has not impaired Tom's quiet enjoyment of the premises. However, if these are residential premises, the landlord may be statutorily or judicially required to furnish heat in winter. In that event, Lil's failure breaches an implied obligation to Tom and entitles him to terminate the tenancy if the failure is sufficiently serious.

Illustration: Tom wants to convert the warehouse he leased from Lil into a movie theater. Under the building code, he must install an additional washroom on the premises if he wants to open the theater to the public. Because Tom's proposed special use of the premises creates this requirement, Lil is not required to satisfy it. Therefore, Tom cannot compel Lil to add a washroom and cannot terminate the lease if she fails to do so.

When a landlord evicts a tenant, the tenant's obligation to pay rent is entirely suspended even if he has not been completely removed from the premises. Based on this doctrine of partial actual eviction, some tenants have argued for a doctrine of partial constructive eviction. They claim that the entire rent obligation should be suspended even though they have not entirely quit the premises. However, this argument has not persuaded any court. Therefore, a tenant must leave the premises completely to succeed on a claim of constructive eviction.

Illustration: Lil shuts off the air conditioning at 5:00 p.m. each day, which makes the premises unusable until the next morning. Tom does not move out, but he refuses to pay rent on the basis that he suffers a partial constructive eviction after 5:00 p.m. each day. Under traditional rules, the claim will fail. Tom's rent obligation is excused only if he moves out and terminates his lease. He cannot stay and refuse to pay rent.

Illustration: Lil fails to repair a leak and, as a result, the basement is continuously flooded and unusable. Tom continues using the rest of the house but refuses to pay rent on the basis that he has suffered a partial constructive eviction from the basement. Under traditional concepts of constructive eviction, Tom's only right is to leave the premises entirely if he wishes to terminate his rent liability. However, Tom can argue that he has been partially actually evicted.

Constructive eviction not only ends the tenant's rent liability, but also may provide a cause of action against the landlord for breach of covenant. The action is based on the covenant to repair, if the lease contains one, or on the covenant of quiet enjoyment.

A tenant who claims constructive eviction and leaves the property is still liable under the lease if a court subsequently holds that the claim was unfounded. In that case, the tenant has merely abandoned the premises and is subject to all the liability that an abandoning tenant incurs.

E. RIGHT TO RENT REDUCTION (ABATEMENT)

In some jurisdictions, a tenant can reduce or withhold rent if the premises fall into disrepair.

1. Landlord's Covenant to Repair

If the landlord has given a covenant to repair and breaches it, the tenant generally is not entitled to withhold or to reduce rent. If the tenant seeks a monetary remedy for the landlord's breach, it may be limited to the cost of repairs or for the reduction of rental value.

2. Repair-and-Deduct Statute

Some statutes that require landlords of residential premises to keep them in habitable condition authorize the tenant to repair the premises and to deduct the cost from his rent. These statutes do not permit the tenant to pay a reduced rent based on the premise's reduced rental value.

3. Implied Warranty of Habitability

Since 1970, over forty states have created an implied warranty of habitability in residential leases. In some states, the implied warranty was judicially created. In other states, the warranty was statutorily created. Under the warranty, the landlord has the duty to maintain the premises, often in compliance with the local housing codes or a statutory standard. When a landlord violates the warranty, the tenant has a cause of action to recover the decreased rental value resulting from the violation.

Litigation between a landlord and tenant under the implied warranty of habitability usually begins when the tenant withholds rent. When the landlord brings an action to dispossess the tenant for nonpayment, the tenant defends by arguing that the rent is not due because of the code violations. Because affirmative defenses may be unavailable in a summary dispossession action, the tenant may be required to pay all or part of the rent into court each month while the case is pending as a condition to asserting this defense. At the conclusion of the hearing, the court allocates the escrowed rent between the landlord and the tenant. However, many jurisdictions do not permit rent withholding for breaches of the warranty of habitability.

4. Retaliatory Eviction

By statute or by judicial decision, many states prohibit landlords from evicting a tenant for asserting his rights under the warranty of habitability.

Illustration: Tom, a month to month tenant, withheld one month's rent to make a repair under a repair-and-deduct statute. Lil then gave the requisite notice to terminate the tenancy. If the termination is in retaliation for Tom's assertion of his statutory right, most states will not permit the termination. In some jurisdictions, termination by the landlord within a specified period, such as six months or a year following the tenant's assertion of rights, is presumed to be retaliatory.

Illustration: Tom, a periodic tenant, made the same repair and deduction as in the last Illustration. Lil then served notice that the rent would be tripled the following period. When Tom refused to pay the increase, Lil brought an action to dispossess him. This rent increase constitutes a retaliatory eviction.

Illustration: Tom notified the municipal health inspectors about code violations on the leased premises. As a result, Lil either terminated the tenancy or raised the rent. Either way, Lil has performed a retaliatory eviction, which is not permitted under most states' laws.

F. TORT LIABILITY FOR DISREPAIRS

1. Early Common Law

a. *Landlord's Liability*

Under the earlier common law, a landlord's tort liability for injuries caused by a physical defect in the leased premises was extremely circumscribed in three ways: (1) the scope of the landlord's duty, (2) the requirement for privity of contract, and (3) the recovery amount.

(1) Scope of Landlord's Duty

Traditionally, a landlord was liable for injuries caused by a defect in the premises that existed when the lease began in only the following six situations.

(a) Latent Defect

A landlord has a duty to disclose defects in the premises that are not readily discoverable based on a reasonable inspection (a latent defect). The failure to disclose constitutes fraud by omission. Often, the landlord is liable only if she knew of the defect, but, in some jurisdictions, the landlord is liable if she had reason to know about it. In these jurisdictions, the landlord has a duty to inspect the premises before leasing them. However, the landlord's only duty is to disclose the defect; she need not repair it.

Illustration: When Lil leased an apartment to Tom, she knew that the water in the shower unexpectedly could become extremely hot. She did not tell Tom. She will be liable to Tom if he is injured as a result.

(b) Unreasonable Risk of Harm to Persons Outside the Premises

If a condition on the leased premises creates an unreasonable risk of harm to people who are not on the premises, the landlord is liable for any injuries.

Illustration: When Lil leased the premises to Tom, an awning hook on the building extended over the adjoining sidewalk. If a passer-by is injured by the hook, Lil is liable.

(c) Premises Leased for Public Admission

When a landlord leases property that she knows will be open for public admission, she is liable for injuries caused by a condition that existed when the lease began.

Illustration: Lil leased an arena for a concert. A person attending the concert was injured when a step in a stairwell in the arena broke. If the defect in the step existed before the property was leased, Lil is liable.

(d) Common Areas

"Common areas" include those parts of the premises that are available for use by other tenants and their invitees, such as a building lobby or elevator. Because the landlord retains possession of the common areas, rather than giving exclusive possession to a particular tenant, she is liable for their condition unless the parties contracted otherwise.

(e) Landlord Covenanted to Make Repairs

If a landlord violates her covenant to make repairs in the leased premises, she is liable for any resulting injuries. This duty includes repairs necessary to satisfy the implied warranty of habitability. Absent a duty to inspect the premises, the landlord is liable only if she had notice of the defect and a reasonable opportunity to repair. Moreover, the tenant has a duty to inform invitees of the defect and otherwise to exercise due care.

Illustration: Lil gave a covenant to repair in her lease with Tom. Tom notified Lil that a light switch in the leased premises was defective, but Lil did not repair it.

Tom's visitor was injured when she received a shock from the light switch. She has a cause of action against Tom for failing to warn her of the defect and may have a cause of action against Lil for breach of the covenant to repair.

(f) Landlord's Negligent Repairs

The landlord is liable for injuries resulting from her negligence in making repairs if the tenant did not know and did not have reason to know of the danger. The landlord is liable though she was not obligated to make the repairs but voluntarily undertook to make them.

Illustration: The treads in the stairwell in Tom's apartment were rotting, so Lil replaced them. However, Lil did not properly attach the new treads, and Tom was injured when he stepped on one and it tipped. Lil is liable to Tom.

(2) Privity of Contract Requirement

The earlier common law prohibited recovery from the landlord unless the injured party was in privity of contract with her (i.e. had signed the lease). Therefore, the tenant's invitees and even his family generally would not have a cause of action against the landlord for injuries they suffered as a result of a defect in the premises for which the landlord was responsible.

(3) Recovery Amount

Even when the landlord was liable for a defect in the leased premises, the traditional rule limited the injured party's recovery to the cost of repairing the defect or to the amount by which the defect decreased the property's rental value.

b. Tenant's Liability

A large body of tort law deals with a tenant's liability to persons who are injured due to a defect in the premise's condition. Under the earlier common law, the tenant's liability depended in large part on the injured person's legal status. The tenant owed different duties of care to licensees, invitees, and trespassers.

2. Modern Law

a. Scope of Duty and Privity

Courts increasingly are rejecting the earlier common law restrictions on landlords' and tenants' liability for defects in the leased premises and are applying the usual tort requirements. Therefore, landlords and tenants must act as "reasonable persons" without regard to the injured party's privity or his common law status as a licensee, invitee, or trespasser.

(1) Landlord's Liability for Third Party's Criminal Activities

Generally, landlords are not liable for criminal attacks by other people. However, some courts now hold landlords liable in one or more of the following circumstances.

(a) Known Physical Defect

If the landlord knows of a physical defect in the premises that foreseeably increases the risk of a criminal attack, such as broken door or window locks, the landlord can be liable for the attack, even though she did not commit it.

(b) Providing Security

When a landlord provides security, she will be liable for a criminal attack if she removes the security or if it is provided in a negligent manner. It is irrelevant whether the landlord covenanted to provide security or provides it gratuitously.

Illustration: Lil hired a security guard to sit at the front door of her apartment building to prevent entry by unauthorized people. If she discontinues that service or if the security guard does not exercise reasonable care and a tenant is criminally attacked as a proximate result, Lil is liable.

(c) High Crime Area

In some jurisdictions, a landlord is liable for foreseeable criminal attacks even if they are not caused by a physical defect in the premises.

Illustration: Lil owns an apartment building in an area with a high crime rate. She may be liable if she fails to take precautions to prevent criminal attacks in the building even if such precautions are not required by the housing code or other legal duty. For example, she may be liable if she does not adequately secure the doors to the building, even if she is not otherwise required to do so.

b. Recovery Amount

Today, landlords are liable for all damages caused by a defect in the premises for which she is responsible. Courts have awarded damages for personal injury, decrease in rental value caused by the defect, property damage, relocation expenses, and emotional distress. A landlord also can be liable for punitive damages when her breach was willful and wanton or fraudulent.

c. Exculpatory Clauses

A landlord may attempt to insulate herself from liability by including an exculpatory clause in the lease. The clause may state that the landlord will not be liable for willful and wanton, reckless, or negligent conduct. Although such clauses generally are enforceable in commercial leases, at least with respect to negligent conduct, today they normally are unenforceable in residential leases.

In earlier cases, courts held that an exculpatory clause that bound a tenant also bound his invitees, but courts in more modern cases hold that an invitee cannot be bound because he was not a party to the lease.

Illustration: Tom's lease states that Lil is not liable for any negligent maintenance of the building. The clause is not a valid defense for Lil in a tort action brought by Tom's guest for injuries caused by Lil's negligent maintenance of the common hallway. The clause also may not protect Lil in a suit brought by Tom if he is injured as a result of Lil's negligent maintenance.

Illustration: Tom's lease covenants that he will hold Lil harmless against any liability imposed on her as a result of the premises' condition (an indemnity clause). The clause is not a valid defense for Lil against a third party suing her in tort. But, if the third party recovers a judgment against Lil, she may proceed against Tom based on the indemnity clause to recover the amount she had to pay the third party.

V. TRANSFER OF TENANCY

A. DISTINCTION BETWEEN ASSIGNING AND SUBLEASING

A lease assignment is the tenant's (assignor's) outright transfer of his entire remaining leasehold interest to an assignee. In contrast, a sublease is a leasing (subletting) of the tenant's estate by the tenant (sublessor) to another (subtenant or sublessee). Whether a transfer constitutes an assignment or a sublease is not determined by how the parties label the document. A court may declare that an assignment has occurred even though the parties have called it a sublease or vice versa. Under the original common law rule, the tenant must retain some part of the leasehold estate for the transfer to be a sublease. The more modern view makes the assignment/sublease distinction depend on the parties' intent, rather than on whether the tenant has transferred his entire estate or only some part of it.

Illustration: Tom has a lease with five years remaining in the term. He transfers the right to possess for the next four years to Sue. Traditionally, a court would hold that this is a sublease, because Tom has a reversion of one year after Sue's term expires.

Illustration: Tom has a lease with five years remaining in the term. Sue and he execute a document entitled "Sublease" that gives Sue the exclusive right to possess one room on the premises for the remaining five years. Under the traditional common law rule, this is not a sublease, but rather a partial assignment, because Tom has no reversion in that room. The length of the estate, rather than the size of the property, controls.

Illustration: Tom has a lease with five years remaining in the term. He transfers the entire balance of the term to Ann, who agrees to pay Tom $50 more per month than Tom owes to Lil. This is an assignment, despite the additional consideration, because Tom has no reversion. The court would characterize the additional $50 per month as deferred payment for the assignment, rather than as additional rent payable to Tom.

Illustration: Tom has a lease with five years remaining in the term. He transfers the entire balance of the term to Ann. The assignment document provides that Tom may re-enter and terminate Ann's estate if she fails to perform any lease obligation. In some states, this is treated as a sublease, because Tom retained a right of re-entry. Courts in other states more strictly follow the common law system of estates and hold that this is an assignment because the right of re-entry is not a common law estate. Thus, the entire estate has been transferred to Ann.

B. ASSIGNMENT'S EFFECT

1. Effect on Tenant

After an assignment, the original tenant remains in privity of contract with the landlord, because they signed the lease. Therefore, the tenant remains bound on all promises made to the landlord in the lease, unless the landlord releases him from liability. If the original tenant is held liable to the landlord for the assignee's default, the original tenant can exercise the landlord's rights against the assignee based on the doctrine of subrogation.

Illustration: Tom assigned his lease to Ann. Even if Lil accepted Ann as an assignee, Tom is still liable for the rent if Ann fails to pay it based on his promise to pay in the original lease. However, if Tom has to pay Lil, he can subrogate to Lil's right against Ann and sue her for the amount he had to pay.

2. Effect on Assignee

A lease assignment transfers the tenant's rights under the lease to the assignee, which creates privity of estate between the landlord and assignee. Based on privity of estate, the landlord and assignee can enforce the real covenants in the lease against each other. Real covenants are covenants that directly affect the land or the tenancy. For that reason, they "run with the land." If the lease includes any personal covenants (covenants that do not directly affect the land or the tenancy), the assignee is liable for them only if she "assumed" personal liability for the tenant's lease obligations. If the assignee assumes the tenant's lease obligations, the landlord is a third party beneficiary of the assumption agreement and can enforce it against the assignee. If the landlord was a party to the assumption agreement, she is in privity of contract with the assignee.

Illustration: Tom's lease contained a covenant that he would insure the premises. Under the applicable state law, this covenant does not run with the land. Tom assigned to Ann who did not assume. If Ann does not insure the premises, Lil has no recourse against her. But because Tom remains liable on his original promise to insure, Lil may obtain relief against him.

Illustration: Tom's lease contained a covenant that he would insure the premises. Under the applicable state law, this covenant does not run with the land. Tom assigned to Ann who assumed. If Ann fails to insure, Lil may enforce the assumption agreement against her either as a third party beneficiary or based on privity of contract. Lil also may sue Tom on the covenant in the original lease. If Lil sues Tom, Tom can sue Ann for breach of the assumption agreement.

Illustration: In Tom's lease, he gave a covenant to repair, which runs with the land. Tom assigned the lease to Ann who did not assume. If Ann does not repair, Lil may sue Tom and Ann. Lil may sue Tom because the original lease between them created privity of contract. Lil may sue Ann because the assignment created privity of estate between them and because the covenant runs with the land. If Lil sues Tom, he can recover from Ann. Although no privity exists between Tom and Ann, Tom can enforce the landlord's rights against Ann by subrogation.

3. Effect on Landlord

When the tenant assigns the lease, the assignee can enforce the landlord's real covenants against her, and the landlord can enforce the real covenants against the assignee.

Illustration: Tom's lease contained a covenant by Lil to make repairs, which is a real covenant. Tom assigned to Ann. Lil failed to make necessary repairs. Ann may enforce the covenant against Lil.

4. Effect of Second Assignment

An assuming assignee has the same duties to the landlord as the original tenant and, thus, remains liable on the lease covenants even after assigning her interest to a new assignee. In contrast, a nonassuming assignee is liable only while he has the right to possess. Once the nonassuming assignee assigns, no risk of future liability exists because he no longer has privity of estate with the landlord.

Illustration: Tom's lease contained a covenant that he would insure the premises. Under the applicable state law, this covenant does not run with the land. Tom assigned to Ann who assumed. Ann then assigned to Bob who assumed. If Bob does not insure the premises, Lil may sue Tom, Ann, or Bob. Ann's liability under the assumption does not end when Ann assigns, just as Tom's liability continued after he assigned.

Illustration: The same facts as in the previous Illustration, except that Bob did not assume. If Bob does not insure, Lil may sue Tom or Ann but not Bob.

Illustration: The same facts as in the first Illustration, except that neither Ann nor Bob assumed. If Bob does not insure, Lil's only remedy is against Tom.

Illustration: The same facts as in the first Illustration, except that Ann did not assume, but Bob did assume. If the assumption agreement is valid, Lil can sue Tom or Bob. However, courts in some states hold that Bob assumed no obligation because Ann was not personally responsible. In these jurisdictions, Lil could sue only Tom.

Illustration: Tom's lease contained his covenant to repair, which runs with the land. Tom assigned to Ann who did not assume. Ann then assigned to Bob who also did not assume. If Bob does not repair, Lil may sue Tom or Bob but not Ann. Tom is liable on the lease (privity of contract). Bob is liable because the covenant runs with the land, and he now owns the leasehold (privity of estate). Ann is not liable because she never assumed (no privity of contract) and because she no longer has an interest in the land (no privity of estate).

C. SUBLEASE'S EFFECT

A sublease does not transfer the tenant/sublessor's rights or duties to the subtenant. Instead, the sublessor remains the landlord's tenant and has privity of estate and privity of contract with her. As the sublessor's tenant, the sublessee and sublessor have privity of estate and privity of contract. The subtenant does not become the landlord's tenant, and no privity exists between them. Therefore, neither can directly enforce lease obligations against the other based on privity. However, some states have enacted a statute that enables a landlord to sue a sublessee.

Illustration: Tom sublet to Sue. The original lease contained Tom's covenant to insure, which runs with the land under the applicable state law. If Sue does not insure, Lil can proceed against Tom but not against Sue unless a state statute authorizes an action against her. Even without such a statute, Lil can terminate the tenancy for the failure to insure, which will also terminate Sue's subleasehold.

Illustration: Tom sublet to Sue. In the sublease, Sue covenanted to insure the premises. If Sue does not insure, Tom can enforce the covenant against her, but Lil cannot unless a state statute enables her to do so.

Illustration: Tom sublet to Sue. The original lease contained Tom's covenant to insure, and Sue assumed that obligation. If Sue fails to insure, Lil may sue her, because Lil is a third party beneficiary of Sue's assumption agreement or is in privity of contract with her if Lil was a party to the assumption agreement.

D. RESTRICTIONS ON TENANT'S RIGHT TO TRANSFER

Because a tenancy for a term or a periodic tenancy is freely alienable, the tenant may assign or sublease without the landlord's consent. Therefore, landlords often restrict a tenant's right to assign or sublet by a lease provision. The landlord has a sufficient interest in the property to justify this restraint on alienation, although courts generally construe such lease provisions as narrowly as possible. If a tenant assigns or subleases without the landlord's consent, the conveyance is valid as a matter of common law. However, most consent clauses are written as forfeiture restraints, which enable the landlord to terminate the lease if the tenant transfers his interest without the landlord's consent. The tenant also is liable to the landlord for any damages that she suffers as a result of the transfer.

1. Landlord's Right to be Unreasonable

Most lease provisions that restrict assignments and subleases state that the tenant shall not assign or sublet without the landlord's consent. If the provision does not expressly state that the landlord cannot withhold consent unreasonably, most courts will not add such a requirement. However, some courts impose an obligation on the landlord to act in good faith even if it is not expressed in the lease. Courts disagree whether the landlord may condition her consent on receiving a rent increase. A court may regard such a demand as unreasonable unless the lease specifically permits it. In jurisdictions that require a landlord to mitigate damages after a tenant abandons, a court effectively may impose a duty to consent to a reasonable transfer if the landlord would have to accept that transferee in mitigation of the tenant's damages.

Illustration: Tom proposes to assign to Ann, but Lil unreasonably refuses to consent. Lil's arbitrary refusal may be valid unless the no-assignment clause requires her to act reasonably. However, if Tom now abandons and offers Ann as a tenant again, Lil's second refusal to accept Ann may constitute a failure to mitigate damages. In a state where Lil has a duty to mitigate, her second refusal may terminate Tom's continuing liability for rent.

2. Effect of Consenting to First Assignment

Pursuant to the Rule in Dumpor's Case (1603), if a landlord consents to one assignment, she waives any right to prohibit subsequent assignments. Thus, the assignee subsequently can assign without consent. Many courts today have rejected the Rule. In jurisdictions that still follow it, a lease provision can negate it. For example, the original lease may provide that consent to one assignment does not constitute consent to further assignments, though the assignee may not be bound by that provision because he was not a party to the lease. Alternatively, the landlord can condition her consent to the first assignment on the assignee's agreement to seek consent before assigning to a new assignee. Some courts that apply the Rule to assignments do not apply it to subleases.

VI. TERMINATION OF TENANCIES

A. TERMINATION ACCORDING TO TYPE OF TENANCY

1. Tenancy for a Term

Because the lease specifies a termination date, the tenancy for a term automatically ends on that date. No notice is required, unless the lease provides otherwise. The tenancy ends when the term ends.

2. Periodic Tenancy

This tenancy automatically renews until timely notice of termination is given by the landlord or by the tenant. Usually, such notice must be given at least one period in advance. Thus, a tenancy from week to week usually requires one week's notice of termination, and a tenancy from month to month usually requires one month's notice. The tenancy from year to year required only six months' notice of termination at common law. Some state statutes alter these common law notice periods.

The notice usually must coincide with the rental period, i.e. a tenancy from month to month commencing on the first day of each month can only be terminated by a notice effective on the first day of a month. Some states permit the parties to agree to a shorter notice period, such as seven days' notice for a month to month tenancy. On the other hand, some states require longer notice periods than the common law, such as one month's notice to terminate a weekly tenancy or sixty days' notice to terminate a monthly tenancy.

3. Tenancy at Will

This estate terminates when either party gives notice to that effect to the other. At common law, the notice could take effect immediately. Today, many states impose a waiting period, thereby making the tenancy at will very much like a periodic tenancy in this regard. When the agreement gives one party the option to terminate early, the estate may be treated as a defeasible term, rather than as a tenancy at will, such as a term for years subject to defeasance by the landlord or tenant at an earlier time. In other jurisdictions, courts will give both the landlord and the tenant the right to terminate despite a more restrictive lease provision.

A tenancy at will also terminates when the landlord or tenant dies or when either party attempts to assign its interest. The tenancy also can terminate if the tenant commits waste.

4. Tenancy at Sufferance

The common law does not require any notice to end this tenancy, because the original termination date has passed. However, some states statutorily require notice. If the holdover becomes a periodic tenant by virtue of the landlord's election, this estate must be terminated in the same manner as all other periodic tenancies.

B. OTHER WAYS OF TERMINATING A TENANCY

1. Destruction of Premises

At common law, destruction of the premises did not terminate the tenancy. The tenant still had a nonfreehold estate in the land even if it hardly could be used. Today, many states provide by statute that destruction of all or a material part of the premises automatically terminates the tenancy or gives each party an option to terminate. Most leases also provide for this contingency.

2. Tenant's Breach—Doctrine of Independent Covenants

At common law, the tenant's failure to perform covenants under the lease did not entitle the landlord to terminate the estate. Covenants in leases were independent, so that nonperformance by one did not excuse performance by the other. Thus, even though the tenant was not paying rent, the common law landlord had to let the tenant retain possession. The landlord's remedy was to enforce the particular covenant involved. For example, if the tenant did not pay rent, the landlord could sue to recover the rent or could seek the old remedy of distress to levy on the tenant's chattels.

Today, either by statute or by lease provision, a landlord can terminate the tenancy if the tenant defaults in the performance of any major covenant, including the obligation to pay rent. Most leases make the tenant's performance of all his lease covenants a condition for continuance of the estate. This provision enables the landlord to terminate the lease (usually called a right of entry) incident to her reversion. After default by the tenant, the landlord usually is required to give notice that the tenant must correct the breach or quit the premises. If the tenant fails to do either, the landlord may commence summary proceedings to terminate the tenancy and to recover possession (unlawful detainer action).

3. Landlord's Breach—Covenant of Quiet Enjoyment

As for the tenant, the landlord's lease covenants were independent. Therefore, the tenant was obligated to continue paying rent even if the landlord failed to perform her lease covenants. One exception was the covenant of quiet enjoyment, which is the landlord's promise that she will not disturb the tenant's possession. This covenant is implied into every lease. If the landlord breaches this covenant, the tenant is entitled to terminate the tenancy.

Eviction by the Landlord—Illustration: Tom has a tenancy for a term with six months remaining. However, Lil changed the lock on the door, thereby locking Tom out. Tom may now treat the tenancy as being terminated and may stop paying rent. Tom also may treat the lockout as a tort—either a trespass or a forcible entry—and may sue for damages. Finally, Tom can sue to recover possession.

Eviction by Third Parties—Illustration: Tom has a tenancy for a term with six months remaining. An intrusion by third parties makes it impossible for Tom to possess the premises. Tom may not terminate his lease obligations, because Lil has not breached. The landlord's covenant of quiet enjoyment applies only to acts of Lil or her agents. She does not insure Tom's possession against third parties. This reasoning also justified the common law rule that destruction of the premises did not terminate the tenant's lease obligation, unless the landlord caused the loss.

Eviction by Other Tenants—Illustration: Other tenants in the building disturb Tom's possession. In some jurisdictions, Tom may terminate under these circumstances. In many other jurisdictions, however, the landlord is not responsible for the other tenants' actions, unless those actions violated their leases. If so, Lil's power to prevent Tom's neighbors from violating their leases may entitle Tom to treat her as responsible for the disturbances they cause.

Eviction by Paramount Title—Illustration: Lil failed to pay her mortgage, and the mortgagee foreclosed and evicted Tom. This is an eviction by paramount title. Lil's covenant of quiet enjoyment protects against that contingency. Therefore, Tom may treat the lease as terminated.

a. Mortgages and Leases

If the landlord mortgages the property and then leases it, the tenant's interest is inferior to the mortgage. The mere existence or assertion of a mortgage or any other adverse claim does not constitute a breach of the covenant of quiet enjoyment. There first must be an "eviction." If the mortgagee forecloses, the tenancy is destroyed because the leasehold, as well as the reversion, was subject to the mortgage. An eviction has now occurred, and the tenant may stop paying rent and quit the premises even if the mortgagee desires to preserve the tenancy. For mortgage foreclosures, see Chapter 12.

On the other hand, if the landlord first leases the property and then mortgages it, the lease is paramount to the mortgage. In this case, a foreclosure sale transfers only the reversion and makes the purchaser the tenant's new landlord. Because the tenancy is not destroyed, no eviction has occurred and the covenant of quiet enjoyment is not breached.

Most mortgagees will not accept a mortgage that is subject to outstanding leases. Therefore, leases commonly provide that they will be subject to mortgages executed either before or after the lease (subordination clause).

b. Constructive Eviction

At early common law, lease covenants were independent. Therefore, when the landlord defaulted, the tenant could sue for breach but could not terminate the lease. However, if the landlord's failure to perform a covenant virtually destroyed the tenant's ability to enjoy the premises, the landlord was in breach of the covenant of quiet enjoyment. When that covenant is breached by an actual eviction, the tenant always can terminate. By analogy, when the landlord has breached indirectly by failing to perform a covenant, a constructive eviction has occurred, and the tenant may terminate.

4. By Agreement—Surrender

The parties always can agree to terminate a tenancy before it would end normally. Unlike a contract, surrender is not accomplished simply by agreeing to terminate. Because the lease conveyed an estate in property to the tenant, he should reconvey that estate to the landlord by a surrender deed if the estate is long enough to come within the Statute of Frauds. However, surrender by operation of law sometimes occurs when the tenant abandons the property and the landlord re-enters. Surrender by operation of law eliminates the need for a writing. A conveyance of the landlord's reversion to the tenant is by release deed.

5. Eminent Domain

The government has the power to acquire private property for public use. When leased property is taken, the government acquires the tenant's, as well as the landlord's, interest, which has the effect of terminating the lease.

The government is required to pay just compensation (i.e. the fair market value of the property), and both the landlord and the tenant may share in the condemnation award. If the value of the tenant's leasehold was equal to his rent burden, he has no claim to any part of the award because his loss (future use of the premises) is offset by an equivalent gain (termination of future rent liability). But if his leasehold had a value in excess of his rent, some of the award belongs to him.

Illustration: Tom leased property for five years at $1,000 per month. Because neighborhood conditions have improved, the fair rental value of the property is now $1,200 per month. If the government takes the property, Tom should receive the lost bonus value of his lease, which is $200 for each month remaining in the lease term, reduced to the present value. Lil will receive the land's fair market value, less the amount of Tom's award. Lil's interest is worth less than it would be otherwise because of the depressing effect of Tom's lease. If her property would be worth $100,000 if it was not leased to Tom, the fact that Tom pays $200 per month below the current market rent means that any buyer of the property would require that the purchase price be reduced to cover that shortfall in rent.

When the government takes property only temporarily and for a shorter duration than the remainder of the tenancy, the lease is not terminated, and the award goes entirely to the tenant. However, the tenant must continue to pay rent to the landlord. When a physical part of the property is taken, most courts hold that the tenant's rent liability is unaffected. Therefore, the tenant is entitled to receive both the future rent owed for the part taken and its bonus value. The balance goes to the landlord.

C. LANDLORD'S REMEDIES FOR CONTINUED POSSESSION AFTER LEASE TERMINATES—HOLDOVER TENANTS

The tenant's possession should end when the leasehold ends. If a tenant holds over after the term expires, the landlord has a choice of remedies.

1. Double or Treble Damages

Statutes in many states permit the landlord to recover two or three times the regular rent for the time that the tenant actually holds over. This remedy sometimes is limited to willful or malicious holdovers.

2. Increased Rent

The lease may specify a higher rent for any period of holding over, or the landlord may notify the tenant before the end of the term of this consequence. Courts generally uphold this type of lease provision or notice if the rent increase is reasonable. However, if the tenant already has begun holding over, an attempt to increase the rent thereafter may be invalid.

3. Eviction and Damages

In every state, a landlord may evict a holdover tenant and recover damages for the fair rental value of the premises during the holdover period.

4. Self-Help

Although a landlord may be entitled to evict a holdover tenant, the landlord may not enter the premises without a court order or use self-help to oust the tenant, such as changing the locks. In many states, such acts make the landlord guilty of forcible entry because the tenant is a peaceable, albeit wrongful, possessor. A landlord's right to evict is primarily the right to bring judicial summary dispossession proceedings against the tenant.

5. Renewal of Tenancy for Additional Term

The landlord may elect to renew a holdover's tenancy for another term, usually equal to the length of the original term, regardless of how long the tenant actually held over. However, the new term usually may not exceed one year because of the Statute of Frauds. In most states, the tenant becomes a periodic tenant. In others, the tenant becomes a tenant for a term.

Illustration: Tom had a one year lease and held over for five days after its expiration. Lil may elect to make Tom stay another period, either as a periodic tenant (majority rule) or as a tenant for a term (minority rule). If Tom becomes a periodic tenant, some states treat him as a tenant from year to year because the original term was a year. Other states will treat him as a tenant from month to month if the rent was paid on a monthly basis.

Illustration: Tom was a tenant from month to month. Either Lil or Tom gave thirty days' notice of intent to terminate the tenancy effective the following month. However, Tom held over for three days after the termination date. As a result, Lil can hold Tom liable for the entire month, either as a tenant from month to month or as a tenant for a term (a month).

a. Consequence of Tenant for a Term Becoming a Periodic Tenant

A tenant for a term who holds over may, at the landlord's election, be converted into a periodic tenant. Because periodic tenancies are terminated only by giving the necessary notice, the tenancy may be continued for a third period, even though the tenant did not hold over after the second period, if he does not give timely notice of intent to terminate during the second period.

Illustration: Tom had one year lease that began on January 1, 2008 and ended on December 31, 2008. Tom held over until January 5, 2009, and Lil elected to renew Tom's tenancy. Under the applicable state law, Tom became a tenant from year to year. On December 31, 2009, Tom vacated. If Tom did not give timely notice to terminate the tenancy at the end of 2009, Lil can hold him liable for the next year (2010) because the tenancy from year to year that was created in 2009 automatically renewed in 2010.

b. Increased Rent

Most states require that the landlord give a rent increase notice as far in advance as a termination notice. Therefore, a landlord may be unable to increase the rent owed by a holdover tenant unless notice of the increase was given in a timely manner.

Illustration: Tom held over after the end of his tenancy. Lil then notified him that, if he stayed, he would owe a higher rent. Unless she gave this notice sufficiently in advance of the date of the increase, the increase is invalid.

D. CONSEQUENCES OF A TENANT ATTEMPTING TO SURRENDER THE ESTATE BEFORE THE END OF THE TERM – ABANDONMENT AND SURRENDER

In a tenancy for a term and a periodic tenancy, the tenant has an estate that continues for a certain length of time. The estate's duration is unaffected by the tenant's possession or failure to possess. The estate is possessory whether the tenant actually possesses. Consequently, even a nonpossessing tenant owes rent for the entire lease term.

1. Failure to Pay Rent

A tenant does not terminate the tenancy simply by failing to pay rent. Under the early common law doctrine that lease covenants are independent, the landlord could not terminate the estate merely because the tenant failed to perform the rent covenant. Today, a landlord generally may terminate the tenant's estate for nonpayment of rent. However, nonpayment does not automatically terminate the estate. Termination requires the landlord's affirmative act.

2. Failure to Retain Possession and to Pay Rent

If a tenant abandons the leased property and stops paying rent, the tenancy is not automatically terminated. The landlord can treat the lease as continuing and can sue for the rent due for each succeeding period.

Illustration: Tom is a tenant for a term of five years at a rent of $100 per month. After one year of possession, Tom abandoned the property and paid no more rent. Among her other alternatives, Lil can sue Tom for $100 each month thereafter, entirely ignoring Tom's abandonment. Lil also may wait three months and then sue for $300 in back rent or wait six months and sue for $600. Only the statute of limitations dictates how long Lil may wait. Lil may sue for rent only when it becomes due. She cannot sue for the rent for the balance of the term immediately upon Tom's abandonment. Even if the lease has a rent acceleration clause, which makes all the rent due when Tom breaches, a court usually would not grant Lil this extreme form of relief.

Illustration: Tom is a tenant from month to month. Tom paid January's rent, which was due on January 1. He abandoned the premises on January 20 and paid no rent thereafter. Lil filed suit on May 15. In this action, Lil can recover rent for the months of February through May. A periodic tenancy is terminated only by notice, and Tom gave no notice. Therefore, the tenancy is still alive, and rent is due for each month it continues. Although Tom's abandonment and rent default gave Lil the option of terminating the estate, she was not required to do so. She may continue to hold Tom liable for rent until he properly terminates the tenancy.

a. *Duty to Mitigate*

The two previous Illustrations assumed that a landlord is entitled to leave the premises vacant and to hold the tenant liable for rent. This had been the majority rule in the United States. However, a growing number of jurisdictions compel the landlord, by statute or by judicial decision, to mitigate damages by looking for a new tenant. Even under the rule that a landlord must mitigate, the abandoning tenant is liable for the rent specified in his lease if the landlord is unable to find a new tenant.

b. *Surrender by Operation of Law*

If a tenant abandons the property and stops paying rent, the landlord may treat the tenant's conduct as an offer to surrender the leasehold estate. The landlord can accept this offer by re-entering the premises and retaking possession. Re-entry terminates the tenancy and the tenant's rent liability.

Illustration: Tom was a tenant for a term with eight months remaining on his lease. Tom stopped paying rent and abandoned the property. Lil immediately re-entered, remodeled, and began using the premises. These acts terminated the tenancy and Tom's liability for the remaining rent.

Because the lease conveyed an estate in land to the tenant, the early common law provided that the estate could be terminated only by a reconveyance to the landlord by a surrender deed. To solve the practical problems posed by the tenant's abandonment, the courts created the fiction that the tenant's abandonment constituted an offer to surrender the leasehold estate and that the landlord's re-entry was an acceptance of that offer. In this way, the tenant's estate was surrendered by operation of law, rather than by surrender deed.

3. Tenant's Failure to Pay Rent or to Perform Other Lease Covenants

Today, either by statute or by lease provision, a landlord normally can bring judicial proceedings to evict a tenant after default. In these proceedings, the court usually both terminates the tenancy and orders the tenant's physical eviction. Consequently, the tenant's liability for future rent also terminates.

Illustration: With six months remaining on the lease, Tom fails to pay rent, and Lil brings a summary dispossession action against him. In the action, Lil prays to have Tom's tenancy terminated. The suit will give Lil possession of the premises and will terminate Tom's liability for future rent.

a. Dispossession Without Termination

Some states permit a landlord to dispossess a defaulting tenant without terminating the leasehold estate. When this is permitted, the tenant is denied possession but remains liable for rent for the balance of the term. This fairly inequitable combination is rare.

4. Reletting for Tenant's Account

When the tenant abandons the premises, the landlord may have a third remedy that is midway between the choices of terminating the tenancy and of permitting the premises to stay vacant and suing for the rent. The landlord may re-enter and relet the premises as the tenant's agent or for the tenant's account, so that the tenant's liability is limited to the rent due before a new tenant was found, plus any rent differential if the new tenant pays a lower rent.

Illustration: Tom abandoned when his lease had one year remaining at a monthly rent of $1,000. Lil re-entered and, one month later, relet the premises for a monthly rent of $900. At the end of that year, Lil can sue Tom for $1,000 (for the month that the premises were vacant), plus $1,100 ($100 per month loss for the remaining eleven months).

In some states, this remedy is unavailable to the landlord unless the lease provides for it or unless the landlord notifies the tenant of her intent to pursue this remedy. However, the tenant's consent generally is not required.

Because re-entry and reletting are possessory acts, a danger exists that a court will treat them as a retaking of possession for the landlord's own account, thereby causing the lease to terminate.

Generally, the landlord must make it plain throughout that she has acted solely for the tenant's account. But sometimes the acts themselves may defeat contrary statements of intent, such as when the landlord entirely reconstructs the premises to suit a new tenant who agrees to rent for a much longer period than the balance of the original term. In such a case, a court may hold that a surrender has occurred, despite the landlord's assertion that she is acting solely as the tenant's agent.

5. Difference Value Damages

When a tenant abandons, courts increasingly award the landlord the difference between the property's fair rental value and the rent amount in the tenant's lease. This measure of damages protects the tenant from liability for the full rent and benefits the landlord by allowing suit to be brought immediately after abandonment, rather than when the term ends. When this measure applies, alternative measures of recovery often are prohibited.

Illustration: Tom had one year remaining on his lease when he abandoned. The rent reserved under the lease is $1,000 per month, but the fair rental value of the premises is only $900. If permitted in the jurisdiction, Lil may sue immediately for $1,200, which is the difference between $900 and $1,000 for the remaining twelve months (12 x $100). This may be the only remedy available to Lil.

Illustration: Tom had one year remaining on his lease when he abandoned. The rent reserved under the lease is $1,000 per month, but the fair rental value of the premises is $1,100 per month. Lil can recover no damages, because Tom's abandonment benefited her. Before Tom's abandonment, Lil was renting premises worth $1,100 per month for only $1,000 and was losing $100 a month for every month that Tom stayed.

Illustration: Tom had one year remaining on his lease when he defaulted in his rent. Lil sued to terminate his estate. The rent reserved under the lease is $1,000 per month, but the fair rental value is $900. In addition to terminating Tom's interest in the land, Lil may recover $1,200 (the difference between $900 and $1,000 over twelve months), plus any unpaid back rent. It is irrelevant that Lil, rather than Tom, terminated the tenancy. Her damages are the same.

CHAPTER FIVE

EASEMENTS, PROFITS, AND LICENSES

I. NATURE OF EASEMENTS

A. EASEMENTS DISTINGUISHED FROM POSSESSORY INTERESTS

An easement holder is known as the dominant tenant (represented by "Dita" in the Illustrations). The dominant tenant does not have the right to possess the property but has only a right to make some limited use of it. Property subject to an easement always is owned by someone other than the dominant tenant. In this context, the owner is known as the servient tenant (represented by "Steve" in the Illustrations).

1. No Right to Exclude

Ownership and the right to possess generally include the right to exclude others from the property. Because an easement is a nonpossessory interest, normally it does not include the right to exclude others or to stop them from also enjoying the property. However, an "exclusive" easement gives the dominant tenant the right to prevent the servient tenant from permitting others to use the easement.

Illustration: Steve owns a parcel of land in fee simple absolute. He granted Dita a right of way on a road across it. She has an easement, not a possessory interest, in Steve's property. She may use the road but cannot stop others from also using it, except to the extent that their use interferes with hers. In contrast, Steve, as possessor, may exclude everyone except Dita from crossing his property, even though their crossings constitute no real injury to Steve. As possessor, Steve also may continue to use the road himself, so long as he does not interfere with Dita's use. If Steve leased or sold the road to Dita, thereby transferring full possession to her, she could exclude him and all others from using the road even without showing that their use interfered with hers.

Illustration: Lil leased her property to Tom for ten years. The lease restricts Tom to residential uses of the property. Tom has a possessory interest in the property and not just an easement. While Tom's possessory interest is limited in its use, Lil did not retain any possessory rights. Otherwise, she could run a business on the property so long as it did not interfere with Tom's residential use. Because Tom has the exclusive right to possess, he may exclude all others, including Lil.

B. EASEMENTS DISTINGUISHED FROM OTHER NONPOSSESSORY INTERESTS

1. Profits

The owner of a profit has the right to enter the servient estate to remove some part or product of the soil. The early common law profits included (a) turbary—the right to remove turf for use as fuel, (b) piscary—the right to fish, (c) estovers—the right to cut timber for fuel, and (d) pasture—the right to graze animals. Contemporary interests in land that sometimes are called profits are the right to mine coal or other minerals, to drill for oil or gas, or to cut timber.

Virtually no difference exists between the laws governing easements and profits. Both generally come under the same rules. Under the Restatement of Property (Third), easements and profits are categorized together as "servitudes" and generally are subject to the same rules.

2. Natural Rights in Land

By virtue of possession alone, a possessor has certain rights in neighboring lands. But these "natural rights" are different from an easement. No person acquires an easement in another's land merely by virtue of owning or possessing some other land. An easement must be created.

Illustration: Martin owns Lot 1, and Nora owns the adjacent Lot 2. Merely by virtue of owning Lot 1, Martin can prevent Nora from excavating her land so close to the lot line that the natural support her lot provides to his lot would be removed.

Illustration: The owner of a downstream lot may be able to enjoin the owners of upstream lots from polluting the stream or from taking more than their fair share of water.

3. Licenses

Easements may be categorized according to their duration in the same manner as estates. For instance, easements can be created to last indefinitely, for life, or for a certain term. However, there is no easement equivalent to the tenancy at will. When a use of land is terminable at the will of the servient tenant, it is a license, rather than an easement. The primary distinction between a license and an easement is that the former is terminable at will and the latter is not. A license is a revocable nonpossessory right to use land for a limited purpose, such as parking a car in a parking lot or dining at a restaurant.

II. TYPES OF EASEMENTS AND PROFITS

A. APPURTENANT v. IN GROSS

An appurtenant easement benefits a particular parcel of land (the dominant estate or dominant tenement), even if title to the land is transferred after the easement is created. In contrast, an in gross easement benefits a particular individual regardless of whether she owns any land. The land that is subject to an appurtenant or in gross easement is called the servient estate or servient tenement.

Illustration: Steve granted Dita the right to swim in a pond on his property. Dita is not a neighbor. If this is not a license, it probably is an easement in gross. Dita may swim in the pond regardless of what property she owns or whether she owns any property at all.

Illustration: Dita owned a large parcel of land adjacent to a stream. She sold the part of the property directly contiguous to the stream to Steve but reserved an easement to cross from her remaining property to the stream. Unless Dita reserved this right just for herself, her easement is appurtenant. It was created to benefit her retained parcel. When she sells the retained parcel, she no longer can use the easement, but the new owner can.

An appurtenant easement is connected to the dominant estate even if the dominant and servient parcels are not adjacent.

Illustration: Dita owns a parcel of land far upstream from Steve's land. Steve granted Dita the right to flood his property. The easement is appurtenant if it is connected to ownership of the upstream parcel, rather than a right granted just to Dita.

1. No Dominant Tenement when Easement is in Gross

An appurtenant easement always benefits some land held by the dominant tenant. An in gross easement does not necessarily benefit any particular parcel of land. An in gross easement is intended to benefit only its holder, though it incidentally may enhance her use of a parcel of land. Thus, when an easement is in gross, there is no dominant estate though there is a dominant tenant.

2. Profits

A profit may be appurtenant or in gross according to the same criteria as for easements.

Illustration: Steve granted Dita a profit to mine coal on his land. This profit is probably in gross because Dita may enjoy the privilege of mining regardless of what property she owns.

Illustration: Steve granted Dita a profit to drain water from a lake on his land to irrigate her land. This profit is appurtenant if it is for the benefit of Dita's land even when she no longer owns it.

B. AFFIRMATIVE, NEGATIVE, OR SPURIOUS

An easement is affirmative when it entitles the dominant tenant to use the servient estate for a particular purpose. It is negative when it entitles the dominant tenant to prevent the servient tenant from using the property in a particular way.

Illustration: Steve granted a right of way to Dita. Without this easement, Dita would be guilty of trespass if she walked across Steve's land. With the easement, however, Dita may cross without being liable for trespass. This easement is affirmative.

Illustration: Steve granted Dita an easement of view over his property. Without this easement, Steve could build on his property in a way that blocked Dita's view. After granting the easement, Steve no longer has this right. Dita has a negative easement.

The term "spurious easement" is sometimes used when the servient tenant agrees to perform an affirmative obligation. However, as its name indicates, it is not really an easement. Instead, its enforcement usually must be based on some theory other than easement law. One reason that these cannot be easements is that courts do not permit private parties to create "novel interests" in land. Easements can be created only for uses authorized by the courts or legislature.

Illustration: Steve agreed with Dita that he would plant and care for a tree on his property. Dita does not have an easement in Steve's property. A negative easement would permit Dita to restrain, not compel, Steve from some use. Nor is this an affirmative easement, because Dita does not have the right to enter Steve's property to plant or care for the tree herself.

III. CREATION OF EASEMENTS, PROFITS, AND LICENSES

A. BY EXPRESS WORDS — GRANT AND RESERVATION

The usual way to convey an easement is by a deed or other written conveyance ("I grant you a right of way across my land."). When a landowner transfers his land and wishes to retain certain rights in it, he normally gives a deed that conveys title to the land but reserves an easement in it ("I grant Lot 1 to you but reserve a right of way across it from Lot 2 to the road."). The Restatement of Property states that words of contract, as well as words of conveyance, may create an easement. Restatement (Third) of Property (Servitudes) § 2.1 (1998) (hereinafter "Restatement of Servitudes"). Thus, pursuant to the Restatement, a contractual agreement providing for one party to have a right of way over the property of another is as effective as a deed.

At common law, the grantor had to "reserve," rather than "except," the easement, because only physical parts of the property could be excepted. In most jurisdictions, the grantor can reserve an easement only for herself and not for a third party. If she wants a third party to have the benefit of the easement, she has to convey it directly to that person. Alternatively, she can reserve it to herself and then transfer it to the third party if it is transferable. The Restatement of Servitudes, if followed by the jurisdiction, permits a servitude to be reserved for the benefit of a third party. Restatement of Servitudes § 2.6.

1. Formalities and Failure to Comply with Them — Licenses

Creation of an easement generally requires the same formalities as the transfer or creation of other interests in land. Usually, a writing, signature, and delivery of the document are necessary. When an attempt to create an easement fails because of noncompliance with the necessary formalities, the grantee acquires a license. A license is revocable unless the licensee has a defense prohibiting it. See Section VIII of this Chapter.

Illustration: Steve orally granted Dita a right of way across his property for ten years. The relevant Statute of Frauds requires a signed writing to convey an interest in land that exceeds one year. As a result, Steve's grant did not give Dita an easement, but it did give her a license to cross his land. Therefore, Dita will not be trespassing when she crosses Steve's land, but he may revoke her privilege to do so at any time.

2. Formal Creation of Licenses

Not all licenses arise because of inadequate attempts to create an easement. A revocable privilege of use may be precisely what the parties intend.

Illustration: Steve delivered to Dita a written and signed instrument that states: "You may walk across my property until I change my mind." Even if the document complies with all the formalities for a conveyance, it creates only a license because it expressly makes the interest revocable.

3. Other Revocable Rights to Use

A license can arise not only from a failed attempt to create an easement or from an express declaration of revocability, but also because the parties have created an interest too limited to be characterized as an easement.

Illustration: Steve invited Dita to a party at his house. The invitation gave Dita a license, even if it was written and says that it is irrevocable. The right to enter land that is created by a party invitation is too slight to be an easement.

Illustration: Steve sold Dita a ticket to watch a sporting event on his property. Despite the enforceable contract underlying the ticket, it created only a license. If Steve breaches the contract by refusing Dita admission, she has only an action for damages.

B. BY IMPLICATION

Two types of implied easements are legally recognized — an easement by necessity (also known as a way by necessity) and a quasi-easement (also known as an easement implied by past use). These easements are implied based on the grantor's and grantee's presumed intent. An implied easement will be created only if an express easement could have been.

1. Easement by Necessity

An easement by necessity (also known as a way by necessity) is implied when a parcel of land is subdivided in such a way that one or more of the subdivided lots do not have access to a public road (i.e. are landlocked). In this situation, courts presume that the buyer and seller of the landlocked lot must have intended to create an access easement for it. Otherwise, the lot would be virtually unusable. A public policy to enhance the productive use of land also supports the implication of an easement. However, the owner of the landlocked lot can waive the creation of an implied access easement.

Three elements must be satisfied to imply an easement by necessity: (1) The dominant and servient estates were owned by the same person; (2) The need for an access easement was created by the subdivision of the commonly owned land; and (3) The easement is necessary to use the dominant estate.

a. Common Ownership

The dominant and servient estates must have been owned by the same person before the need for access to the dominant estate arose.

Illustration: Dita and Steve own neighboring lots, both of which adjoin a public road. The portion of the road adjacent to Dita's lot was closed permanently, and she has no other access to a public road. She cannot get a way by necessity across Steve's land.

b. Need Created by Subdivision

A way by necessity is implied only when the grantor conveys a part of the property she owns or when she divides the entire property among separate grantees. In either case, an earlier ownership has been severed into multiple ownerships.

In the following Illustrations, assume that Owen owned a large parcel of land with a house on the rear half and a public street adjoining the front half.

Illustration: Owen conveyed the rear half to Dita and retained the front half. An easement can be implied in favor of Dita's half across Owen's half.

Illustration: Owen conveyed the rear half to Dita and the front half to Steve. An easement can be implied in favor of Dita's half across Steve's half.

Illustration: Owen conveyed the entire parcel to Dita. A driveway from Owen's house crosses a neighboring parcel. If Owen did not have an easement across the neighboring parcel, he could not have conveyed an express easement to Dita, and an implied easement cannot be created. Conversely, if Owen had an appurtenant easement over the neighboring land, the transfer of his lot to Dita automatically would transfer the existing easement to her, even if the deed did not mention it. It would not be created by implication.

Illustration: Owen conveyed the front half to Steve. Because of circumstances existing when Owen made the conveyance, an implied easement in favor of the rear half was not implied. Owen later conveyed the rear half to Dita. An implied easement cannot be created as a result of this second conveyance regardless of the circumstances, because the severance of ownership already had occurred. When Owen conveyed the rear half to Dita, he could not create an express easement over the front half for her because he no longer owned that portion of the property.

(1) Implied Grant and Implied Reservation

An implied easement can be created by grant or by reservation.

Illustration: Dita owned a parcel of land with a house on the rear half and a public street adjoining the front half. Dita sold the front half of the lot to Steve. If an easement is implied from the circumstances of this conveyance, the easement was *reserved* for Dita's retained parcel.

Illustration: Steve owned a parcel of land with a house on the rear half and a public street adjoining the front half. Steve sold the rear half of the lot to Dita. If an easement is implied from the circumstances of this conveyance, the easement was *granted* to Dita together with the rear half of the lot.

(2) Implied from Plat

When a real estate developer acquires a parcel of land to subdivide into smaller lots, he or she will prepare a map (plat) that shows where each home and street in the subdivision will be located. If the map shows that a buyer's home will be built adjacent to a street, she has a legitimate expectation that the developer will construct the streets and open them for public use. Courts enforce this expectation by creating an implied easement of access over the streets shown on the map. Some courts imply the easement over all the streets in the subdivision (beneficial or full enjoyment rule), whereas others limit the easement to those streets necessary for access from the property to the nearest public way (narrow or necessary rule). An intermediate rule makes the easement's scope as extensive as necessary to protect the market value of the buyer's property. The Restatement of Servitudes provides that mapped streets imply an easement to use the street and that mapping of amenities, such as parks and beaches, implies the creation of servitudes in those lands for that purpose. Restatement § 2.13. For the implication of other servitudes from a general plan, see Chapter 6.

c. Necessity

Courts in some jurisdictions require absolute or strict necessity for a way by necessity, but others require only that the easement is necessary to provide reasonable access. Some states have enacted a statutory standard.

Illustration: Owen owned a peninsula. He conveyed the land at the end of it to Dita. Her parcel is surrounded by water on three sides and by Owen's retained land on the fourth side. A court that applies the strict necessity standard may deny Dita a way by necessity across Owen's retained land because she has access by water. A court that applies a reasonable necessity standard could determine that the need for vehicular access is an adequate justification for implying an easement.

2. Quasi-Easement

A quasi-easement (also known as an easement implied by past use) is created when four elements are satisfied. Two elements are the same as for easements by necessity — the same person must have owned the dominant and servient estates, and a parcel split must have created the need for the easement. The other two elements are (1) apparent and continuous use of the easement before the parcel split, and (2) the easement's reasonable necessity for use of the dominant estate.

a. Prior Use

An easement is implied when a parcel is severed only if the use existed before the severance. Such prior use was not an easement because the user owned the parts of the property that were burdened and benefited by the use, so that the right to use did not exist as a separate interest in another's property. The term "quasi-easement" refers to a use that would have been an easement if the dominant and servient properties had been owned separately. Thus, for an easement to be created by implication, a quasi-easement must have existed before severance.

Illustration: Dita owned a parcel of land with a house on the rear half and a driveway running from the house across the front half of the lot to the street. Dita sold the front half to Steve. Because the driveway and Dita's use of it existed as a quasi-easement before Dita conveyed to Steve, a court may imply an easement in her favor.

Illustration: Dita owned a parcel of land with a house on the rear half. After Dita sold the front half of the parcel to Steve, she first began to drive across it. A quasi-easement did not exist before the conveyance. Consequently, a court will not imply an easement in Dita's favor.

(1) Apparent

Because the basis for implying an easement is an assumption that the parties would have created one by express language had they considered the matter, the quasi-easement generally must be apparent to justify such an inference. However, "apparent" does not necessarily mean visible. Uses that are discoverable by a reasonable inspection also can be apparent.

Illustration: When Dita sold the front half of her property to Steve, a paved driveway ran across it to Dita's house on the rear half. Although Dita was not actually driving over the driveway when Steve purchased, the driveway is apparent, and an easement over it may be implied in Dita's favor.

Illustration: Owen owns two houses that are on one parcel of land. Both houses are connected to a public sewer by a sewer pipe that runs under the front house. Although the sewer pipe is underground, an inspection by a plumber would reveal that fact. Consequently, a court may hold that the pipe is apparent. Thus, when Owen sells either house, an easement under the front house in favor of the rear house may be implied. The Restatement of Servitudes goes further than the traditional common law rule and provides that underground utilities serving either parcel need not be apparent or known in order to create an easement by implication. Restatement § 2.12, comment g.

(2) Continuous

Unless circumstances indicate that the pre-existing use was permanent and would continue after the severance, no basis exists for assuming that the parties would have created an easement had they thought about it. Thus, courts require that use of the quasi-easement be continuous. The Restatement of Servitudes incorporates this requirement by stating that the prior use must not be "merely temporary or casual." Restatement § 2.12.

Illustration:　Before Dita sold the front half of her property to Steve, she occasionally drove across it to reach her house on the rear half. However, there is no driveway or other indication of use. Because no evidence exists that Dita regularly used the front half of the lot for passage to the rear half, an easement of passage will not be implied.

Illustration:　Dita paved a road from her house on the rear half of her property across the front half to a public street. When she sold the front half to Steve, an easement of passage might be implied because the paved driveway is a continuous burden on the front half in favor of the rear half.

b.　Reasonable Necessity

Recognition of an implied easement not only conveys a property interest to the dominant estate owner, it also takes an interest from the servient estate owner. Therefore, courts are reluctant to recognize an implied easement unless it serves a significant purpose. They require that the easement be necessary or beneficial to the owner of the prospective dominant estate.

Courts generally require only reasonable necessity or convenience to *grant* an implied easement to a grantee. In contrast, courts frequently require strict necessity to *reserve* an implied easement for the grantor's benefit. An easement by implied reservation gives the grantor an easement in property he granted even though, as the deed drafter, he had the ability to reserve an easement expressly. Moreover, deeds often contain covenants of title that warrant the title to be free of any easement not expressly disclosed in the deed. Thus, courts are more reluctant to imply an easement in a grantor's favor than in a grantee's favor.

Illustration: Steve's house on the rear half of his lot is connected to a driveway that runs across the front half to the street. Steve sold the rear half to Dita. Even though Dita could build a new driveway on her property that runs to a different street, a court may imply an easement by grant in her favor because of the cost to build a new driveway.

Illustration: Dita's house on the rear half of her lot is connected to a driveway that runs across the front half to the street. Dita sold the front half to Steve. Although Dita could build a driveway on her retained property that runs to a different street, it would be expensive. Courts that require strict necessity to create an implied reserved easement will not create the easement because Dita can gain access by other means, albeit at a heavy cost.

C. BY PRESCRIPTION

The doctrine of prescriptive easements is analogous to the doctrine of adverse possession.

Most of the rules and concepts applicable to adverse possession apply to prescription as well. Therefore, those principles will be discussed only briefly in this section.

Adverse possession is based on the statute of limitations for possessory actions (ejectment). Unlike adverse possession, an ejectment action is unavailable for adverse use. Therefore, the doctrine of prescriptive easements arises only by judicial analogy to adverse possession or by express legislation.

The original judicial rationale for prescriptive easements was the fiction that a use that had continued for long enough probably commenced with the grant of an easement that since had been lost (a "lost grant"). The possessor's failure to stop the adverse use was taken as proof that the possessor had given permission to the user long ago. Courts generally have abandoned this theory, although in some cases a few of the standards of prescription derive from that old view. For example, some courts require the use to be "peaceable." Today, most states strictly analogize prescriptive easements to adverse possession and only modify the rules to conform them to easements' special characteristics.

The Restatement of Servitudes § 2.17 states that prescriptive use should include actions taken pursuant to the terms of "an intended but imperfectly created servitude," such as when the absence of a writing defeats the creation of a legal easement but the intended beneficiary thereafter used the property as if she were entitled to do so.

1. Prescriptive Use v. Prescriptive Possession

Many activities can be viewed as either use of the property or possession of the property. Thus, a long continued activity may create either ownership by adverse possession or a prescriptive easement. The property owner's behavior during the prescriptive period may be the controlling factor.

Illustration: Dita regularly grazes her cattle on Steve's land. Her use could ripen into either ownership of the property by adverse possession or a prescriptive easement to graze. The outcome probably depends on whether Steve also uses the property during the same time period. If Steve is also using the property, Dita cannot claim title by adverse possession because her possession is neither exclusive nor uninterrupted. But, under these same circumstances, Dita can claim a prescriptive right to graze. On the other hand, if Steve does not use the land and if it is primarily grazing land, Dita's same acts could give her title by adverse possession

2. Elements of Prescription

a. *Adverse and Hostile*

These requirements, borrowed from adverse possession, have the same meaning in this context. The user must act without the owner's permission. In some jurisdictions, an owner may establish that all uses are permissive by posting a sign on the property to that effect, which may be easier than constantly monitoring the property. In some jurisdictions, an owner is presumed to have given permission to others to use unenclosed and unimproved land.

b. *Payment of Taxes*

Many states limit adverse possession to situations in which the possessor has paid property taxes during the limitations period. However, because easements are rarely assessed or taxed separately, tax payment usually is not required for prescription.

c. *Exclusive*

Adverse possession requires that the claimant's possession be exclusive. Although courts frequently state that a prescriptive easement also requires exclusive use, the exclusivity requirement for prescription differs from that for adverse possession. Unlike a fee title owner, an easement owner does not have the right to exclude others from the land. He merely has the right to prevent others from interfering with his use. As long as he does that, he has satisfied the exclusivity requirement for prescription.

d. Uninterrupted

Adverse possession is interrupted when the owner or someone else actually or judicially takes possession. However, another's possession does not necessarily conflict with an adverse use and will not automatically interrupt a ripening prescriptive easement. Only the actual interruption of the use is sufficient to prevent prescription.

Illustration: Dita consistently walked across Steve's property for twenty-five years. During that time, Steve also used the property for various purposes, such as walking and grazing cattle. Steve's use and possession of the property did not interrupt Dita's use, so she may claim a prescriptive easement.

Illustration: Dita walked across Steve's property until he erected a fence barring her before the time for prescription had run. The fence interrupts Dita's use and may prevent her from acquiring a prescriptive easement.

(1) Ineffective Interruptions

An interruption stops prescription only if it effectively interrupts the use. However, under the lost grant theory, even an ineffectual interruption could bar prescription by refuting the inference of a lost grant.

Illustration: Dita consistently walked across Steve's property. Steve built a fence to stop her, but she knocked it down and continued crossing. Steve did not interrupt Dita's use.

Illustration: Dita consistently walked across Steve's property. Steve informed Dita that she could continue to do so. Steve's grant of permission did not stop the statute of limitations. Steve cannot eliminate the adverseness of Dita's use by unilaterally consenting to it.

3. Prescriptive Easements as Appurtenant or in Gross

Depending on the circumstances, a prescriptive easement can be either appurtenant or in gross.

Illustration: Dita consistently walked from her property across Steve's property to get to the road. Dita acquired an appurtenant easement.

Illustration: Dita consistently walked across Steve's property to get to the road. Dita does not live near Steve and changed residences several times during the prescriptive period. Dita probably acquired an in gross easement.

a. *Negative Prescriptive Easements*

Generally, acquiring a negative easement by prescription is impossible because the alleged dominant tenant has not conducted an activity that wronged the servient tenant.

Illustration: Dita has looked out from her windows over Steve's land for thirty years. She now seeks to enjoin him from building in a manner that will interfere with her claimed easement of view. Dita will fail because her enjoyment of the view did not interfere with Steve's ownership. As a property owner, Dita was privileged to look over Steve's property, and he could not have enjoined her from doing so. Her privileged act cannot ripen into a right to stop Steve from engaging in his privileged act of building. Steve has no duty to refrain from building solely because he did not build in the past. The English doctrine of "ancient lights" dictates a contrary result, but that doctrine has not been adopted in this country. However, under the Restatement's use of prescription to cure imperfectly created servitudes, Steve's oral grant of an easement of view, coupled with Dita's thirty years of viewing, could ripen into a prescriptive easement.

Illustration: Dita erected a building on her land twenty-five years ago. The building is so heavy that it would have subsided if Steve had excavated on his adjoining land. Dita has not thereby acquired an easement of support in Steve's land. Steve has not had a cause of action against Dita for the past twenty-five years. She was privileged to build her building, and he was privileged to excavate. His failure to exercise his privilege for the past twenty-five years has not caused him to lose it. Steve is under no duty to support her building by not excavating. See Chapter 15 on support.

IV. TRANSFER OF EASEMENTS

A. TRANSFER OF EASEMENT'S BURDEN

When the servient estate is transferred, the burden of the easement transfers with it because an owner cannot convey more than she has. Thus, the easement's burden always "runs with the land." However, this doctrine is subject to the operation of the recording acts. See Chapter 10.

B. TRANSFER OF EASEMENT'S BENEFIT

An appurtenant easement always benefits a dominant estate, but an in gross easement has no dominant estate. It has only a dominant tenant. Thus, the rules for transfer of an easement's benefit differ according to the easement's nature.

1. Transfer of In Gross Easement's Benefit

Originally, an in gross easement's benefit was nontransferable. It was regarded as conferring a relatively small benefit compared to the burden on the servient estate to warrant the extensive clouding of title that transferability would entail. However, because in gross easements of a commercial nature do provide a significant benefit, the modern view is to permit them to be transferred. A noncommercial in gross easement also can be transferred if the parties did not intend it to be usable only by the original dominant tenant.

2. Transfer of Appurtenant Easement's Benefit

An appurtenant easement's benefit is automatically transferred with the dominant estate even if it is not mentioned in the deed that transferred the estate. Thus, an appurtenant easement "runs with the land." However, if the deed expressly provides that the easement is not transferred with the dominant estate, the transferor may retain it, or it may be destroyed.

Illustration: Dita had an appurtenant right of way easement across Steve's property. When Dita sold her land, the buyer obtained both the land and the easement, even if the deed did not expressly grant the easement.

Illustration: Dita had an appurtenant right of way easement across Steve's property. When Dita sold her property, she expressly excepted the right of way from the grant. The easement was either extinguished or converted into an in gross easement held by Dita. The result depends on whether the easement's creator intended that it could exist independently of the former dominant estate.

Illustration: Dita had an appurtenant right of way easement across Steve's property. She purported to grant the right of way to Ann without conveying the dominant estate to her. Ann did not acquire the right of way over Steve's property, because the easement would be changed impermissibly from appurtenant to in gross.

3. Transferability Affected by Creating Language

The parties can modify the foregoing rules by providing otherwise in the instrument by which the easement was created. A transferable easement can be made nontransferable, and a nontransferable easement can be made transferable.

Illustration: Steve's deed to Dita said: "I give you the right to walk from your property across my property. However, if you ever convey your property, this right will expire." This easement is not transferable even if it is construed to be appurtenant.

Illustration: Steve's deed to Dita said: "I give you the right to swim in my lake, wherever you reside. You may transfer this right to other members of your family." Although this is a noncommercial easement in gross, it is transferable under the circumstances specified in the deed.

V. SUBDIVISION OF EASEMENTS AND PROFITS

A. SUBDIVISION OF BURDEN

When the servient estate is subdivided, each part remains subject to the easement, unless the easement is located on only some parts of the servient estate. A servient owner has no greater power to extinguish an easement or profit by subdividing the property than he does by transferring it.

Illustration: Steve's property was subject to an easement of passage that crossed the property from east to west. Steve subdivided his land into western and eastern parcels. Both parcels remain subject to the easement.

Illustration: Steve's property was subject to an easement of passage that crossed the property from east to west along its northerly boundary. Steve subdivided his land into northern and southern parcels. The northern parcel is subject to the easement, but the southern parcel is not because that part of the property was never subject it.

B. SUBDIVISION OF BENEFIT

1. Easements

The distinction between appurtenant and in gross easements is relevant to this issue, as it is to the transfer of an easement's benefits.

a. *Subdivision of In Gross Easement's Benefit*

In jurisdictions where in gross easements are nontransferable, the easement's benefits may not be subdivided or apportioned. In jurisdictions where transfers are allowed, no clear standard governs the easement's subdivisibility. The terms of the grant may provide guidance as to the parties' intent. For prescriptive easements, a court must determine whether the servient tenant's original acquiescence reasonably can be enlarged to encompass use by more than one dominant tenant.

b. Subdivision of Appurtenant Easement's Benefit

When the dominant estate is subdivided, each part is entitled to the benefit of a pre-existing appurtenant easement, unless the original grant prohibits subdivision, the subdividing grants expressly negate a transfer of the benefit, or the subdivided use would unreasonably burden the servient estate.

Illustration: Steve granted Dita a right of way across his property. Dita subdivided her lot into three parcels and conveyed one each to Ann, Bob, and Cathy. Ann, Bob, and Cathy all have rights of way across Steve's property.

Illustration: Steve granted Dita a right of way across his property from her existing house. Dita subdivided her land into three parcels and conveyed one each to Ann, Bob, and Cathy. Ann received the parcel with the house. Only Ann has a right of way across Steve's property.

Illustration: Steve granted Dita a right of way across his property. Dita subdivided her lot into three parcels and conveyed one each to Ann, Bob, and Cathy. In the deeds to Bob and Cathy, Dita expressly excepted the right of way across Steve's property. Only Ann has a right of way.

Illustration: Steve granted Dita a right of way across his property from her existing house. Ann sold the property to a company that demolished her house and built a large factory. Trucks constantly drive across the right of way to and from the factory and have damaged the right of way. A court may prohibit continued use of the right of way because it constitutes an unreasonable burden.

2. Profits

Some courts apply different standards to the subdivisibility of an in gross profit. In some jurisdictions, a profit in gross is subdivisible if it is admeasurable, i.e. quantifiable. In others, the Rule of Mountjoy's Case is applied to permit subdivision of a profit only if it will continue to be worked as a common stock.

Illustration: Dita has the right to mine fifty tons of coal a month from Steve's land. Because this is an admeasurable profit, some states will permit her to subdivide the right, so long as no more than fifty tons of coal are removed per month. In other jurisdictions, Dita may subdivide the profit only if all the takers mine the coal jointly and not through separate operations.

VI. SCOPE OF USE

This section addresses the variety of activities that are permitted to the dominant and servient tenants with regard to the easement.

A. USES BY DOMINANT TENANT

No grant or reservation of an easement precisely and completely states the exact nature of the dominant tenant's permitted use. Consequently, courts frequently must determine whether some new activity is within the easement's scope. The following Illustrations indicate some ways in which a dominant tenant may seek to vary an easement's benefit.

Location of Benefit — Illustration: Dita has a right of way from her house across Steve's land. She wants to relocate the house elsewhere on her property and continue to use the right of way.

Enlargement of Benefit — Illustration: Dita has the right to run water in a ditch across Steve's property to irrigate her land. She now seeks to run water in the ditch to irrigate the parcel adjacent to her land as well.

Location of Burden — Illustration: Dita has a right of way located along the northern boundary of Steve's property. She now wants to cross along the southern boundary of Steve's property instead.

Activity on Dominant Estate — Illustration: Dita has a right to run water in a ditch across Steve's property to water her cattle. She now seeks to run water in the ditch for irrigation instead.

Activity on Servient Estate — Illustration: Dita has a right of way over Steve's property. She now seeks to (1) drive, rather than walk, across the property, (2) cross at night instead of during the day, (3) cross twice a day instead of once a day, or (4) permit friends to use the right of way to visit her.

1. Standards for Determining Whether Use can Change

a. When there is Explicit Language

If the easement's terms are explicit as to any matter, the dominant tenant cannot deviate from those terms.

Illustration: Steve granted Dita a right of way ten feet wide along the northern border of his property. Dita cannot widen the path or relocate it even though the change would not harm Steve.

Illustration: Steve granted Dita the right to run water in a ditch across his property for irrigation purposes only. Dita cannot use the water for any non-irrigation purposes, even though Steve would not be injured by the change.

b. When there is not Explicit Language

Even without explicit language, the dominant estate cannot be enlarged.

Illustration: Dita has the right to run water in a ditch across Steve's property to irrigate her land. If she acquires additional land, she cannot irrigate it with water from the ditch across Steve's land.

When an easement's terms do not specify whether a new activity is allowed, no single rule exists. Some courts consider a variety of factors, including the circumstances of the original grant, the consideration paid for it, and the prior and subsequent uses of the servient estate. Others follow a "rule of reason," which permits only reasonable rights and burdens. Both approaches attempt to do what the parties would have done had they considered the matter and acted reasonably about it.

Illustration: Dita has a right of way across Steve's property. The grant of the right of way does not specify a mode of transportation. Dita originally rode a horse across Steve's property but now seeks to drive a car instead. Some authorities would look at the circumstances of the grant (whether the parties had cars at the time, whether the road was paved), how much Dita paid for the easement, and whether a car was ever driven over the road before or after the easement was given. Courts applying the rule of reason would assess whether driving a car is a reasonable activity for Dita and whether it would be unreasonably burden the servient estate.

An implied easement is the most difficult to interpret with regard to scope. In general, the circumstances that were considered to determine whether the easement should be created will determine its nature and extent.

c. When Easement is Prescriptive

With a prescriptive easement, the only factor to consider is the previous use, because there is no writing. However, courts agree that the use is not limited to the precise original use. Rather, the prescriptive use is a guide to determine whether the servient tenant would have acquiesced to the new use, as well as to the original use.

Illustration: Dita walked across Steve's property at 5 p.m. every day for twenty-five years. Now she wants to walk across his property at 6 p.m. Based on Steve's failure to stop Dita at 5 p.m., a court might conclude that Steve would not have stopped her at 6 p.m. Thus, Dita may now cross at 6 p.m.

Illustration: Dita walked across Steve's property every day for twenty-five years. Now she wants to drive a car across his property instead. A court might conclude that Steve would have stopped Dita from crossing if she had driven, rather than walked. Thus, Dita will not be allowed to drive.

2. Changes Caused by Development of Dominant Estate

Courts generally hold that an easement's use can change when the dominant estate is developed if the development is normal and reasonable and if the new activity is reasonably required by the dominant tenant. This holding is based on the assumption that, when the easement was created, the parties must have anticipated that changes would occur and would have agreed in advance to changes in the easement's use if they had thought about it. However, while a reasonable servient tenant probably would agree to normal development of the dominant estate, he probably would not consent to a change that unreasonably burdened his own property, even if it were the result of normal growth of the dominant estate.

Illustration: Steve granted a right of way to Dita when she used her land as a farm. The entire area is now becoming residential. Dita has built several houses on her property and seeks to use the right of way for access to all the houses. This use should be allowed, because this development of Dita's property is reasonable, the right of way is reasonably required for access to the houses, and the new use does not unreasonably increase the burden on the servient estate.

Illustration: Steve granted a right of way to Dita when she used her land as a farm. Valuable minerals now have been found on Dita's land and on other nearby properties, and extensive mining activity has begun. Dita wants to use the right of way for trucks to carry the ores. Although mining may be a reasonable use of Dita's land, the additional noise and disruption caused by the trucks substantially increase the burden on the servient estate. Therefore, a court should enjoin this new use. However, many courts consider only Dita's use and do not consider the burden on the servient estate. In return, the dominant tenant, rather than the servient tenant, is obliged to keep the easement in repair, though injured third parties still may be able to recover against the servient tenant because he possesses the land.

B. USES BY SERVIENT TENANT

1. Nature of Dominant Tenant's Rights

An easement holder has the right to use, rather than the right to possess. Therefore, a dominant tenant may not sue in trespass or ejectment if others use the easement area. Instead, the dominant tenant is limited to a cause of action for unreasonable interference with the easement. Therefore, harm is a far more essential element to protect an easement than to protect possession.

Illustration: Dita has a right of way over a road on Steve's land. Ann has started walking on the same road without anyone's consent. Dita can obtain judicial relief against Ann only if Ann's activity unreasonably interferes with Dita's right of way. But Steve can recover from Ann in trespass without showing any direct injury from her activity.

2. Nature of Servient Tenant's Rights

By granting a particular use to a dominant tenant, the servient tenant does not lose the right to use the property in the same way or in any other way, as long as he does not unreasonably interfere with the dominant tenant's use.

Illustration: Dita has a right of way over a road on Steve's land. Steve may continue to walk on the road and to do any other act he pleases on the road, as long as it does not unreasonably hinder Dita's right of passage.

a. Third Parties' Rights

Because the servient tenant retains the right to use his property in any way that does not interfere with the easement, he may permit others to use the property in similar ways.

Illustration: Steve gave Dita a right of way on a road across his property. Steve may permit Ann to use the same road as long as her use does not unreasonably hamper Dita's use. Both Dita and Ann are dominant tenants.

VII. TERMINATION OF EASEMENTS AND PROFITS

As described in this section, easements and profits can be terminated in a variety of ways.

A. TERMINATION BY LANGUAGE IN THE GRANT

An easement or profit may be created for a limited or conditional duration. When the time passes or the condition occurs, the easement or profit ends.

Illustration: Steve granted Dita the right to cross his property for so long as she lives in the house next door. Once Dita moves, the easement ends.

Illustration: Dita's ten-year lease of a house included the right to walk across the adjacent lot owned by her landlord, Steve. When the lease expires, the easement terminates.

Illustration: Steve granted Dita the right to park in his garage. A fire destroyed the garage, and Steve elected not to rebuild. Dita's easement ended, because it was implicitly conditioned on the continued existence of the structure that was the servient tenement.

B. MERGER

When the dominant tenant acquires the servient estate, the easement or profit merges into the fee title and is extinguished because an owner cannot hold an easement or profit in her own property. Similarly, when the servient tenant of an appurtenant easement acquires the dominant estate, the easement is extinguished by merger.

Illustration: Dita had a right of way across Steve's land. She then bought Steve's land. As the owner of the servient estate, she has the right to cross it without owning an easement. Therefore, the easement is extinguished.

1. Temporary Merger or Reseparation

If the dominant tenant acquires only a temporary possessory interest in the servient estate, the easement is merely suspended until the possessory interest ends. On the other hand, if the easement was extinguished by a complete merger of the parcels, it is not revived if they subsequently are separated again. However, a new easement may be implied from the severance.

Illustration: Dita had a right of way across Steve's land. Dita then rented Steve's land for five years. During the lease term, Dita did not have an easement, but the easement resumed when the term expired.

Illustration: Dita acquired a right of way easement across Steve's land. She then purchased Steve's land and later sold her original parcel to Ann. The deed to Ann did not expressly convey a right of way over Dita's retained parcel. Ann did not acquire an easement because it was extinguished when Dita acquired the servient tenement. However, an implied easement might have been created if an apparent, continuous, and necessary quasi-easement existed when Dita conveyed to Ann or if Ann's parcel otherwise would be landlocked.

C. RELEASE AND ABANDONMENT

A release deed from the dominant tenant to the servient tenant extinguishes an easement. The deed transfers the easement to the servient tenant, and it merges it into the larger possessory estate. All the formalities necessary to create an easement apply to its release. Therefore, the dominant tenant's oral statement that the easement is terminated or is transferred to the servient tenant is ineffective for lack of compliance with the Statute of Frauds. However, under principles somewhat similar to the abandonment and surrender of leaseholds (see Chapter 4), easements can terminate by operation of law under certain circumstances.

1. By Words Alone

A mere oral attempt to terminate an easement is ineffective, because it violates the Statute of Frauds.

2. By Nonuse Alone

The dominant tenant's nonuse of an easement also does not terminate it. The holder of a property right does not have to exercise it to keep it alive. However, in some jurisdictions, a prescriptive easement will terminate if it is unused for a period equal to the limitations period for creating such easements.

3. By Words and Nonuse

The dominant tenant's oral statements signifying her intent to abandon the easement, followed by nonuse, may terminate it. The nonuse must continue long enough to verify the intent to abandon. Easements can be terminated in such cases because their destruction creates no void in ownership. The servient estate is merely freed from the easement's burden.

4. By Words and Inconsistent Acts

The dominant tenant's oral statements signifying her intent to abandon the easement, coupled with significant actions that are inconsistent with its continuance, may terminate it.

Illustration: Dita had a right of way on a road across Steve's property. She told Steve that she would no longer use the road and then built a fence blocking her access to the road. Dita's statement and acts are sufficient to extinguish the easement.

5. By Inconsistent Acts Alone

The dominant tenant's actions may be so permanent and so inconsistent with the easement's continuation that her intent to abandon may be inferred, thereby terminating the easement.

Illustration: Dita had an easement of view across Steve's property. She tore down her house and erected a permanent windowless building on her property. Although Dita made no statements, her intent to abandon may be inferred, which terminates the easement.

6. By Words of Dominant Tenant and Acts of Servient Tenant — Estoppel

The dominant tenant's oral statement may terminate the easement if the servient tenant foreseeably and detrimentally relies on the statement. However, the servient tenant's acts alone cannot prove the dominant tenant's intent to abandon.

Illustration: Dita told Steve that she was giving up her right of way across his land. In reliance on this statement, Steve erected a building across the road. Dita is estopped to assert that the easement was not terminated.

Illustration: Dita stopped using her right of way across Steve's land, and Steve plowed up the road. Dita is not estopped from claiming her easement, because she made no statements that induced Steve's action and because Steve will not be harmed if Dita resumes using the right of way.

D. ADVERSE USE

The dominant tenant has a cause of action for the servient tenant's or any third party's unreasonable interference with her use of the easement. However, if the dominant tenant does not assert this cause of action in a timely fashion, it may be lost by adverse possession or by prescription.

Illustration: Dita had a right of way across Steve's land. Steve erected a fence barring Dita from access for twenty-five years. Dita lost her easement.

Illustration: Dita had a right of way across Steve's land. Steve walked across the same road for twenty-five years. Dita has not lost her easement unless Steve's actions unreasonably interfered with her passage.

Illustration: Dita had a right of way across Steve's land, but she has not used it for twenty-five years. Nonuse alone does not destroy the easement. Steve must have acted adversely to her interest during the period of nonuse to destroy it.

Although some courts hold that an easement in a building is destroyed when the servient tenant intentionally destroys it, the majority view is that termination occurs only if the destruction was accidental or if the structure had become so obsolete that the servient owner was forced to destroy it. The building's continued existence was an implied condition to the easement (i.e. "You may cross through my building so long as there is a building.").

E. INVALIDITY

Like other interests in land, easements and profits are invalid if they violate the Rule Against Perpetuities, especially if they are in gross and, therefore, not tied to the duration of a dominant tenement. However, the Restatement of Servitudes (§ 3.3), the Uniform Common Interest Ownership Act (§ 2–103), and the Uniform Condominium Act (§ 2–103) propose that the Rule be inapplicable to servitudes and to the power to create them. The rule against restraints on alienation also may invalidate easements and profits, although public purposes such as historic preservation may make the restrictions reasonable.

F. SALE OF SERVIENT ESTATE TO BONA FIDE PURCHASER

If a purchaser of the servient estate does not have notice of the easement, the easement can be terminated. Even if the purchaser does not have actual notice of the easement, she has constructive notice if it is recorded in the public property records or if it is discoverable by a reasonable inspection of the land. Because implied and prescriptive easements are not created by a writing, they are not subject to the recording requirement, and a purchaser generally will take subject to them even if she is unaware of them. However, some courts have held that a purchaser is not bound by an implied easement if it is not apparent.

G. TERMINATION OF NECESSITY FOR IMPLIED EASEMENT

Because an implied easement is created by necessity, it generally will terminate when the need for it ends. However, some courts have held that a way by necessity is not terminated when a public road is built adjacent to a formerly landlocked parcel.

H. FORFEITURE BY MISUSE

If an easement holder misuses it in a manner that cannot be corrected, the easement is forfeited.

Illustration: Dita had an appurtenant right of way easement across Steve's land. She subsequently acquired land adjoining the dominant estate and constructed an office building on the combined parcels. Because limiting use of the right of way to people going only to the part of the building on the original dominant estate would be very difficult, if not impossible, a court could hold that Dita forfeited the easement.

VIII. TERMINATION OF LICENSES

A. IRREVOCABLE LICENSE

A license usually terminates when the licensor revokes it. However, the license is irrevocable if the licensor knew that the licensee would expend time or money in reasonable reliance on it. Consequently, it cannot be terminated at the licensor's will. The Restatement of Servitudes treats reasonable reliance as an exception to the Statute of Frauds (§ 2.9) or as creating an easement by estoppel (§ 2.10).

Illustration: Steve orally granted Dita the permanent right to maintain a sewer pipe under his land. In reliance on Steve's grant, Dita installed the pipe. The grant created a license because it was oral. But Dita's expenditure of time and money made the license irrevocable. Steve is estopped to revoke Dita's interest.

Illustration: Steve executed a written grant to Dita that stated: "You may drive across my property until I change my mind." Dita then paved the road on Steve's property. Steve may revoke, because Dita's expenditure of money was not made in reasonable reliance on a permanent grant. The grant's express language made it a revocable license.

A license that is irrevocable because of estoppel may be terminated when conditions have changed or when the licensee has recovered the value of her reliance.

B. LICENSE COUPLED WITH AN INTEREST

When a license authorizes the licensee to leave personal property on the licensed land, the license cannot be revoked until the licensee has had an opportunity to recover her property.

Illustration: Dita parked her car in a parking ramp. Her license to park in the ramp cannot be revoked, thereby making her a trespasser, until she can recover her car.

CHAPTER SIX

REAL COVENANTS AND EQUITABLE SERVITUDES

An interest "runs with the land" when it benefits or burdens subsequent owners. Thus, an appurtenant easement runs with the land because it burdens the servient estate even after it has been transferred and continues to benefit the dominant estate even after it has been transferred. Therefore, a landowner may have the right to walk across another's land based on an easement between their predecessors in title, regardless of whether the current owners ratified it. In contrast, an in gross easement's benefit cannot run with land because there is no dominant estate, but its burden can run with the servient estate.

Covenants (promises) respecting land may run with the land in a roughly similar manner to easements. When a covenant runs with the land, the land remains burdened or benefited by it even though the parties to the covenant no longer own the affected parcels. Thus, running covenants transfer duties and rights in a way not permitted by traditional contract law.

Illustration: Ann covenanted with Bob that she would not sell liquor on her property. Ann sold her property to

Cathy. If the requirements for a covenant to run with the land are met, Cathy may not sell liquor on the property though she neither made nor assumed the covenant. However, if the covenant does not run with the land, Cathy is not bound by it.

I. REAL COVENANTS COMPARED TO OTHER INTERESTS THAT BIND FUTURE OWNERS

A. EASEMENTS

Although easements run with the land, the types of activities for which an easement can be created have always been somewhat limited, and courts have resisted attempts to create new kinds of easements. Restrictions that are too novel to qualify as easements or that are "spurious" (see Chapter 5) cannot be characterized as easements. Thus, courts had to create a different type of interest — the covenant running with the land — to make these types of agreements enforceable between subsequent owners of the affected properties.

Generally, parties creating an easement use conveyancing language, such as "I grant" or "I reserve." In contrast, parties creating a covenant use promissory language, such as "I promise" or "I agree." However, regardless of the language used, a court is free to determine the real character of the interest regardless of the creating language. The

Restatement of Servitudes permits a servitude to be created "by contract or conveyance." § 2.1.

A duty to refrain from acting in a particular way can be either a negative easement or a covenant, but an affirmative obligation can only be a covenant and not an easement. A covenant, whether affirmative or negative, can never be acquired prescriptively. To avoid confusion, easements and covenants will be treated in this Chapter as distinct property interests, though the Restatement categorizes them both as a "servitude."

Illustration: Ann promised Bob that (1) she would not build any structures in her garden that blocked Bob's view, (2) Bob could enter the garden to smell the flowers, and (3) Ann would water the plants regularly. In the above examples, (1) is a negative easement of view that prohibits Ann from building certain types of structures on her land, (2) is an affirmative easement that entitles Bob to perform an otherwise unprivileged act on Ann's land, and (3) is a covenant because it imposes a duty on Ann to perform an act. Without a writing, Bob could acquire only the second right by prescription.   Bob cannot adversely possess the easement of view or Ann's obligation to water, because Bob has not physically possessed those rights. However, once granted, all of Bob's rights may be lost by prescription.

B. DEFEASIBLE ESTATES

The owner of a defeasible estate owns her land subject to a condition, and she cannot convey the land free from that condition. In that sense, the condition on her estate runs with the land. However, the benefit of the condition is itself an interest in land and generally is transferable. It does not run with any other land.

Illustration: Owen conveyed land to Ann in fee simple so long as liquor is not sold on the premises. Ann has a fee simple determinable. If Ann conveys the property to Bob, Bob will have the same estate and cannot sell liquor there. Owen has a possibility of reverter, which he can transfer. However, if the conveyance's language is ambiguous, a court may construe the restriction as a covenant, rather than as a condition, to avoid the harsh forfeiture remedy. In this way, the promise will run with the land but with a less drastic remedy.

C. CONTRACT ASSIGNMENT AND ASSUMPTION

Courts accepted the concept of real covenants running with the land before contract law permitted rights to be assigned and duties to be delegated. When contract law had evolved to incorporate these concepts, courts continued to recognize covenants running with the land. The most important difference between these two sources of rights and duties is that contract law requires the remote purchaser of the burdened land to agree to the burden. In contrast, a purchaser of land encumbered by a covenant is bound even if he does not agree to it.

Illustration: Ann covenanted that she would not use her land to compete with Bob's business. Bob then sold his land and business to Cathy. If the covenant's benefit does not run with the land, the benefit transfers to Cathy only if Bob assigns it to her. If the covenant's benefit does run with the land, it automatically transfers to Cathy along with the property without the need for an assignment.

Illustration: Ann agreed to water Bob's lawn every day. Ann then sold her property to Cathy. If the covenant's burden does not run with the land, Cathy must water Bob's lawn only if she assumes the covenant ("Cathy hereby assumes the obligation of the covenant"). If the covenant's burden runs with the land, Cathy is bound even if she did not expressly assume it.

II. REQUIREMENTS FOR COVENANT TO RUN WITH THE LAND

A covenant runs with the land only if (1) it is legally enforceable, (2) the parties intended that it run with the land, (3) it touches and concerns the land, and (4) privity of estate exists.

A. COVENANT MUST BE AN ENFORCEABLE PROMISE

Originally, a covenant was a promise made under seal. Although most states have eliminated the requirement for a seal, contract law has many other important rules concerning the enforceability of promises. For example, consideration must be given, and the promise cannot be for an illegal purpose. If the covenant is unenforceable between the covenanting parties, it cannot bind their successors. In a majority of jurisdictions, covenants that run with the land must be in writing. However, the doctrines of estoppel and part performance may excuse the absence of a writing. When the covenant is in a deed, it is enforceable against the grantee if she accepted the deed even though she did not sign it.

B. PARTIES MUST HAVE INTENDED THAT THE COVENANT RUN

A covenant will not run unless the original covenantor and covenantee intended that it should. The parties need not manifest their intent in any particular manner. However, the court in Spencer's Case (1583) held that a covenant concerning something not yet in esse (not yet in existence) will not run unless the "assigns" of the parties are specifically mentioned. A reference to the covenantor "and his assigns" or "his successors and assigns" is a common method today for expressing the intent that the covenant run with the land.

Illustration: Ann covenanted to build and to maintain a fence between Bob's and her lots. Because the fence does not yet exist, this covenant would not run under Spencer's Case unless Ann expressly stated in the covenant that she covenanted for herself and for her assigns. However, if the fence already existed and the covenant only concerned maintenance, any language indicating intent that the covenant burden her successors would be sufficient.

C. PROMISE MUST TOUCH AND CONCERN LAND

Courts will enforce a covenant against future owners only if it "touches and concerns" the land. In one case, the court stated that the covenant "must affect the nature, quality, or value" of the land or its use. Another commonly cited standard is that a covenant must increase or decrease the promisor's or promisee's legal relations concerning land. The promise must make ownership more or less valuable. However, several courts have noted that this standard is more question-begging than helpful.

1. Burden v. Benefit

A covenant concerning the use of land consists of two parts. It burdens the covenantor's land, and it benefits either the covenantee's land or some third person. Therefore, the question whether the covenant touches and concerns land may be a two part question: (1) Does the covenant's burden touch and concern land; and (2) Does the covenant's benefit touch and concern land? Just as an easement may be appurtenant (burdens the servient estate and benefits the dominant estate) or in gross (burdens the servient estate but does not benefit a dominant estate), a covenant may only burden land, may only benefit land, or may burden and benefit separate parcels. In general, a burden that can be performed only by the owner or possessor of the burdened land touches and concerns that land. Conversely, only a benefit that will be enjoyed by the current owner or possessor of the benefited land touches and concerns that land.

Illustration: Ann covenanted with Bob that she would not sell liquor on her land. She made this promise because Bob has moral objections to alcohol. The covenant's burden touches and concerns Ann's land, because it deprives her of an otherwise available use. But the covenant's benefit does not necessarily touch and concern another parcel of land.

Illustration: Ann covenanted to water Bob's lawn every day. The covenant touches and concerns Bob's land because it benefits the land, rather than Bob as an individual. The owner of the benefited land is the only person interested in enforcing the covenant. But the covenant's burden does not touch Ann's land, because Ann can perform this covenant regardless of whether she owns any property.

a. Requirements for Burden to Run

Under one view, a covenant's burden runs if it touches and concerns the covenantor's land even if it does not benefit the covenantee's land. This "liberal" view has the virtues of simplicity and directness. It focuses only on the covenant's qualities to determine whether the burden runs. A different view is that the burden runs only if both the burden and the benefit touch and concern land. This more restrictive view derives from the old English prohibition against easements in gross and the policy that one parcel of land should not be restricted unless some other parcel is proportionally benefited. It is easier to identify and locate subsequent owners of benefited land than subsequent owners of a covenant in gross who may not own any land in the vicinity of the burdened land.

Covenant not to Compete — Illustration: To avoid competing with Bob's tavern, Ann promised not to sell liquor on her land. Courts in many states hold that the covenant's benefit does not touch and concern Bob's land because it does not enhance his physical enjoyment of his land, but merely increases the amount of money that he can make on it. On the other hand, the burden clearly touches and concerns Ann's land, because it restricts her use. Thus, the covenant may be characterized as a burden that touches and concerns the land but a benefit that does not. Under the more liberal rule, the burden may run. Under the more restrictive rule, it may not.

b. Requirements for Benefit to Run

A benefit will run even if the burden does not touch and concern land, because the benefit's running does not hamper the benefited land's alienability or utility.

Illustration: Ann covenanted to water a tree on Bob's property. This benefit touches and concerns Bob's property. Therefore, it runs to and is enforceable by future owners of Bob's property, though the covenant's burden does not affect any land owned by Ann.

Illustration: Bob operates a grocery store on his land. Ann covenanted with him that she would not operate a grocery store on her land. In some states, this covenant's benefit is not considered to touch and concern Bob's land and, therefore, will not run with it. A benefit never runs if it does not touch or concern the land.

2. Covenants to Pay Money

In the early common law, courts held that covenants to pay money did not touch and concern land. Today, however, most courts recognize that payments of money can be a substitute method for performing an act that does touch and concern land. For example, a covenant in a private subdivision to pay assessments for maintenance of the common areas may be a substitute for a covenant by a lot owner to maintain them himself. Courts today look at the purpose for the money covenant to determine whether it touches and concerns land.

D. PRIVITY OF ESTATE

Three types of privity of estate exist — mutual, horizontal, and vertical. Since courts first held that a covenant could run with the land, they have required one or more types of privity of estate as a prerequisite.

The Restatement of Servitudes entirely eliminates the privity requirement for the creation of a servitude. § 2.4. It also provides that prescription may cure the absence of privity if state law requires it. § 2.17.

1. Mutual Privity

In the earliest cases concerning the running of covenants, courts required mutual privity. The covenanting parties had to have a tenurial relationship, which probably exists today only between a landlord and tenant. Under a slightly less strict view of mutual privity, the covenanting parties both had to have interests in the same land. Thus, they may co-own the property or be dominant and servient tenants of an easement on the property. Mutual privity rarely is required today.

2. Horizontal Privity

Horizontal privity exists between the grantor and grantee of an estate in land. Under the stricter traditional view, the horizontal privity requirement was satisfied only if the covenantor gave the covenant at the same time that the covenantee transferred fee title to the covenantor. Under the more liberal rule, horizontal privity is satisfied if the covenant is given in exchange for the conveyance of any interest in land.

Illustration: Ann and Bob own adjoining parcels of land on a lake. They exchange covenants that they will not build on their respective parcels in a manner that will interfere with the other's view of the lake. Under the traditional view, this exchange of covenants does not constitute horizontal privity, because the covenants were not given when the fee title was transferred. However, this exchange does satisfy the requirement of the more liberal view.

Some states require horizontal privity for the covenant's burden to run but not for the covenant's benefit.

Illustration: Ann and Bob are neighbors. They agree that Ann will not erect any structure on her land over thirty feet high. Because they are not in horizontal privity, the burden of this covenant may not run at law to bind Ann's successors, but the benefit may run to Bob's successors. Therefore, Ann would be bound by the covenant even after Bob transfers his land, but her successors in interest would not be bound even while Bob still owns his land.

3. Vertical Privity

Vertical privity focuses on the chain of conveyances of both the burdened and benefited parcels. An unbroken chain of conveyances must exist from the original covenantor to the current owner of the burdened land and from the original covenantee to the current owner of the benefited land. The chain of conveyances is broken when an adverse possessor or a person who does not have notice of the covenant (bona fide purchaser) acquires the land.

Illustration: Ann owned a parcel of land and sold half to Bob. The deed to Bob included his covenant to build and to maintain a fence on the lot line between Ann's and his lots. Ann later sold her lot to Cathy. Cathy lost her ownership of the lot to an adverse possessor, Dave. Bob sold his lot to Edna. If Edna does not perform the covenant, Dave cannot enforce it if the jurisdiction requires vertical privity. Although vertical privity exists for the burdened land, Dave's adverse possession destroyed the vertical privity for the benefited land.

a. Transfer of Lesser Estate

A special issue arises when the possessor of the burdened or benefited land has a lesser estate than the original covenantor or covenantee.

(1) Burdened Land

In many jurisdictions, the current possessor of the burdened land is not bound by the covenant if he has a lesser estate than the original covenantor. In other jurisdictions, the current possessor is bound by negative covenants, which restrict the ability to use the land, but not by affirmative covenants, which require performance of an action. However, the possessor is bound by a negative covenant only if she had notice of it.

Illustration: Ann owned a parcel of land and sold half to Bob. The deed to Bob included his covenant to build and to maintain a fence on the lot line between Ann's and his lots. If Bob leases his lot to Cathy, she is not bound by this affirmative covenant, because her tenancy is a lesser estate than Bob's fee title.

Illustration: Ann owned a parcel of land and sold half to Bob. The deed to Bob included his covenant to use the land for residential purposes only. If Bob leases his lot to Cathy, courts in some jurisdictions would hold that she is not bound by the covenant. However, courts in other jurisdictions would hold that she is bound if she had notice of it, because it is a negative covenant.

(2) Benefited Land

Courts generally will enforce a covenant though the possessor of the benefited land has a lesser estate than the original covenantee.

Illustration: Ann owned a parcel of land and sold half to Bob. The deed to Bob included his covenant to use the land for residential purposes. If Ann leases her lot to Cathy, Cathy can enforce the covenant though her tenancy is a lesser estate than Ann's fee title.

III. EQUITABLE SERVITUDES

A. POLICY UNDERLYING EQUITABLE SERVITUDES

The legal requirements for a covenant to run with the land are sufficiently difficult that they often defeat the covenanting parties' attempts to bind successors. For example, in England, where the privity requirement is satisfied only by tenurial relationships, land cannot be transferred with enforceable restrictions in the deed. In the United States, privity requirements often prevent neighbors from making binding agreements. One reason these legal rules have survived despite their undesirable effects is that an alternative enforcement device has long been available — enforcement in a court of equity.

In 1848, the English Court of Chancery decided Tulk v. Moxhay, 41 Eng. Rep. 1143 (Ch. 1848), which involved a covenant in a deed that the grantee would not build on the granted property. When the defendant acquired the burdened land, he refused to comply with the covenant. Because the original covenanting parties did not have a landlord-tenant relationship, they were not in mutual privity, which was required in England. Therefore, the covenant did not run at law to bind the successor of the burdened land. However, the court held that the defendant was equitably bound to comply with the covenant because he knew about it when he acquired the land. The equitable interest that the court created is called an equitable servitude.

The court in *Tulk* gave two reasons for subjecting the defendant to the burden. First, if the successor was not bound, the original grantee-covenantor could sell the land for appreciably more than he had paid for it. Thus, the grantee-covenantor would be unjustly enriched. Second, if the successor could acquire the land free of the covenant though he knew about it, he would destroy a benefit for which the original grantor-covenantee had contracted. Thus, the court also was concerned about a wrongful interference with a contractual relationship. Therefore, the court held that the covenantee had an equitable right in the covenantor's property that bound any future owner who acquired the property with notice of it.

B. RULES CONCERNING EQUITABLE SERVITUDES

1. Applicability of Rules for Covenants Running at Law

The legal requirements of privity and of touch and concern have limited or different application to equitable enforcement of a servitude.

a. *Privity*

After *Tulk v. Moxhay,* the covenantor and covenantee need not have been in privity of estate for a burden to be enforceable in equity against subsequent owners, and the successor-owner need not have acquired the covenantor's entire estate.

Illustration: Ann covenanted with her neighbor, Bob, that she would use her property only for residential purposes. Ann then sold her land to Cathy, who knew about the covenant. Although Bob could not enforce the covenant against Cathy at law, it is enforceable against her in equity.

Illustration: Ann covenanted with her neighbor, Bob, that she would use her property only for residential purposes. Ann then leased the property to Cathy, who was aware of the covenant. Bob may enforce the promise in equity against Cathy though she did not acquire Ann's entire interest.

b. *Touch and Concern*

Courts differ on the touch and concern requirement for equitable servitudes. In England, an equitable servitude's burden will not run with the land, unless its benefit also touches and concerns land. In the United States, courts often do not require the benefit to touch and concern land for either the benefit or the burden to run. However, if the burden does not touch and concern land, a court probably will hold that it does not run.

Illustration: Ann covenanted with her neighbor, Bob, that she would not use her land in competition with his use of his land. This covenant does not satisfy the privity of estate requirement for a real covenant. Ann then sold her property to Cathy, who knew about the covenant. In many jurisdictions, the covenant's benefit is deemed not to touch and concern Bob's land, although its burden touches and concerns Cathy's land. Therefore, in England, the burden would not bind Cathy, even in equity. But, in the United States, Cathy probably would be bound by an equitable servitude.

Illustration: Ann covenanted with her neighbor, Bob, that she would not use her land in competition with his use of his land. This covenant does not satisfy the privity of estate requirement for a real covenant. Bob then sold his land to Cathy. If Ann and Bob intended that future owners of Bob's lot could enforce Ann's promise, Cathy probably can enforce it as an equitable servitude though the benefit does not touch and concern her land.

Illustration: Ann covenanted with Bob that she would maintain his garden. This covenant does not satisfy the privity of estate requirement for a real covenant. Ann then sold her property to Cathy, who knew about the covenant. Because the burden does not touch and concern land, Cathy probably is not bound by an equitable servitude.

2. Special Equitable Requirements

Although the traditional legal requirements for a covenant to run are eliminated or attenuated for an equitable servitude, equity adds some special requirements before it will enforce a servitude against a remote owner.

a. Notice

Equity imposes a servitude's burden only if the promisor's successor took with notice of it. The notice may be actual or constructive.

b. Negative Promises Only

In a few jurisdictions, equity will not enforce affirmative promises (promises that require the promisor to perform an act). Only negative promises (those that prohibit the promisor from acting in a certain manner) are enforceable. However, most modern courts do not make this distinction and will enforce either kind of promise, as a real covenant or as an equitable servitude.

IV. ENFORCEMENT OF NEIGHBORHOOD RESTRICTIONS

Subdivision developers often insert use restrictions in all or most deeds to individual lots in the subdivision. Once the developer has sold all the lots, it no longer can enforce the restrictions. Instead, the subdivision lot owners have that right, often through a homeowners' association. This section addresses the problems that lot owners may confront when enforcing restrictions against each other. In the Illustrations in this section, "CG Company" refers to the common grantor, a corporation that sold all the lots in the subdivision in numerical order to alphabetically listed buyers.

A. ENFORCEMENT BY LATER GRANTEES AGAINST EARLIER GRANTEES — RUNNING OF BENEFIT

When a prior grantee gave a covenant restricting her lot, a later grantee from the same common grantor usually can enforce the covenant. The benefit of the earlier covenant touched and concerned the common grantor's retained land and ran with the part that the common grantor conveyed to the subsequent grantee.

Illustration: CG Company conveyed Lot 1 to Ann, who covenanted to restrict it to residential purposes. CG Company then conveyed Lot 2 to Bob. Bob may enforce the covenant against Ann. Ann's covenant benefited CG's retained land, which included Lot 2. The benefit of Ann's covenant ran with Lot 2 when CG conveyed it to Bob.

B. ENFORCEMENT BY EARLIER GRANTEES AGAINST LATER GRANTEES — ALTERNATIVE THEORIES

A prior grantee sometimes can enforce restrictions against a subsequent grantee from the same common owner. The prior grantee's enforcement right rests on one of three theories, depending on whether the covenant was given by the common owner, the subsequent grantee, or the prior grantee.

1. Enforcement of Common Owner's Covenant to Prior Grantee — Running of Burden

When the common owner covenants with the prior grantee to restrict all its retained property for the benefit of the prior grantee's lot, the covenant burdens all of the common owner's retained land and binds subsequent grantees. This theory does not apply to land that was not in the subdivision when the covenant was made. Because that land was owned by someone else when the covenant was given, the covenantor probably did not intend that the prior grantee should receive the benefit of a covenant that later burdened that property.

Illustration: CG Company conveyed Lot 1 to Ann and covenanted that it would restrict all its remaining land in the subdivision to residential purposes. CG then conveyed Lot 2 to Bob. Ann may enjoin Bob from using his lot for nonresidential uses if he took with notice of CG's covenant. If Lot 2 was not part of the subdivision when CG gave Ann its covenant, she may not enforce it against Bob.

2. Enforcement of Subsequent Grantee's Covenant to Common Owner — Third Party Beneficiary

A prior grantee may enforce a subsequent grantee's covenant to the common owner if the covenant was intended for the prior grantee's benefit. Because the prior grantee is not the promisee or a successor to land owned by the promisee when the covenant was given, the covenant's benefit did not run with the land to the prior grantee. Instead, the prior grantee is a third party beneficiary of the covenant if it was intended to benefit prior grantees.

Illustration: CG Company conveyed Lot 1 to Ann. CG Company then conveyed Lot 2 to Bob, who covenanted for the benefit of all lots in the subdivision that he would use his land for residential purposes only. Ann may enforce Bob's covenant as a third party beneficiary. She is an intended beneficiary of his promise and need not show that either the burden or the benefit of Bob's covenant runs with the land.

a.   When Third Party Beneficiary Theory Applies

Many deed covenants specify the burden but fail to specify what property is to be benefited by it. When a prior grantee seeks to enforce such a covenant, he must show that he "impliedly" was intended to be a third party beneficiary of the covenant. Courts in some states will not allow a prior grantee to make this showing, perhaps due to the old common law prohibition against reserving conditions in favor of strangers. However, courts in other states grant third party beneficiary status whenever adequate extrinsic evidence supports it.

Illustration: CG Company conveyed Lot 1 to Ann. CG Company then conveyed Lot 2 to Bob.   Bob covenanted to restrict his land to residential purposes, but the covenant did not state what land was intended to receive the covenant's benefit.   Witnesses testify that CG told Bob that the covenant was intended to benefit all other lots in the subdivision and that Bob agreed. Under these circumstances, some courts will permit Ann to enforce the covenant, though she is not expressly designated as the covenant's beneficiary.

3.   Enforcement of Restriction when Prior Grantee Covenanted with Common Owner — Implied Reciprocal Servitudes

Some courts hold that, when a grantee covenants to restrict his land in some manner, a reciprocal restriction is created by implication against the grantor's retained land in favor of the grantee's land. Thus, an "implied reciprocal servitude" burdens the retained land and binds subsequent owners with notice of it.

Illustration: When CG Company conveyed Lot 1 to Ann, she covenanted to restrict it to residential uses. CG then conveyed Lot 2 to Bob without a restriction. Ann may be able to limit Bob to residential uses based on an implied reciprocal servitude. A court might hold that, when Ann covenanted with CG, CG impliedly covenanted to Ann that its retained land also would be restricted. The reciprocal burden that attached to Lot 2 ran with the land to Bob, if he took with notice of the burden.

a. Prior Grantee's Reliance

Some courts hold that reciprocal servitudes can be implied only if the prior grantee purchased in reliance on similar restrictions being imposed on the remaining lots. For these courts, reliance furnishes the basis for implying a reciprocal servitude.

C. SIGNIFICANCE OF COMMON PLAN

A neighborhood development scheme (a common plan) may be essential to the recognition of third party beneficiary status or of an implied reciprocal servitude.

1. To Provide Notice

Even if a purchaser does not have actual notice of a common plan, the plan may provide notice in two other ways. First, a recorded map or plat that shows uniform restrictions on lots in the subdivision may provide *record notice* of the restrictions. Second, the mere existence of uniform structures or landscaping may provide *inquiry notice* as to the cause for such uniformity.

2. To Apply Third Party Beneficiary Theory

In some jurisdictions, a prior grantee cannot enforce a covenant against a subsequent grantee if a common plan does not exist. In these jurisdictions, only subsequent grantees can enforce the covenant. The Restatement of Servitudes provides that each lot included in the common plan is impliedly benefited from all the servitudes it creates. § 2.14(1).

3. To Imply Reciprocal Servitudes

A subsequent grantee may not be bound by an implied reciprocal servitude unless a common plan exists. Without a common plan, a subsequent grantee is subject only to express covenants.

4. To Burden Benefited Lots

Courts in some jurisdictions hold that a prior grantee is not bound by a covenant if the lack of a common plan prevents a reciprocal covenant from being implied in her favor against subsequent grantees.

Illustration: CG Company conveyed Lot 1 to Ann, Lot 2 to Bob, and Lot 3 to Cathy. The deeds to Ann and Bob include building restrictions, but the deed to Cathy does not. If no general building plan exists in the neighborhood, Cathy's lot is not subject to an implied reciprocal servitude. If Cathy's lot is not burdened, Bob's lot also may not be burdened because it is not benefited. Thus, Ann cannot enforce the restriction against either Bob or Cathy.

Illustration: CG Company conveyed Lot 1 to Ann with a restriction in her deed, then conveyed Lot 2 to Bob with no restriction, and then conveyed Lot 3 to Cathy with a restriction similar to Ann's. Ann can enforce the restriction against Bob if a court implies a reciprocal servitude against him, which may depend on the existence of a common plan. Ann also can enforce the restriction against Cathy, either as an implied reciprocal servitude or as a third party beneficiary of Cathy's promise to CG, which also may require the existence of a common plan. Bob can enforce the restriction against Ann as the successor to a lot benefited by Ann's covenant, though he may have to show a common plan because his lot is not similarly restricted. Bob also can enforce the restriction against Cathy under a third party beneficiary theory. He cannot use the implied reciprocal argument against Cathy, because he did not make a promise from which a reciprocal servitude may be implied. Similarly, he cannot claim to be the beneficiary of a reciprocal servitude implied from Ann's covenant to CG. As the owner of Lot 3, Cathy can enforce the restriction against Ann, because Lot 3 is benefited by Ann's covenant. Cathy cannot enforce the restriction against Bob, because he did not give a covenant. A court probably would not treat Cathy as a third party beneficiary of any reciprocal servitude implied against Bob from Ann's promise. A court also is unlikely to retroactively imply a reciprocal servitude against Bob based on Cathy's promise to CG.

D. ENFORCEMENT BY HOMEOWNERS' ASSOCIATION

If the developer wants to create a homeowners' association and to grant it power to enforce the common restrictions, the developer can convey a parcel of land to the association, such as for a community club house, and then state in each deed to a lot in the subdivision that the restrictions are for that parcel's benefit, as well as for the other lots. If the developer has not yet created the association, the designated parcel still can be benefited by express deed restrictions. When the common owner creates the association and conveys the designated parcel to it, the benefit of the deed restrictions will run with the parcel. Even without owning a benefited parcel, the association may be able to enforce the restrictions as the original covenantees' agent. However, it may have difficulty enforcing covenants against successor owners if the jurisdiction requires it to own land that is touched by the covenant's benefit.

Once the developer has sold all the land in the subdivision, a court probably would hold that it no longer can enforce, release, or modify the covenants.

E. EFFECT OF OMISSION IN LATER DEEDS

If the restriction was recorded in the public property records, future purchasers of the property are bound or benefited by it even if the deed by which they acquired title did not mention it. The recorded document provides constructive, if not actual, notice of the restriction.

V. TERMINATION OF RESTRICTIONS

A. TERMINATION BY COVENANTING PARTIES' ACTS

1. Restricted Duration

If the covenant is expressly limited, such as for twenty years or until termination by a majority vote of the affected property owners, expiration of that time period or a majority vote terminates the restriction. Statutes also may limit the life of such interests.

2. Release

The beneficiary can terminate a covenant's obligations by release (retransfer of the interest) or by rescission (cancellation of the agreement). The release only binds the releasor. Other beneficiaries are not bound by the release or rescission.

Illustration: CG Company conveyed Lot 1 to Ann with a covenant that it would restrict all retained lots to residential use. CG then conveyed Lot 2 to Bob and obtained his covenant to restrict his parcel to residential use. CG later released Bob from his covenant. Ann still can stop Bob from using his property for a nonresidential use. CG's release terminates only its right to enforce Bob's obligation. Bob still has a duty to Ann based on CG's covenant to Ann, which ran with the land to bind Bob.

3. Merger

Covenants are destroyed when the same person owns the benefited and burdened parcels, in the same way that easements terminate by merger of the dominant and servient estates.

4. Abandonment

A common grantor who initially includes restrictions in deeds but then fails to include them in deeds for the remaining lots may be deemed to have abandoned the common plan, thereby terminating the covenants that were created. Even when covenants were included in all the deeds, widespread and tolerated noncompliance by the lot owners may have the same effect.

5. Prescription

A covenantor or his successor may be sued by the covenantee or her successor if he refuses to honor the covenant. Like other lawsuits, this type of action is subject to the statute of limitations. Therefore, a covenant that has been violated for too long may be lost by prescription.

6. Estoppel

Covenants may be terminated by estoppel in the same fashion as easements. This defense, like laches, unclean hands, acquiescence, and changed conditions, is equitable and may merely prohibit enforcement by injunction without necessarily prohibiting a legal remedy for damages.

7. Laches

A court will deny equitable relief when the plaintiff seeking to enforce a covenant has waited too long to enforce it to the detriment of the burdened property's owner.

8. Unclean Hands

A court will deny equitable relief to the owner of a benefited parcel if he has violated a similar covenant imposed on his land.

9. Acquiescence

A court will deny equitable relief to the owner of a benefited parcel if she has permitted too many other lot owners to breach their covenants.

B. TERMINATION RESULTING FROM EXTERNAL ACTIONS

1. Changed Conditions

Most courts will not enforce a covenant, at least in equity, when changed neighborhood conditions have substantially diminished the covenant's benefits. However, the changed conditions normally must have occurred within the neighborhood that is subject to the covenants. Changes outside the restricted area are an insufficient justification to terminate the restriction for lots at the outer edge of the restricted area. Otherwise, if the covenants burdening the lots at the outer edge are terminated, the covenants burdening the lots next to the outer edge lots will terminate, and the domino effect will continue until all the lots in the neighborhood are unrestricted. A change in the restricted parcels' zoning classification does not constitute an adequate changed condition unless the new zoning ordinance prohibits the uses permitted by the covenant.

Illustration: When Ann agreed with Bob to restrict her adjacent property to residential uses, the entire neighborhood was residential. Neighborhood conditions now have changed. Her house is the only remaining residential structure, and her lot would be worth substantially more for a commercial use.   Under the circumstances, the slight benefit to Bob no longer may justify the heavy burden imposed on Ann. Therefore, a court might not enforce the covenant against her.

2. Government Acquisition

If the government acquires burdened property by eminent domain, it takes title free of all private restrictions.   As a result, compensation may be owed not only to the owner of the burdened lot for loss of her fee title, but also to the owners of the benefited lots for the loss of their covenant rights in the land that is taken.

When the government sells the property at a tax sale because the owner failed to pay the property taxes, courts are split as to whether the new owner is subject to the pre-existing restrictive covenants.

C. LEGAL INVALIDITY

Like easements and profits, covenants that violate the rule against unreasonable restraints on alienation are invalid.   Covenants also are invalid if they violate the Rule Against Perpetuities, though the Rule is less likely to be applied to servitudes than to estates in land. Covenants are invalid if they restrain trade in violation of the antitrust laws, such as covenants not to compete and tying arrangements that force members of a subdivision to pay for common recreational facilities even if they do not want them. Courts increasingly are applying modern rules against unconscionability to agreements affecting land. Restatement of Servitudes § 3.7. Finally, covenants are invalid if they discriminate against classes of people protected by federal, state, or local law.

PART TWO
CONVEYANCING

INTRODUCTION

Part Two addresses problems incident to the transfer of interests in land. Landlord-tenant law could be regarded as a branch of conveyancing, because it involves the transfer of a leasehold estate from landlord to tenant. However, it has been treated as a separate topic because the problems involved in that context generally deal with the parties' relations after the lease has been executed. The creation and transfer of easements also could be treated as a conveyancing topic. However, the conveyancing aspects of easements generally are incidental to other issues. Adverse possession is not a question of conveyancing at all, because the title acquired by the adverse possessor is an original title, rather than one conveyed by the former owner.

CHAPTER SEVEN
REAL ESTATE BROKERS

I. BROKER'S ROLE

A. BROKER'S ECONOMIC FUNCTION

Property can be sold without a broker's assistance, but the buyer and seller generally find it to be more convenient to have a broker assist them. Therefore, most real estate sales involve a broker. Unlike many other retail industries, the broker does not carry her own inventory. Rather than buying and selling land herself, she normally acts as an agent for the buyer or seller.

In most cases, the seller retains the broker, which is the assumption in all the Illustrations in this Chapter. For rental properties, the landlord usually retains the broker. Even when the buyer or tenant retains the broker's services, she still may receive her commission from the seller or landlord.

B. WHO MAY ACT AS A BROKER

A broker must be licensed by a state regulatory agency. To obtain a license, a broker must possess certain minimum academic credentials, such as some college education, must pass a qualifying exam, and must satisfy character and fitness requirements. The broker also may have to satisfy continuing education requirements and have a certain amount of experience in real estate marketing. Real estate salespersons hold inferior licenses that entitle them to perform broker services only under the supervision of a licensed broker. The educational requirements for a salesperson's license are less than for a broker's license.

Engaging in brokers' activities without a license may trigger criminal or civil liability and prevents the agent from collecting the commission that otherwise would be due. A "finder" exception permits an unlicensed person to recover compensation for introducing a buyer and seller to one another. However, any additional activity, such as participating in the negotiations, makes one a broker, rather than a finder, and requires a license.

C. BROKERS' SERVICES

A property owner hires a broker to market the property. Thus, the broker is the seller's agent. The broker locates potential buyers and presents their purchase offers to the seller, which he can accept or reject. The broker normally does not have authority to sign a sales contract on the seller's behalf or to transfer title to the property to the purchaser.

This Chapter deals with the contract between the broker and the seller or buyer. The contract between the seller and the buyer is covered in the next Chapter. The two contracts often are confused. For instance, a property owner may employ a broker and agree to pay her a commission if she finds someone who will offer the seller $200,000 for his house. If the broker finds such a person, the seller can reject the offer, but he may owe the broker a commission because she performed her part of the contract.

D. BROKERS' OTHER LEGAL OBLIGATIONS

1. Discrimination

Federal, state, and local civil rights and licensing laws prohibit brokers from discriminating against prospective purchasers or renters based on factors such as race, sex, and religion. Brokers are prohibited from (1) discriminating in rendering services or in advertising, such as advertising an apartment building as being "a Christian building," (2) steering (directing prospective buyers or renters to certain areas or away from other areas based on factors such as their race or religion), and (3) blockbusting (attempting to trigger panic sales by spreading rumors in a neighborhood that members of a protected class are moving into the area). Sanctions may include damages, fines, censure, and loss or suspension of the broker's license.

2. Practicing Law

Brokers generally may not practice law by giving legal advice or by drafting contracts, deeds, mortgages, and other documents. However, in many jurisdictions, brokers are permitted to fill out simple legal forms incidental to the services they have rendered as a broker.

3. Antitrust

Brokers may not conspire to fix commission rates or otherwise to eliminate competition. A local multiple listing service's refusal to admit "discount brokers" and other efforts to discourage competition also may violate federal or state antitrust statutes.

II. LISTING AGREEMENTS AND COMMISSIONS

The employment contract between a broker and her principal is called a listing agreement. In the listing agreement, the seller authorizes the broker to act as his agent in advertising the property for sale and showing it to potential purchasers. Many states require that listing agreements be in writing, although the Statute of Frauds does not apply because a listing agreement is an employment contract and does not convey an interest in land.

A. TYPES OF LISTING AGREEMENTS

Listing agreements are classified according to the circumstances under which the seller must pay a commission to his broker.

1. Open (Nonexclusive) Listing

A broker earns a commission under an open listing agreement only if she is the "procuring cause" of the purchase. Thus, she is not entitled to a commission if the seller or someone else finds the buyer. "Procuring cause" is a question of fact. In some states, the standard is satisfied if the broker was the first person to notify the buyer or someone connected with the buyer about the property's availability. In other states, the broker must play a more significant role to be considered the procuring cause.

2. Exclusive Listing

If the broker is entitled to a commission even when someone else is the procuring cause of the purchase, the agreement is an exclusive listing. If the seller is not liable for a commission if he finds the buyer, the agreement is an "exclusive agency" listing. If the seller is liable even if he finds the buyer, the agreement is an "exclusive right to sell" listing.

B. EARNING A COMMISSION

Under most listing agreements, the broker earns the commission when a "ready, willing, and able purchaser" has been presented to the seller. The agreement usually does not define the adjectives "ready, willing, and able," but they are commonly understood to describe a person who wants to purchase the property on the terms specified in the listing agreement and who is capable of performing the contract of sale, such as by paying the purchase price.

1. Sale Closing as Condition Precedent

If the broker earns her commission by finding a ready, willing, and able buyer, she is entitled to the commission even if the sale is not completed. She may demand her commission from the seller even though the buyer subsequently defaults. To avoid this result, some states require that the buyer actually must purchase the property before the broker's right to a commission vests. These states reason that this result is consistent with sellers' expectations, especially because sellers normally anticipate paying the commission from the sale proceeds. The seller and broker always can include a condition of closing in the listing agreement.

a. *Closing as Condition or Mere Calendar Event*

Many sales contracts between sellers and buyers contain a provision that revises the broker's commission right by providing for its payment at the closing. This type of provision is valid if the broker also signs it, but a court then has to determine whether the provision abrogated the broker's earlier entitlement to a commission for having produced a ready, willing, and able buyer or whether it merely postponed the time of its payment to the closing.

2. Lesser and Contingent Offers

When a prospective buyer makes an offer that satisfies the terms in the listing agreement, the broker has earned the commission even if the seller does not accept the offer. But it is rare for a buyer to make a perfect offer. If the offer is for less than the asking price, no commission is yet earned because the purchaser is not "ready, willing, and able" to purchase on the seller's terms. However, if the seller accepts the offer, the broker is entitled to her commission.

If the buyer's offer is contingent on getting a mortgage loan, selling her current house, or some other condition, she is not yet "ready, willing, and able" to purchase, and no commission is yet due. Even if the seller accepts the offer, whether the buyer will complete the deal is unknown. Thus, until the contingency is removed, the broker has not earned the commission.

III. BROKER LIABILITY

Because brokers are involved in complicated legal relations with sellers and buyers, they frequently are involved in litigation with them. The more common legal theories behind such lawsuits are listed below.

A. CONTRACT

The listing agreement usually is written as a bilateral contract between the broker and the seller to prevent the seller from revoking just before the broker completes her performance. However, to make it bilateral, the broker must make some promise to the seller. She cannot promise success because that is too unpredictable, but she can promise to use diligence or best efforts to find a buyer. Lack of diligence then may make her liable, perhaps in an amount equal to the harm suffered by the seller because a timely sale was not made.

B. LICENSING STANDARDS

Licensing statutes frequently provide standards of conduct for brokers to retain their licenses. Courts may treat such statutory standards as grounds for imposing civil liability when the broker's violation causes harm. Thus, a broker's lack of "honesty," a common statutory standard, may cause not only suspension or revocation of a broker's license, but also may subject her to economic liability to the injured party.

C. NEGLIGENCE AND FRAUD

As professionals, brokers are held to a high standard of care and will be liable for malpractice when their conduct falls below that standard. If the broker is the seller's agent, she clearly owes him a duty of care, but lack of privity between the buyer and broker may limit her liability to the buyer to cases of fraud or deceit.

Illustration: The broker did not advise the seller to insist that the buyer's promissory note to him be secured by a mortgage and did not advise the buyer to test the soil for contamination before buying, and both parties were injured as a result. The broker is liable to the seller if a jury decides that due care required her to give him such advice. But, in many states, she is liable to the buyer only if the buyer can show that the broker knew of the contamination and intentionally concealed it or failed to disclose it.

D. AGENCY

An agent owes fiduciary duties of loyalty, integrity, and good faith to her principal. Thus, as the seller's agent, the broker is prohibited from putting the buyer's interests or her own interests above the seller's. She may not side with the buyer against the seller in the negotiations. Furthermore, she cannot acquire the seller's property for her own account unless her involvement in any such acquisition is fully disclosed to him beforehand.

1. Whose Agent is the Broker?

It has been assumed in this Chapter that the broker is the seller's agent because he retained her services and will pay her commission, which are the usual grounds for an agency relationship. After entering into the listing agreement, the broker may put the listing into a "multiple listing file" for distribution to all other brokers who belong to the same service and possibly to the public. Under the rules of the multiple listing service, the broker then must split her commission with any other broker who finds a purchaser for the property. A buyer generally assumes that the "showing broker" with whom he has been working is his agent, while the "listing broker" is the seller's agent. But because the showing broker will receive his share of the commission from the seller and received his authorization to act from the listing broker, courts normally characterize the showing broker as the seller's subagent, rather than as the buyer's agent. Despite what the buyer thinks, the showing broker's fiduciary duties are owed to the seller! To avoid this situation, many buyers now enter into buyer's broker agreements, by which the showing broker expressly agrees to be the buyer's agent.

CHAPTER EIGHT

CONTRACT OF SALE

When a seller and buyer agree to the terms of a sale, they normally sign a contract of sale (also known as a purchase agreement or as an earnest money contract). In the contract, the seller promises to convey the land, and the buyer promises to pay for it. The contract provides a date for the "closing" (the consummation of the sale) that is usually several weeks after the contract is signed to give the buyer time to arrange financing, have the title examined, inspect the property, and take the other steps necessary to complete the transaction. At the closing, the seller delivers a deed to the buyer, and the buyer pays the purchase price. On escrow closings, see Chapter 9. This Chapter is concerned with the parties' relationship after they sign the contract of sale but before the sale is closed.

I. CONTRACT FORMATION — STATUTE OF FRAUDS

The seller-buyer relationship begins when the parties enter into a binding contract of sale. Because the contract involves the transfer of an interest in land, it is subject to the Statute of Frauds and must be in writing. To satisfy the Statute of Frauds, the writing must include at least the parties' names, a property description, the purchase price, words that demonstrate intent to buy and sell, the terms of the sale, and the signatures of the parties to be charged.

As with other contracts that are subject to the Statute of Frauds, an oral agreement for the sale of land may be enforceable in equity for specific performance and sometimes at law for damages based on estoppel (inducing detrimental reliance) or part performance. Courts disagree as to what constitutes sufficient part performance to take a case out of the Statute. In order of increasing judicial acceptance, courts have found adequate part performance when: (1) the buyer has paid all or part of the price; (2) the seller has delivered possession to the buyer; (3) the seller has delivered possession, and the buyer has paid all or part of the price; and (4) the seller has delivered possession, and the buyer has made improvements to the property. In all these situations, the parties' actions tend to prove that a contract was made, because they probably would not have been undertaken otherwise.

A. DISCRIMINATION BY SELLER

Federal, state, and local laws prohibit sellers from refusing to sell to particular buyers based on factors such as race, color, religion, national origin, handicap, sex, age, or marital status. Some laws exempt owners of single family homes from some or all of these requirements, and commercial properties may be regulated differently than residential properties. A seller who violates these laws may be forced to pay damages to the aggrieved buyer and to comply with the law by selling to that buyer.

II. MARKETABLE TITLE (MERCHANTABLE TITLE)

Because of land's special nature, the question of title to any particular parcel always has been a more important and more difficult question than for personal property. The variety of permissible estates in land, the fact that ownership may be subject to leases, easements, restrictive covenants, and other interests, the potential for adverse possession, and the technical formalities for title transfer all make the condition of the seller's title a matter of great concern to any prospective buyer. This subsection is concerned with the problems that arise when a question exists about the seller's title.

A land buyer generally does not investigate the title before the contract of sale is signed. The buyer does not want to invest the time and money for a title search before she knows whether the seller and she will agree on the terms of the sale. To enable the buyer to withdraw from the contract if the title is flawed, every contract includes a representation concerning the quality of the seller's title. Even if the contract does not include an express representation, the law implies a representation that the seller's title is "marketable." Of course, the contract can expressly negate any representation by the seller about his title, but a buyer would be very unwise to enter into that contract.

A. WHAT IS MARKETABLE TITLE?

In this context, the term "marketable" is not used in the layperson's sense that the title is saleable. Instead, as a matter of law, a seller has marketable title if it is free of any encumbrance and free of any doubt. Thus, a title is unmarketable if (a) the seller lacks all or part of the claimed title, (b) the title is subject to an encumbrance, or (c) a reasonable possibility exists that (a) or (b) is true. For this reason, if the buyer has agreed to acquire title subject to an encumbrance, such as a utility easement, the contract should so specify.

1. Vendor's Title

Unless the contract indicates otherwise, the buyer is entitled to receive fee simple absolute title to the property. If the seller does not have that title, the buyer may withdraw from the contract. The seller is often said to lack a marketable title in such cases, though it could also be said that the seller merely has a marketable title to less than what he promised to convey.

Illustration: Sam and Barb signed a contract for the sale of Sam's land. Barb then discovered that Sam does not own the entire fee interest. He is only a cotenant with someone else. Barb is not obligated to purchase Sam's interest.

Illustration: Sam and Barb signed a contract for the sale of forty acres. Barb then discovered that Sam has title to only twenty-five acres of the parcel. Because Sam lacks marketable title to the forty acres he agreed to convey, Barb is not obligated to complete her purchase.

Illustration: Sam and Barb signed a contract for the sale of Sam's land. Barb then discovered that Sam has only a life estate in the land, rather than fee simple absolute. Barb is not obligated to purchase.

Illustration: Sam and Barb signed a contract for the sale of Sam's land. Barb then discovered that Sam previously had given Ann an option to purchase the land that has not yet expired. Sam's title is not marketable. If Barb accepted his deed, she would be compelled to sell the property to Ann if Ann exercised her option.

2. Title Free From Encumbrances

An "encumbrance" is a lien or other nonpossessory interest or a tenancy. A marketable title is not subject to any encumbrances. Thus, if the title is subject to an encumbrance, it should be stated as an exception to the marketable title standard in the contract of sale.

a. Easements

Illustration: Sam and Barb signed a contract for the sale of Sam's land. Barb then discovered that Sam's fee simple title is subject to an easement that was not disclosed in the contract for sale. Barb is not obligated to purchase.

(1) Exception for Visible and Beneficial Easements

In many states, easements that are visible and beneficial, such as utility easements, are an implied exception to the marketable title requirement. Courts assume that the purchaser observed the easement before she offered to purchase and wants to take title subject to it.

b. Covenants and Servitudes

Illustration: If Sam's title is subject to a restrictive covenant or an equitable servitude, his title is not marketable.

(1) Exception for Superfluous and Unenforceable Covenants

A covenant does not render title unmarketable if it merely compels the owner to do what the law itself requires (as when both a covenant and the zoning ordinance impose the same prohibition against commercial activity) or if it is no longer enforceable.

c. Leases

Illustration: If Sam's title is subject to an existing lease, his title is unmarketable even if the lease is economically advantageous.

d. Money Obligations

Illustration: If Sam's title is subject to a mortgage, judgment lien, assessment lien, mechanic's lien, or any other monetary charge, his title is unmarketable.

3. Title Free From Doubt

The buyer need not prove that the seller's title actually is bad. A title is unmarketable if any reasonable doubt exists concerning its marketability. A buyer is not required to accept a title that may require a quiet title action.

Illustration: The chain of title to Sam's land (i.e. the series of deeds by which previous owners acquired title to it) includes a deed from Ann Smith to Paul C. Jones. However, the next deed in the chain is signed by Paul Jones, rather than by Paul C. Jones. A risk exists that Paul Jones is someone other than Paul C. Jones, which, if true, means that Sam does not have title. Barb is not required to prove that Paul Jones is not Paul C. Jones. Sam's title is unmarketable merely because this question exists.

Illustration: A release of a mortgage on Sam's title was recorded, but the acknowledgment on the release was defective. If this defect creates a reasonable doubt whether the mortgage still encumbers the property, the title is unmarketable.

4. Circumstances not Affecting Marketability

A title may be marketable though the property itself is undesirable. Property that is subject to termite infestation, flooding, bad soil conditions, or other physical problems nevertheless may have a marketable title. Zoning and similar governmental restrictions on the use of property do not affect the title's marketability, though in some jurisdictions an existing zoning or code violation may render title unmarketable.

B. EFFECTS OF UNMARKETABLE TITLE

1. Seller's Right to Cure Defects

The seller is not obligated to have marketable title until the closing. Thus, the buyer is not entitled to terminate the contract of sale as soon as she discovers a title defect. In many states, the buyer must give the seller notice of the defect and a reasonable opportunity to cure. If the contract does not make time of the essence, the seller's time to cure may extend for a reasonable time beyond the closing date. If the contract does make time of the essence, the seller must cure the defect by the closing, unless the buyer did not give adequate advance notice of the defect or waived the marketable title requirement.

Illustration: On January 1, Sam and Barb entered into a contract for the sale of Sam's property. The sale was to be consummated on March 1. On February 1, Barb discovered that Sam's title was subject to an easement. Barb may not terminate the contract on February 1. Instead, she must notify Sam of the defect. If Sam eliminates the easement by March 1, Barb is obligated to complete the sale.

Illustration: On January 1, Sam and Barb entered into a contract for the sale of Sam's land. The sale was to be consummated on March 1. On February 1, Barb discovered that Sam's title was subject to an easement and notified him. Sam diligently worked to remove the easement but did not succeed by March 1. If time is not of the essence, a court may hold that Barb is not yet released from the contract and that Sam has a reasonable time to clear his title. If time is of the essence, Sam's failure to have marketable title on the closing day entitles Barb to terminate the contract.

Illustration: On January 1, Sam and Barb entered into a contract for the sale of Sam's land. The sale was to be consummated on March 1. On February 1, Barb discovered that Sam's title was subject to a mortgage and notified him. Sam took no action to remove the mortgage before March 1 but instructed the closing agent to pay the mortgage from the sale proceeds so that Barb would acquire title free of it. Barb is obligated to complete the sale. Unless specifically prohibited by the contract, the seller normally can use the sale proceeds to remove monetary liens even though, technically, he gets the purchase money before transferring marketable title to the buyer.

2. Seller's Right to Specific Performance with Abatement

If the title defect is insignificant, a seller may be able to get specific performance of the contract. However, the purchase price will be abated if the defect reduces the land's value.

3. Buyer's Right to Terminate

If the seller does not tender marketable title at the closing, the buyer can terminate the contract and can recover any consideration she paid to the seller unless the seller has not had a reasonable time to cure the title defect. However, the buyer can terminate before the closing date if the seller clearly cannot obtain marketable title.

4. Buyer's Right to Damages

A buyer who withdraws from the contract because of an unmarketable title can recover her down payment and any out-of-pocket expenses incurred in preparing to purchase. Many states also permit the buyer to recover loss of bargain damages.

5. Buyer's Right to Specific Performance

If a buyer is willing to accept an unmarketable title, the seller may not refuse to convey based on his flawed title. Thus, the buyer can obtain specific performance of the contract.

a. Specific Performance with Abatement

Generally, if the defect is small and quantifiable, a decree of specific performance against the seller will include an abatement of the price. However, if the defect is substantial, the buyer cannot force the seller to sell at a drastically reduced price.

C. WAIVER OF RIGHT TO MARKETABLE TITLE

A contract for the sale of land should expressly specify the required quality of the seller's title. If it does not, the marketable title requirement is implied.

1. Complete Waiver of Marketable Title

When the parties are unsure about the seller's title, they may waive the marketable title requirement. This often occurs when a landowner is buying a doubtful claim against his own title. Although some courts have held that a buyer's agreement to accept a quitclaim deed from the seller eliminates the marketable title requirement, the better authority is to the contrary.

2. Waiver of Particular Defect

A buyer may be willing to acquire title subject to certain title encumbrances, such as utility easements. To evidence the buyer's willingness, the contract of sale should specify that title will be conveyed subject to those encumbrances. This contract provision eliminates the buyer's right to argue that the seller's title is unmarketable because of the specified encumbrances.

Illustration: Barb's offer to buy Sam's property stated that "the title is to be free of all liens, except recorded building restrictions that are uniform throughout the neighborhood." After Sam accepted the offer, Barb learned that his lot is subject to a set-back requirement that also applies to all other lots in the neighborhood. Although a restrictive covenant normally would make Sam's title unmarketable, Barb cannot terminate the contract because she expressly agreed to take subject to it.

3. Alternative Title Standards — Insurable and Good

Rather than require the seller to transfer marketable title, a contract of sale may require the seller to transfer only an "insurable" or "good" title.

a. Insurable Title

As its name indicates, the insurable title standard requires the seller to transfer a title that a title insurance company is willing to insure. For title insurance, see Chapter 11. This standard generally provides less protection for the buyer than the marketable title standard. Like other types of insurance companies, title insurance companies are in the business of charging premiums to indemnify an insured from loss. In the case of title insurance, the insurer generally will reimburse an insured if she suffers a loss because the seller did not have title or because the title is subject to an encumbrance or other defect that was not disclosed in the policy. However, title insurance policies are subject to numerous exceptions, title insurance companies go out of business, and most land purchasers prefer to have the title they expected, rather than an insurance payment, especially if the defect interferes with their use of the property or causes them to lose the property completely.

b. Good Title

The good title standard provides a purchaser with the least protection. It requires only that the seller, in fact, has the title that he contracted to convey. Even if the title is subject to question, the good title standard is violated only if the defect is valid, even if a quiet title action is required to eliminate the defect.

4. Waiver by Acceptance of Deed — Merger

If the buyer purchases the property and accepts the seller's deed, the buyer no longer can enforce the title standard in the contract of sale. When the sale is completed, the contract provisions "merge" into the deed, and the buyer's rights against the seller thereafter depend on the deed's title covenants, if any.

III. EQUITABLE CONVERSION

Because each parcel of land is unique, a buyer can specifically enforce a contract of sale against a seller that has changed his mind about selling. For this reason, a contract of sale effectively gives the buyer an interest in the land, as well as contract rights against the seller. Therefore, in 32 states, when the contract becomes binding, equitable conversion causes the buyer to become the land's equitable owner and the seller to retain mere legal title. Because the seller's right under the contract is to receive the purchase price, he holds the property title only as security for payment.

Equitable conversion is limited in two ways. First, it normally does not affect the right to possession. Even after a binding sales contract has been executed, the buyer may not enter the property until the seller has transferred the legal title to her or has given her permission to enter before then. Second, the requirement of a specifically enforceable purchase agreement means that an option to purchase or a right of first refusal does not trigger equitable conversion. Equitable conversion occurs only after the purchaser exercises an option or pre-emptive right.

The following sections address the most important consequences of equitable conversion.

A. SELLER'S OR BUYER'S DEATH

If the seller or buyer dies before the closing, the sale still will be consummated. If the seller dies, because his interest in the land became personal property when the contract was signed, the people who inherit his personal property get the purchase price from the sale, but those who inherit his real property must execute the deed to the buyer. Similarly, if the seller married after contracting to sell the land and then died, the surviving spouse could not claim a marital interest because, when the marriage occurred, the seller held the legal title in trust for the buyer. Conversely, if the vendee dies, the purchase price is paid from the personal estate, and the people who inherit his real property will get the land.

B. ACTIONS FOR PROPERTY DAMAGE

If a third party injures the property during the contract period, the doctrine of equitable conversion entitles the buyer to sue him. The seller may sue only if the buyer does not. In contrast, damages for trespass depend on the right to possess, rather than on title, so standing to sue depends on possession. Finally, a buyer may sue a seller who has possession of the property for waste, and a seller may sue a buyer who has possession for impairing the security if she damages the property.

C. RISK OF LOSS FOR INJURIES CAUSED WITHOUT FAULT

In the absence of a contrary contract provision, courts allocate the risk of innocent loss during the contract period in one of three ways.

1. Majority Rule — Risk on Buyer

Under a strict application of the doctrine of equitable conversion, the buyer bears the risk of loss during the contract period because she became the land's owner when the contract was signed. Therefore, she cannot withdraw from the contract if the property is damaged before the closing and must pay the full purchase price specified in the contract.

Illustration: On January 1, Sam and Barb contracted for the sale of Sam's property. The sale was to close on March 1. On February 1, lightning started a fire that destroyed the premises. Under the majority rule, Barb still is obligated to complete the contract and pay the entire price, and Sam may seek specific performance or damages if she fails to do so.

2. Minority Rule — Risk on Seller

The minority (or Massachusetts) rule is that failure of consideration occurs if the seller cannot deliver the premises on the closing day in their original condition. Jurisdictions that follow this rule treat the buyer's obligation to perform as being subject to the implied condition that the property's physical condition is the same as on the contract date. Under this rule, the buyer can terminate the contract or can obtain specific performance with a possible abatement of the purchase price if the property is damaged before the closing.

Illustration: On January 1, Sam and Barb contracted for the sale of Sam's property. The sale was to close on March 1. On February 1, a fire caused $3,000 damage. If Sam does not repair by March 1, Barb can terminate the contract or can sue for specific performance with a price abatement of $3,000.

3. Uniform Vendor and Purchaser Risk Act

Some states have enacted the Uniform Vendor and Purchaser Risk Act, which assigns the risk of innocent destruction during the contract period to the seller unless the buyer has taken possession of the property.

4. Contrary Agreements

Regardless of which rule the jurisdiction follows, the parties are free to allocate the risk of loss in the contract.

a. Insurance Provisions

Both parties can purchase insurance to protect their interest in the property. If the sales contract provides that the buyer will insure the property until the closing, a court might interpret the provision as assigning the risk of loss to her. However, because a buyer can insure her interest even when the seller bears the risk of loss or vice versa, carrying insurance or agreeing to do so does not automatically determine who bears the risk of loss.

If the buyer had the risk of loss but the seller insured the property, the seller holds the insurance award in constructive trust for the buyer in most jurisdictions and must use the award to repair the property or to reduce the purchase price. A court may render a comparable judgment when the seller had the risk of loss, but the buyer insured the property.

D. CREDITORS

Once a contract of sale is binding, the seller's creditors can recover from the unpaid balance of the purchase price, but not from the property itself. However, the buyer's creditors may reach the property to satisfy their claims against her.

IV. DISCLOSURE DUTIES

The common law implied no warranty of fitness. This basic rule generally still applies to real estate. However, sellers now often have greater disclosure duties, and commercial sellers may be subject to an implied warranty of fitness.

A. DISCLOSURE

Every seller of real estate must disclose any material defect known to him and not reasonably discoverable by the buyer (latent defect). If the seller fails to disclose, the buyer can rescind the contract of sale, sue for damages, and possibly recover for personal injuries suffered as a result of the defect. Brokers, lenders, attorneys, escrow officers, and inspectors also may have a duty to disclose latent defects known to them and perhaps even defects they may have suspected or should have known about.

B. IMPLIED WARRANTY OF HABITABILITY

More than forty states now impose an implied warranty of habitability on sellers of new homes. The warranty provides a home owner with a cause of action for physical defects that affect the home's habitability, such as a faulty foundation or roof or inadequate plumbing or heating. The warranty also covers defective conditions in the land, such as improperly compacted soil. The states that recognize the implied warranty differ on a number of its particulars.

1. Plaintiffs

The first purchasers of a home always can enforce the warranty, unless they knew of the defect when they purchased the home. However, only ten states permit subsequent purchasers to enforce it.

2. Defendants

Originally, the warranty applied only to builder-sellers of mass-produced homes, but it now includes anyone who builds houses for sale. In some states, the warranty also applies to a seller that did not build the home if the seller is a real estate developer, such as the developer of a subdivision. However, the warranty normally does not apply to builders that did not sell the property, such as the contractor that the developer employed.

3. Disclaimers

Most states allow a seller to disclaim the warranty of habitability if the disclaimer is clear and conspicuous, but courts in these states strictly construe disclaimers. States that refuse to recognize disclaimers do so on the ground that disclaimers violate public policy.

4. Damages

If the defect cannot be corrected or can be corrected only at prohibitive cost, the usual measure of damages is the difference in the property's value without the defect and with the defect. Otherwise, the measure is the cost of repair. Some jurisdictions also award damages for personal injuries and may allow rescission if the defect makes the house unsafe or otherwise unfit for habitation.

5. Statute of Limitations

States differ on when the statute of limitations to enforce the warranty of habitability begins to run. In some states, it starts to run when construction is completed or when the home is sold. Other states have adopted the "discovery rule." In these states, the statute does not begin to run until the owner discovers the defect or should have discovered it.

V. PERFORMANCE

The seller and buyer must perform the contract within the time specified in the contract. If the contract does not specify a time or if it is specifies a time but does not provide that "time is of the essence," the parties must perform within a reasonable time. The seller must deliver a deed that conveys title to the buyer, and the buyer must pay the purchase price.

A. INSTALLMENT LAND CONTRACTS (CONTRACTS FOR DEED)

In the ordinary contract of sale considered so far, delivery of the deed and payment of the purchase price are concurrent conditions, because both must be performed at the same time. However, the parties instead may enter into an installment land contract at the closing, whereby the buyer pays the price in installments over a period of time, such as five years, before the seller is required to deliver a deed. Under an installment land contract, the buyer normally has the right to possess the property even before delivery of the deed. In reality, this arrangement is a form of mortgage financing, and some states apply mortgage law to it. However, courts in other states enforce installment land contracts according to their terms, which has significant implications. For example, the seller has to have marketable title only when the deed must be delivered, and the buyer is not entitled to the same protections as a mortgagor, such as the right to a foreclosure sale upon default and a statutory right to redeem. Instead, if the buyer defaults on the installment land contract, the seller can take back the land and keep all the buyer's payments, even if they exceed the land's rental value for the time that the buyer had possession. This seller remedy is called forfeiture.

VI. NONPERFORMANCE

A. BY SELLER

If the seller breaches the contract of sale, the buyer can (1) terminate the contract, recover her down payment, and receive a lien on the property until she is repaid, (2) bring an action for specific performance with an abatement of the price for minor defects, or (3) sue for damages in the amount of her expenses and benefit of the bargain damages (the difference between the contract price and the property's market value), where permitted. Courts sometimes limit benefit of the bargain damages to cases in which the seller acted in bad faith.

B. BY BUYER

If the buyer breaches the contract of sale, the seller can (1) terminate the contract and resell the property, (2) bring an action for specific performance, though this remedy is of little use against a buyer who cannot perform and is less readily available to a seller than to a buyer because the seller generally can be made whole by damages, (3) sue for actual damages in the amount of his expenses and benefit of the bargain damages if the land's value has decreased, or (4) retain the purchaser's down payment as liquidated damages if the contract and state law so provide.

CHAPTER NINE

TRANSFER OF TITLE BY DEED

To satisfy the Statute of Frauds, a property owner (the grantor) normally executes a written instrument to transfer title or a lesser interest to a purchaser or donee (the grantee). In this Chapter, the feminine pronoun refers to the grantor, and the masculine pronoun refers to the grantee.

I. DEEDS

A deed is the instrument that a grantor typically uses to transfer title to land. The deed states that the grantor "grants," "conveys," or "quitclaims" title to the grantee. In many states, statutes provide preferred forms and language for deeds. Generally, three types of deeds are used in the United States.

A. QUITCLAIM DEED (DEED WITHOUT WARRANTIES)

A quitclaim deed usually states that the grantor "quitclaims" or "releases" the property to the grantee. By these words, the grantor makes no representation that she has any property to convey. The deed merely states that the grantor conveys whatever interest, if any, she has in the property. This form of deed is useful for quieting title to property by buying potentially adverse claims, because a grantor is not liable if, in fact, nothing was owned or conveyed. Quitclaim deeds also commonly are used to release mortgages and for intrafamily transfers.

B. LIMITED WARRANTY DEED (BARGAIN AND SALE DEED, GRANT DEED, OR SPECIAL WARRANTY DEED)

A limited warranty deed normally states that the grantor "grants," "conveys," or "bargains and sells" the property to the grantee. In many states, such language is statutorily defined as representations that the grantor owns the property and has not encumbered it or conveyed it to anyone else. In the absence of a statutory definition, these representations are expressly included in the deed.

C. GENERAL WARRANTY DEED

A general warranty deed states that the grantor "conveys and warrants" the property to the grantee. In many states, this phrase is statutorily defined to provide broad representations concerning the title being conveyed. In the absence of a statutory definition, the deed must expressly state these covenants concerning the title.

II. EXECUTION OF DEEDS

A. SIGNATURE

The Statute of Frauds requires the grantor to sign the deed. The early common law also required the grantor to affix her seal to the deed, but that requirement has been abolished in virtually every jurisdiction. The grantee need not sign or seal the deed even if it includes covenants by him, because acceptance of the deed is deemed to constitute acceptance of its terms.

B. CONSIDERATION

Because a conveyance is not a contract, consideration is unnecessary. However, deeds commonly state that consideration was paid to rebut any inference of a resulting trust or to qualify the grantee as a bona fide purchaser under the recording act.

C. ESSENTIAL TERMS

To satisfy the Statute of Frauds, a deed must include the parties' names, a legal description of the property, and words of conveyance, such as "conveys" or "bargains and sells," as well as the grantor's signature.

1. Parties

The grantee should be named or adequately described, such as "my present husband." The grantee's name can be left blank to be filled in later. However, if the grantor dies before that occurs, the deed may be invalid. Unless the grantor dies, the grantee usually can insert any name he wants.

The grantor must sign the deed. If her signature was forged, the deed is entirely void. The deed also is void if the grantor's signature is genuine but was obtained by fraud, such as by representing that she was only signing an autograph book. However, if the fraud was collateral to her signature, such as the grantee falsely promising to pay the grantor, the deed is voidable but not void. A subsequent transfer of the title to a bona fide purchaser may defeat the grantor's later attempt to invalidate the conveyance. If the grantor is not the sole owner, her signature alone will only convey her interest in the property. A conveyance of the fee simple absolute title would require the signature of any spouse, cotenant, easement holder, or other interest owner.

2. Property Description (Legal Description)

The legal description must be sufficiently detailed to distinguish the property being conveyed from every other parcel of land. The description can refer to an official survey or to a recorded plat map or can describe each boundary by metes and bounds. Any part of the property that the grantor "excepts" (if an existing interest) or "reserves" (if a new interest) also must be described adequately. The most common methods for describing land are the federal survey system, a recorded plat map, and metes and bounds.

a. Federal Survey System (Government Survey or Rectangular System)

Principal meridian lines (north-south) and base lines (east-west) running across most of the country furnish location points for many parcels. Every six miles, range lines run parallel to the meridian lines, and township lines (east-west) run parallel to the base lines. Each thirty-six square mile parcel that is bounded by range lines and township lines is called a township. Townships are divided into thirty-six sections that are one mile long on each side. They are numbered sequentially from the top right corner of the township across to the top left corner (1 to 6), then down one level and back across to the right (7 to 12), continuing from right to left and then left to right to the bottom of the section. These one square mile sections (640 acres) may be divided into 160 acre quarter sections (e.g. northeast quarter) or into 40 acre quarter-quarter sections (e.g. northwest quarter of the southeast quarter). A description generally reads from the smallest locator to the broadest.

Illustration: "E1/2 of NW1/4 of SW1/4, Sec. 8, T5N, R6W, PB & M" refers to the east half of the northwest quarter of the southwest quarter of Section 8, Township 5 North, Range 6 West of the specified principal base line and meridian. Thus, the property is located in the square mile section bordered by township lines 4 and 5 north of the base line and by range lines 5 and 6 west of the meridian line.

b. Plat Maps

Today, most land development occurs when subdividers acquire agricultural or range land and convert it into smaller residential or commercial plots. For its own convenience and to comply with the state subdivision law, the subdivider has a surveyor prepare a map of the newly subdivided parcels. The map is recorded in the public land records and provides the basis for legal descriptions of the new, smaller parcels, such as "Lot 23 of Block 15 of the New Pines Subdivision, as recorded in volume 9, page 150, Official Records of Jones County, Georgia." Recorded maps of condominium projects ("vertical subdivisions") usually include the height and other dimensions of each unit.

c. Metes and Bounds

A parcel can be described by identifying a point of beginning and then by giving a series of "calls" that give the direction and length (the "bearing") of each boundary. For example, the description might state "beginning at the southwesterly intersection of Oak and Main Streets, then west 25 feet to the fence, then south 100 feet, then northeast approximately 120 feet back to the beginning." This triangle would be described with much more detail and precision in a real deed.

d. Inconsistent Descriptions

In a legal description, a "monument," such as a tree or fence, is inconsistent with a "course" or "distance" (25 feet) or an "angle" (west), when they do not lead to the same place. For example, if one walking 25 feet west from the tree would go beyond the fence in the preceding paragraph, the monument reference prevails over the course reference. In this hierarchy, map references are between monuments and courses. Name or quantity references, such as "known as Smith Ranch, being 1.03 acres," are lowest in the hierarchy. If uncertainty about property boundaries exists between neighbors, rather than between a grantor and grantee, the doctrine of agreed boundaries may furnish a basis of resolution. See Chapter 16.

e. Boundaries with Width

If a boundary is defined by reference to a road or other monument, a presumption exists that the deed refers to the monument's center. However, the presumption does not apply in certain cases, such as when the deed provides otherwise or when the grantor's ownership goes only to the edge.

Illustration: A legal description that states that the property "is bounded on the north by the road" presumably means that the parcel's northern border is the middle of the road, rather than the near (south) or far (north) edge. But if the grantor owns the entire width of the road and no land north of it, the boundary would be the northern edge of the road, rather than the middle. If the grantor owned no part of the road, its southern edge would be the boundary.

f. Water Boundaries

If a river or stream is the boundary, the grantee presumptively takes title to the middle of it. As the stream changes course over time, the party on one side may gain land (accretion), while the party on the other side loses land (reliction) due to the alteration of the boundary line. If the change in the stream is sudden and substantial (avulsion), the boundary does not move but remains where it was before the stream change. Other consequences of owning "riparian" land adjacent to a stream are covered in Chapter 14.

3. Words of Conveyance

The deed must show the grantor's intent to transfer an interest to the grantee. No technical words are necessary, but "grant," "quitclaim," and "convey" are common terms. The grantor should not use words that indicate her intent to convey only at the grantor's death (e.g. "I leave"), or the deed might have to comply with the more stringent formalities for the creation of a will.

4. Description of the Estate

If the deed does not specify the estate being conveyed, it presumptively transfers fee simple absolute. The ancient words of limitation "and heirs" are no longer necessary. Therefore, if a lesser estate is intended, qualifying language must be added, such as "for ten years" or "for life." Similarly, the deed should describe whether multiple grantees are taking as tenants in common, joint tenants, or tenants by the entirety. If the form of cotenancy is not specified, a tenancy in common normally is presumed, unless the parties are married, which, in some states, creates a presumption for a tenancy by the entirety. If the estate being conveyed is subject to encumbrances, such as an easement or covenant, the deed should specify them as exceptions to the title being conveyed.

D. ACKNOWLEDGMENT

Most states do not require that the grantor's signature be acknowledged (notarized) or witnessed. These are common requirements for wills but not for deeds. However, the grantor's signature must be acknowledged for the deed to be recorded in the public property records.

E. RECORDING

In most states, a deed conveys title when it is delivered. Failure to record the deed does not defeat the passage of title, and many deeds are delivered but intentionally left unrecorded. However, recording provides important advantages to the grantee. See Chapter 10.

III. DELIVERY OF DEEDS

A deed is ineffective until the grantor delivers it to the grantee. Before delivery, the deed is merely a piece of paper without any legal effect.

A. WHAT IS DELIVERY?

No specific physical acts are required for effective legal delivery of a deed. Delivery is not necessarily the same as the manual handing over of the document, because a deed may be delivered even though it is not handed over. Conversely, a deed may be handed to the grantee and yet not have been delivered as a matter of law. For example, the grantor may hand the deed to the grantee solely for his review of the document. The physical acts are significant as manifestations of the grantor's intent, which is the essential feature of delivery.

Delivery occurs when the grantor properly manifests an intent that a completed or consummated legal act has occurred. The grantor must intend that, as a result of her binding act, the deed has operated to pass title. What distinguishes a will from a deed is that a will transfers title in the future, whereas a deed immediately transfers title, even if it is title to a future interest.

Illustration: Grace signs a deed, puts it down, and says to those who are present: "Now I have transferred my property to Gene." Even though Grace has not handed the deed to Gene, it may be considered to be delivered. Grace's statement indicates that she regards the deed as already having transferred the title to Gene, i.e. that she has committed a binding legal act.

Illustration: Grace signs a deed, hands it to Gene, and says: "Hold onto this deed for me because later I may want to make you the owner of the property." Delivery has not occurred because Grace's statement indicates that she does not regard handing the deed to Gene as sufficient to transfer title.

A presumption exists that a deed has been delivered when it is in the grantee's possession, and a contrary presumption exists when the grantor retains possession. However, both presumptions are rebuttable, as the above Illustrations indicate. A rebuttable presumption of delivery also exists when the grantor has notarized or recorded the deed. When a deed has been dated and delivered, delivery is presumed to have occurred on the date specified in the deed.

Even after delivery has occurred, the deed is effective to transfer title only if the grantee accepts it. However, acceptance is presumed whenever title would be beneficial to the grantee. Acceptance is presumed to have occurred on the same date the deed was delivered. In fact, the grantee need not even know that delivery has occurred, but he can reject a deed when it would have harmful consequences to him. For example, the property might be contaminated by toxic wastes, which the owner is legally obligated to eliminate.

B. INTENT THAT DEED BE PRESENTLY OPERATIVE

Delivery occurs only if the grantor has a present intent that the deed immediately transfer title. If the grantor intends that the deed transfer title only at some future time, delivery has not occurred.

Illustration: Grace hands Gene her deed and says: "The property is now yours." Delivery has occurred, because Grace intended the deed to transfer title immediately.

Illustration: Grace hands Gene her deed and says: "Record this deed when I die; recording will make the property yours." The deed has not been delivered, because Grace intends it to transfer title in the future, rather than immediately. Her statement indicates a belief that recording is essential to transfer title. Although she may be mistaken, it demonstrates that she does not intend the deed to become effective immediately. She did not intend to perform a completed legal act.

Illustration: The granting clause in Grace's deed to Gene states: "To Gene on his 21st birthday." When

Gene is 19 years old, Grace hands him the deed and says, "I now give you an interest in my property." Grace has *presently* delivered a *future* interest to Gene as evidenced by her use of the present verb tense ("I now give you"). The delivery satisfied the present intent requirement.

1. Effect of Future Events When No Intent Exists to Make Deed Presently Operative

To satisfy the delivery requirement, the grantor must have a present intent that the deed transfer title immediately. If the grantor intends the deed to operate only in the future, there is no delivery. But when that specified future date arrives, the grantor then may have a present intent. At that later time, the deed can be regarded as delivered. Sometimes it is said that the grantor ratified the earlier physical act of delivery.

Illustration: Grace handed her deed to Gene and said: "This deed will make you the owner of the property when you are twenty-one." Grace later attended Gene's twenty-first birthday party and congratulated him on his new ownership of the property. The deed may be regarded as delivered on Gene's birthday. It was not delivered when Grace handed it to Gene, because she then had no present intent. But on his birthday, she intended the deed to operate, i.e. she had a present intent. Because no particular physical acts are required, the deed was delivered that day though Grace did not hand the deed to Gene then.

2. When Future Event is Grantor's Death

A future intent cannot become a present intent when the grantor intends that the deed operate only at her death. When the grantor dies, she cannot have any intent and, thus, cannot deliver a deed. Moreover, a transfer that becomes effective only at the grantor's death normally must comply with the requirements for a valid will.

Illustration: Grace handed Gene her deed and said: "Record this deed when I die, and you will then become the owner of my property." Grace's false belief in the necessity for recording means that the deed was not delivered when she handed it to Gene. As long as Grace is alive, she has no present intent that the deed transfer title, because she does not want title to pass until her death. But when she dies, she obviously has no intent, and delivery cannot occur. As a result, Gene will not obtain title from the deed.

Illustration: Grace's safe deposit box is opened at her death and is found to contain a deed to Gene with the following note: "This deed is for Gene, so that he will be taken care of after I am gone." No delivery occurred. Grace's note indicates an intent that the deed operate only at her death. Therefore, she had no present intent while she was alive to commit a binding legal act.

C. NO CONDITIONAL DELIVERY TO GRANTEE

Under the general rule prohibiting conditional delivery of a deed, a court may reach one of two results if the grantor hands the deed to the grantee and states some conditions. In most jurisdictions, courts hold that the grantor had a present intent to make the deed operative, so delivery occurred free of the condition. In other jurisdictions, the court may hold that the condition negates any intent to make an immediate transfer of title, so that delivery has not occurred.

Illustration: Grace handed her deed to Gene and said: "Record this deed when I die." There are two possible outcomes. The court may hold that present delivery occurred, so that the nonrecordation condition fails and Gene becomes the owner at once with the right to record. Alternatively, the court may hold that Grace did not intend the deed to be operative until after her death, so that the deed was not delivered and Gene receives nothing. Neither resolution effectuates Grace's intent that Gene take the property at her death. She should have left the land to Gene in a will.

D. DELIVERY TO SOMEONE OTHER THAN GRANTEE

1. Grantee's Agent

Delivery to the grantee's agent is the same as delivery directly to the grantee, because the agent is subject to the grantee's control. Therefore, the rule that conditional deliveries are invalid usually still applies.

Illustration: Grace handed her deed to Gene's wife and said: "Please give this deed to Gene when he gets home, but tell him not to record it until next year." If Gene's wife is regarded as his agent, delivery to her is the same as delivery to Gene, and the condition concerning recording may be invalid.

2. Grantor's Agent

The grantor may hand a deed to her agent for delivery to the grantee. In that case, delivery occurs when the agent delivers the deed to the grantee, but only if the grantor had a present intent at that time.

Illustration: Grace handed her deed to her husband and said: "Please give this deed to Gene when you see him at the party tonight." When her husband took the deed, he became Grace's agent. At the party, Grace watched her husband hand the deed to Gene. At that point, the deed was delivered in the legal sense, because Grace's husband had her authority to deliver it to Gene.

Illustration: Grace handed her deed to her husband and said: "Deliver this deed to Gene when I die." Grace died, and her husband handed the deed to Gene. There is no delivery. Grace's husband was her agent, and an agent's power terminates when the principal dies. Thus, he no longer had authority to deliver the deed to Gene.

3. Escrow

A deed may be delivered to a third person who is an agent for neither party. Such a person is called an "escrow," "escrow agent," "escrow holder," or "escrowee." A true escrow agent is not subject to the control of either person acting without the other. The grantor places the escrow agent beyond her control by giving up the right to recall the deed from the escrow. This device permits a valid conditional delivery to be made to take effect in the future, even when the condition is the grantor's death. By waiving the right to recall the deed, the grantor manifests her intent to perform a binding legal act. The escrow agent's authority does not depend on the grantor's continued assent, and the delivery may be completed when the condition occurs.

In the following four Illustrations, assume that the grantor has waived the right to recall the deed and that "Ezra" is the escrow agent.

Illustration: Grace handed her deed to Ezra and said: "Deliver this deed to Gene on his 21st birthday." Ezra delivers the deed to Gene on his 21st birthday. At that moment, valid delivery occurs.

Illustration: Grace handed her deed to Ezra and said: "Deliver this deed to Gene on his 21st birthday." Grace died before Gene turned 21. Ezra delivers the deed to Gene on his 21st birthday. The delivery is valid, even though Grace is dead.

Illustration: Grace handed her deed to Ezra and said: "Deliver this deed to Gene when I die." When Grace dies, Ezra hands the deed to Gene. The delivery is valid.

Illustration: Grace handed her deed to Ezra and said: "Deliver this deed to Gene when he is 21." However,

Grace took the deed back from Ezra when Gene was only 19. Title still passes to Gene on his 21st birthday. Grace's recovery of the deed is irrelevant, because a binding legal act occurred when she irrevocably delivered her deed into escrow.

a. Contingency Certain to Occur

In a few states, a grantor cannot conditionally deliver a deed into escrow unless the condition is certain to occur. This rule has been criticized as confusing an unconditional waiver of the right to recall the deed with an allowable conditional event, as shown in the following Illustrations.

Illustration: Grace handed her deed to Ezra and said: "Deliver this deed to Gene when I die. I waive the right to recall it." All jurisdictions agree that Ezra may complete the delivery at Grace's death. She had no right to recall the deed, and the condition is certain to occur.

Illustration: Grace handed her deed to Ezra and said: "Deliver this deed to Gene when I die, but I reserve the right to recall it." All jurisdictions agree that Ezra may not complete the delivery on Grace's death. The event is certain, but the right of recall prohibits a transfer after her death.

Illustration: Grace handed her deed to Ezra and said: "Deliver this deed to Gene if he outlives me. I waive my right to recall it." Courts in most jurisdictions would hold that Ezra may complete delivery after Grace's death if Gene is still alive because she put the deed beyond her control. But a minority of courts would hold that the condition's uncertainty prevents the deed from being legally delivered despite the unconditional escrow.

b. Underlying Contract

A grantor who wishes to make a gift of land can make a binding delivery into escrow by waiving the right to recall the deed. In contrast, if the land is being sold, courts in most states hold that the grantor can recall the deed from escrow before delivery to the grantee unless an enforceable contract exists between them.

Illustration: Grace orally agreed to sell her property to Gene for $10,000. Grace deposited her deed into escrow with instructions that it be delivered to Gene if he paid the price within one month. Before the month had passed, Grace revoked her instructions and recalled the deed. Courts in most states would permit Grace to do so, because the oral contract was unenforceable under the Statute of Frauds.

Because the grantee's payment is not a certain event, this rule is consistent with the minority view that conditional delivery into escrow cannot occur if the condition is uncertain. The rule also is consistent with the majority view if the grantor did not intend to waive the right to recall, because the escrow agent remains subject to the grantor's control until the grantee pays. As the grantor's agent, the escrow agent must honor the grantor's demand to return the deed. The existence of a binding contract between the grantor and grantee does not change the nature of the escrow.   The contract merely enables the grantee to obtain a decree of specific performance of the contract and to force the grantor to deliver the deed regardless of her state of mind.   Once a grantor signs a specifically enforceable contract, she no longer has the right to change her mind.

Illustration: Grace executed a binding contract with Gene to sell her land to him.   Grace then deposited her deed into escrow with proper instructions but later sought to recall the deed before the time for Gene's performance.   Whether the escrow agent returns the deed to her is irrelevant, because Gene can specifically enforce the contract and compel Grace to convey regardless of her state of mind.   This result is the same as if no escrow had been created.   If Grace refuses to deliver a deed to Gene, a court would compel her to do so, and title would pass regardless of her intent.

c.   Relation Back

Generally, a deed deposited into escrow passes title upon delivery from the escrow agent to the grantee.   But, when necessary to do justice and to effectuate the parties' intent, courts hold that the passage of title relates back to the delivery into escrow.

Illustration: Grace deposited her deed to Gene in escrow but died before the escrow agent delivered the deed to Gene.   Her heirs claim that her title passes to them.   However, to protect Gene, a court will hold that the escrow agent's post-death delivery to Gene relates back to Grace's earlier delivery into escrow, so that Gene owns the property, rather than Grace's heirs.

Illustration: Grace deposited her deed into escrow, but Gene died before the escrow agent delivered the deed to him. A court will hold that the delivery of the deed to Gene's estate relates back to the Grace's delivery into escrow, so that legal title passed to Gene when he was alive and then descended to his heirs. This result avoids the rule that a deed is void if it does not convey title to a living grantee.

Illustration: Grace deposited her deed to Gene into escrow but later gave a deed to the same property to Alice. Alice knew of the deed to Gene. The doctrine of relation back gives Gene priority over Alice though the delivery to her preceded delivery to Gene. However, if Alice had been a bona fide purchaser without notice, she might have prevailed under the state recording act. See Chapter 10.

Illustration: Grace deposited her deed to Gene into escrow. Her creditors then attempted to attach the property. Courts in some jurisdictions hold that Gene prevails over the creditors by virtue of the relation back doctrine, but others hold that the doctrine will not apply when innocent third parties are involved.

E. EFFECT OF DELIVERY AND NONDELIVERY

1. Delivery

Title transfers when the deed is delivered. What subsequently happens to the document is unimportant, because the deed has performed its function of transferring title. Title is not recovered by the grantor if the deed is lost, recalled, or destroyed.

Illustration: Grace delivered her deed to Gene but later changed her mind and asked Gene to return it to her. Even if Gene returns the deed, title will remain with him. Grace's delivery transferred title to Gene. If the parties now wish to retransfer title to Grace, Gene must execute and deliver his own deed to her; returning her deed is not an adequate substitute. Return of the deed does not undo its earlier delivery.

2. Nondelivery

Until a deed is delivered, it has no effect on title. However, based on estoppel, a grantor who negligently permitted the grantee to possess an undelivered deed may lose the title to an innocent purchaser of the property from him.

Illustration: Grace executed a deed to Gene but did not deliver it. Gene obtained the deed without Grace's knowledge and recorded it. Grace still owns the property. Gene acquired no interest in the land and, therefore, has nothing to transfer to a bona fide purchaser, even though he recorded the deed.

Illustration: Grace handed her deed to Ezra and said: "Deliver this deed to Gene if he graduates from college." Gene did not graduate from college, but Ezra gave him the deed anyway. The deed has not been delivered. Grace remains the owner of the property.

IV. TITLE COVENANTS IN DEEDS

Today, property purchasers commonly protect their title by purchasing title insurance. A title insurance policy indemnifies the purchaser if the title is not what it was represented to be. However, title covenants in a deed provide an additional source for recovery if the title is defective. Different types of deeds provide different levels of protection.

A. TYPES OF DEEDS

1. General Warranty Deed

A general warranty deed gives the grantee the greatest possible recourse against the grantor for title defects. This deed contains up to six title covenants that cover title defects that arose at any time before the deed was delivered.

2. Limited Warranty Deed (Bargain and Sale Deed, Grant Deed, or Special Warranty Deed)

The most common type of limited warranty deed includes the same title covenants as a general warranty deed but limits their coverage to title defects that arose during the grantor's period of ownership. More generally, a limited warranty deed is any deed that provides some, but not all, of the protection of a general warranty deed. For example, a warranty deed may be limited because it does not contain all the same title covenants as a general warranty deed, though it applies to defects that arose at any time before the deed was delivered.

3. Quitclaim Deed (Deed without Warranties)

A quitclaim deed includes no title covenants. It merely conveys whatever interest the grantor has in the property, if any.

B. SIX COMMON LAW TITLE COVENANTS

Although some differences exist among the states, a general warranty deed usually includes six title covenants. The first three—seisin, right to convey, and against encumbrances—are "present" covenants. The final three—quiet enjoyment, warranty, and further assurances—are "future" covenants.

1. Covenant of Seisin

This covenant warrants that the grantor owns the estate that the deed is to convey. It is breached if the grantor does not own the land or owns a lesser interest.

Illustration: Grace delivered a warranty deed to Gene that purports to convey the fee simple absolute title. If Grace had only a life estate, she breached the covenant of seisin.

2. Covenant of Right to Convey

This covenant is almost identical to the covenant of seisin but warrants that the grantor has the right to convey the estate described in the deed, rather than that she owns it.

Illustration: Grace delivered a warranty deed to Gene that purports to convey the fee simple absolute title. If Grace had only a life estate, she breached the covenant of right to convey, as well as the covenant of seisin.

3. Covenant Against Encumbrances

This covenant warrants that the property is free from all encumbrances. It is violated if the title is encumbered by a lien (tax lien, assessment lien, mechanic's lien, judgment lien, or mortgage), a lease, or a restriction on use (easement, restrictive covenant, or equitable servitude).

Some courts hold that a visible and beneficial easement, such as a utility easement, does not violate the covenant on the ground that the grantee must have seen the easement and been willing to take title subject to it. A few other courts extend this exception to include any encumbrance actually known to the grantee, but this is a minority view. Generally, any encumbrance "assumed" by the grantee, such as a mortgage, is excluded from the covenant against encumbrances.

4 & 5. Covenants of Warranty and Quiet Enjoyment

Although these covenants traditionally have been listed separately, they are essentially indistinguishable. They cover the same types of defects as the covenants of seisin and against encumbrances. However, unlike those covenants, the covenants of warranty and quiet enjoyment are not breached unless the person who owns the interest that breaches them actually asserts it.

6. Covenant of Further Assurances

Unlike the other five covenants, which provide an action for damages, the covenant of further assurances provides a specific performance action if the grantor's initial conveyance was defective. The grantee can use this covenant to force the grantor to execute a new deed. By virtue of this covenant, the grantor also is obligated to transfer to the grantee any adverse interest that the grantor subsequently acquires. The doctrine of estoppel by deed accomplishes much the same result.

C. ESTOPPEL BY DEED (AFTER-ACQUIRED TITLE)

If a grantor warrants that she is conveying an interest in land that she does not own but subsequently acquires, it automatically passes to the grantee without the need for an additional deed. Because this doctrine operates by estoppel, it applies only if the grantor represented in the deed that she had title. The representation estops the grantor from later asserting her after-acquired title against the grantee. The after-acquired title "feeds" the estoppel. The doctrine does not apply if the grantor gave only a quitclaim deed, because it does not make any warranties concerning the title.

D. BREACH OF TITLE COVENANT

1. What Constitutes Breach

The six title covenants differ in the methods by which they are breached.

a. *Covenant of Seisin*

This covenant is breached if the grantor did not have seisin (title) when she delivered the deed. Technically, it is breached even if the grantor owns the property but if a potential adverse possessor whose claim has not yet ripened is in possession. Conversely, it is not breached if the grantor does not own the property but is wrongfully possessing it as a potential adverse possessor. In this case, the grantor has tortious seisin. The grantee need not be evicted from the land to claim a breach. It is sufficient that the grantor did not have seisin.

b. Covenant of Right to Convey

This covenant is breached if the grantor lacks the right to convey the estate that the deed describes. Someone may have a right to convey without necessarily having seisin, such as a person with a power of attorney to convey on the grantor's behalf. Therefore, lack of seisin alone does not breach this covenant. Like the covenant of seisin, the grantee need not be dispossessed from the premises for a breach to occur.

c. Covenant Against Encumbrances

This covenant is breached if an interest, such as an easement or mortgage, encumbers the title when it is conveyed. The encumbrance need not actually disturb the grantee's possession or title.

d. Covenants of Warranty and Quiet Enjoyment

These covenants are breached if the grantee is "evicted" by a paramount title or interest holder. "Eviction" includes not only a physical ouster, but also a constructive eviction, such as paying a paramount lien to avoid a mortgage foreclosure.

e. *Covenant of Further Assurances*

This covenant is breached if the grantor refuses to execute a new deed if the first deed was defective, to obtain a release of an encumbrance, when possible, or to give the grantee a deed for an interest covered by the after-acquired title doctrine.

2. When Covenant is Breached

Deed covenants are divided into "present" and "future" covenants. Present covenants are breached, if ever, at the moment of the conveyance to the grantee. Future covenants are breached only when an eviction occurs.

a. *Present Covenants*

The covenant of seisin is breached at the moment the grantor delivers the deed if she lacked seisin at that time. The covenant of right to convey is breached at the moment of delivery if the grantor lacked the right to convey the property at that time. The covenant against encumbrances is breached at the moment of delivery if the title is encumbered at that time.

b. *Future Covenants*

The covenants of quiet enjoyment and warranty are breached when a paramount title or encumbrance is asserted against the grantee so that he is actually or constructively evicted. The covenant of further assurances is breached when the grantor refuses to obtain or to supply documents that the grantee needs to perfect the title.

E. SUBSEQUENT GRANTEE'S ENFORCEMENT OF COVENANTS (RUNNING WITH THE LAND)

The distinction between present and future covenants controls which covenants "run with the land" to protect subsequent grantees. Because the present covenants are breached only when the deed is delivered, they do not run with the land and cannot be enforced by a future owner, unless the future owner acquires that right from the grantee whose deed covenant was breached. Future covenants do run for the benefit of future owners because these covenants are not breached until an eviction occurs.

1. Covenants of Seisin and Right to Convey

These two covenants warrant present facts about the grantor's title. If the facts are true, the covenants have not been breached and never will be breached. If they are untrue, the covenants were breached at the moment of the conveyance, and the statute of limitations begins to run then. The cause of action for their breach constitutes personal property, which does not run with the land, except in a minority of states. However, the owner of the cause of action can transfer it to the person who owns the property when the defect is discovered if the statute of limitations has not expired.

Illustration: Grace delivered a deed to Gene that contained only the covenants of seisin and right to convey. However, Grace previously had conveyed the same property to Ann. Gene executed a quitclaim deed of the property to Rita. Rita has no remedy against Grace or Gene, even though she did not acquire title. She cannot sue Gene because he gave no covenants. Although Grace did give covenants, they are both present covenants and do not run with the land to protect Rita. However, courts in a minority of states hold that Gene's deed to Rita impliedly assigned his cause of action against Grace to her. In the other states, Gene can transfer his cause of action against Grace to Rita by a separate assignment. However, the statute of limitations on the cause of action is not extended by the transfer to Rita.

2. Covenant Against Encumbrances

As a present covenant, this covenant does not run with the land. If the property is encumbered when it is conveyed, the grantee has an immediate cause of action against the grantor. But subsequent grantees may not sue that grantor for the encumbrance if it still exists when they acquire the property, unless the cause of action was assigned to them. However, a subsequent grantee may sue her own grantor if the title is encumbered and if her deed included a covenant against encumbrances.

Illustration: Grace conveyed her property to Gene by a deed that included a covenant against encumbrances. At the time of the conveyance, the title was subject to an easement. Gene then conveyed the property to Rita by a quitclaim deed. Rita has no remedy, unless Gene assigns his cause of action against Grace to her and the statute of limitations has not expired. Her deed from Gene contained no covenant against the easement, and Grace's covenant did not run with the land.

3. Covenants of Warranty, Quiet Enjoyment, and Further Assurances

These future covenants run with the land and protect subsequent grantees. The statute of limitations begins to run when an eviction occurs. Once these covenants are breached, they technically no longer run with the land. However, courts often hold that the cause of action arising from the breach is impliedly assigned with each conveyance of the property, thus reaching the same result as if the covenant did run.

Illustration: Grace purported to convey property that she did not own to Gene by a general warranty deed. Gene later gave Rita a quitclaim deed to the same property. The true owner appeared and dispossessed Rita. Rita does not have a cause of action against Grace for breach of the covenants of seisin or right to convey, unless Gene assigns that cause of action to Rita and the statute of limitations has not expired. But Rita may sue Grace for breach of the covenants of quiet enjoyment and warranty after she is evicted. If Rita sells the property to Sam after she is evicted, he will have no cause of action against Grace, because even the future covenants do not run once they are breached. However, Rita may assign her cause of action to Sam.

Illustration: Grace's property was subject to a mortgage when she conveyed it to Gene by a general warranty deed. Gene then conveyed the property to Rita by quitclaim deed. The mortgage was not paid, and the mortgagee foreclosed and evicted Rita from the property. Rita may sue Grace for breach of the covenants of quiet enjoyment and warranty, because those ran with the land and were breached when Rita was ousted. But, unless Rita gets an assignment from Gene, she has no cause of action against Grace for breach of the covenant against encumbrances, because it was breached when Grace conveyed to Gene and did not run with the land. Rita cannot sue Gene because he gave no covenants.

F. MEASURE OF DAMAGES

The covenants differ in their measure of damages. In general, the breaching covenantor is never liable for more than the amount she received when she sold the property. Restitution is the maximum recovery. In some states, however, damages are based on the property's value on the date of breach, rather than on the purchase price. Damages generally do not include the cost of improvements made by the grantee. However, he may be able to make such a claim on an unjust enrichment theory or under an "innocent improvement" statute.

If a subsequent grantee sues a grantor, some courts limit recovery to the amount the plaintiff paid for the property even if it is less than the remote grantor received. If a remote grantee has a cause of action under title covenants made by more than one grantor in the chain of title, the grantee can sue them all but is limited to only one full satisfaction. If a grantor who is sued is the beneficiary of earlier covenants, he has an action against the covenantor for any damages he must pay.

Illustration: Grace conveyed property to Gene by a general warranty deed for $10,000. Gene conveyed it to Rita by a general warranty deed for $9,000. Rita conveyed it by full warranty deed to Sam for $11,000. Grace never owned the property, and the real owner evicted Sam. Sam may sue Rita based on her covenants and recover $11,000. He may sue Gene based on the future covenants in the deed to Rita and recover $9,000 (the amount Gene received). He also may sue Grace on the future covenants in the deed to Gene and recover $10,000. However, Sam's total recovery cannot exceed $11,000 even if he obtains judgments against all three defendants. If Sam recovers from Rita, she may have an action against Gene or Grace. If Sam or Rita recovers from Gene, he may have an action against Grace.

1. Covenants of Seisin and Right to Convey

When these covenants are breached, the grantee can recover the price he paid for the property or for so much of the property as the deed failed to convey. Courts differ as to whether the grantee can retain the property or must tender it to the grantor as a precondition to recovery. If the grantee buys the outstanding title, he can recover the amount paid for it, not exceeding the amount the grantor received when she sold the property. In a minority of jurisdictions, the grantee can recover up to the property's value on the date of the breach.

2. Covenant Against Encumbrances

An encumbrance is either monetary or nonmonetary. If it is monetary, such as a tax lien or mortgage, the measure of damages is the cost to remove it, but not in excess of the land's value. If the encumbrance is nonmonetary, such as an easement or restrictive covenant, the measure of damages is the reduction in the land's market value caused by the encumbrance. If the grantee buys the encumbrance or pays it off, he can recover the amount he paid, but not in excess of the amount the grantor received when she sold the property. In a minority of jurisdictions, the grantee can recover up to the property's value on the date of the breach.

3. Covenants of Warranty and Quiet Enjoyment

For a total eviction, the plaintiff can recover the amount he paid for the property.   For a partial eviction, he can recover a proportionate amount of the price.

4. Covenant of Further Assurances

This covenant normally is enforced by a specific performance action, rather than by an action for damages.

CHAPTER TEN

PRIORITIES: THE RECORDING SYSTEM

Priority problems arise when a property owner (1) grants partial interests in the property to successive transferees, such as when the owner gives a mortgage on the property to one person and then gives a mortgage on the same property to another person, (2) purports to transfer the entire estate to different persons, such as when the owner conveys the property to one person and then conveys the same property to another person, or (3) transfers partial and total interests in the same land, such as when the owner gives a mortgage to one person and then conveys the fee title to another person. The relationship between the transferees is analyzed as a question of priorities—who has the prior and, therefore, superior interest. State recording systems generally decide the priorities.

   In most Illustrations in this section, the transfers are of the entire estate, but the same priority principles generally apply to transfers of partial interests.

I. COMMON LAW PRIORITIES

At common law, most questions of priority were determined according to the principle "first in time, first in right." The party who took first had the superior interest. This principle was supported by the logical notion that, after the owner gave his interest to the first transferee, he had nothing left to give to the second. The same principles applied to the resolution of priorities between equitable claimants, so long as the equities were otherwise equal. The one exception was that a prior equitable claim would be defeated by a subsequent legal claim held by a bona fide purchaser. In this one case, the earlier claim would lose priority.

Illustration—Competing Legal Claims: Owen delivered a deed to his property to Ann and later delivered a deed to the same property to Bob. Ann prevails over Bob in their competing claims to legal title, because her claim was first in time. Ann owns the property.

Illustration—Competing Equitable Claims: Owen executed a contract to sell his property to Ann and later executed a similar contract to sell it to Bob. Both claims are equitable, because Owen retains legal title. As between the competing equitable claims, Ann again prevails because her claim was first in time. Ann has the superior right to buy the property.

Illustration—Prior Legal and Subsequent Equitable Claims: Owen delivered a deed to Ann and later contracted to sell the same property to Bob. Ann's prior legal claim based on her deed prevails over Bob's subsequent equitable claim. Ann owns the property and is not obligated to sell it to Bob.

Illustration—Prior Equitable Claim and Subsequent Legal Claim by a Bona Fide Purchaser: Owen contracted to sell his property to Ann and later delivered a deed of the same property to Bob. If Bob paid value to Owen and had no notice of Ann's claim, he is a bona fide purchaser and will prevail over her even though her claim was prior in time. Bob owns the property and is not obligated to honor the contract and sell to Ann. This was the only type of case at common law for which priority in time was not the controlling factor in determining priority.

Although the common law principle of priority based on time is logical and worked in its time, it is unworkable in a modern, mobile society. If A prevails over B simply because she took first, there is no reasonable way for B to purchase O's property. How can B be sure when he pays his money to O that O has not previously conveyed the property to someone else? A diligent search of the property records regarding O's title would be useless because the common law gives A the title even though she never records her deed.

For this reason, every state has replaced the common law rule with a statutory recording system.

The system creates incentives for transferees to record the document by which they acquired an interest in land. The system also generally protects a subsequent transferee against prior unrecorded transfers. The recording statutes do not mandate that a document be recorded to be effective against the grantor. Rather, they provide that a recorded document makes the document effective against the rest of the world, because recording provides "constructive notice" of its contents to everyone. Conversely, if a document is unrecorded, it will be ineffective against certain protected parties.

II. THE RECORDING SYSTEM—RECORDING STATUTES

The primary purpose of state land records systems is to make documents affecting land titles available for public inspection. Therefore, potential purchasers of an interest in land can check the public property records to ascertain whether the seller actually owns the land and whether the title is subject to encumbrances. A search of the public records is useful only if all title documents have been recorded or if the searcher is protected from previously executed documents that are unrecorded. Therefore, the recording acts take the common law exception that a prior equity is defeated by a subsequent bona fide purchaser of the legal title and apply it to all conflicts, whether involving legal or equitable claimants or both. To qualify as a bona fide purchaser, most state recording acts require the purchaser to take without notice of a conflicting claim and to pay value.

A. TYPES OF RECORDING ACTS

Each state has enacted one of three types of recording acts—notice, race, or race-notice.

1. Notice Acts

Notice statutes provide that an unrecorded instrument is invalid against a subsequent purchaser without notice of it. These acts protect a purchaser who acquires property or an interest in it, such as an easement or mortgage, without notice of prior unrecorded instruments affecting it. In this way, they protect a subsequent purchaser who is "pure of heart." For example, Arizona's notice statute provides in part: "No instrument affecting real property gives notice of its contents to subsequent purchasers or encumbrance holders for valuable consideration without notice, unless recorded as provided by law in the office of the county recorder of the county in which the property is located." Ariz. Rev. Stat. § 33–411(A).

Illustration: Owen deeded his property to Ann, who did not record. Owen then deeded the same property to Bob, who knew about Ann's deed but recorded his deed anyway. Ann prevails because Bob took his deed with actual notice of her deed.

Illustration: Owen deeded his property to Ann, who immediately recorded the deed. After Ann recorded, Owen deeded the same property to Bob. Ann prevails even if Bob did not have actual notice of her deed, because her deed recording gave Bob constructive notice of it.

Illustration: Owen deeded his property to Ann, who did not record. Owen then deeded the same property to Bob, who did not know about Ann's deed. Ann later recorded her deed before Bob did. Bob prevails because he did not have actual or constructive notice of Ann's deed when he accepted his deed from Owen.

Illustration: Owen deeded his property to Ann, who did not record immediately. Owen then deeded the same property to Bob, who did not know about Ann's deed. Ann then recorded her deed, but Bob never recorded. Bob prevails against Ann even if he never records, because he did not have actual or constructive notice of Ann's deed when he accepted the deed from Owen. However, Bob should record his deed to protect his ownership from a purchaser whose claim is subsequent to his.

2. Race Acts

A few states' statutes base priority on the order in which the documents were recorded. The subsequent grantee can prevail even if she knew about the prior conveyance. The sole question is which instrument was recorded first. These statutes protect subsequent grantees that are "fleet of foot."

Sometimes, these statutes are worded in terms of priority. In other cases, they achieve the same effect by making recordation part of the process of delivery, so that a deed will not pass title until it is recorded. For example, Maryland's race statute provides: "[N]o estate of inheritance or freehold, declaration or limitation of use, estate above seven years, or deed may pass or take effect unless the deed granting it is executed and recorded." Md. Code Ann., Real Prop. § 3–101(a).

Ohio, like some other states, has a special recording statute for mortgages. The Ohio statute is a race statute: "All properly executed mortgages shall be recorded in the office of the county recorder of the county in which the mortgaged premises are situated and shall take effect at the time they are delivered to the recorder for record. If two or more mortgages pertaining to the same premises are presented for record on the same day, they shall take effect in the order of their presentation. The first mortgage presented shall be the first recorded, and the first mortgage recorded shall have preference." Ohio Rev. Code Ann. § 5301.23(A).

Illustration: Owen deeded his property to Ann, who did not record. Owen then deeded the same property to Bob, who knew about Ann's deed. If Bob records first, he will prevail. If Ann records first, she will prevail.

Illustration: Owen borrowed money from Ann and gave her a mortgage, which she did not record. Owen then borrowed money from Bob and gave him a mortgage on the same land. Bob knew about Ann's mortgage when he accepted the mortgage from Owen. If Bob records and then Ann records, Owen's title is encumbered by both mortgages, but Bob's mortgage has priority over Ann's. If Ann records and then Bob records, Owen's title is encumbered by both mortgages, and Ann's mortgage has priority over Bob's.

Illustration: Owen deeded his property to Ann, who did not record. Owen then borrowed money from Bob and gave him a mortgage on the same land. Bob knew about Ann's deed when he accepted the mortgage from Owen. Owen then borrowed money from Cathy and gave her a mortgage on the same land. Cathy knew about Ann's deed and Bob's mortgage when she accepted the mortgage from Owen. If Ann records before Bob and Cathy, Ann's title is not encumbered by either mortgage. If the order of recording is Bob, Ann, Cathy, Ann's title is encumbered by Bob's mortgage but not by Cathy's. If the order of recording is Bob, Cathy, Ann, Ann's title is encumbered by both mortgages, and Bob's mortgage has priority over Cathy's. If the order of recording is Cathy, Bob, Ann, Ann's title is encumbered by both mortgages, and Cathy's mortgage has priority over Bob's.

3. Race-Notice Acts (Notice-Race Acts)

Race-notice statutes provide that an unrecorded conveyance is invalid against a subsequent purchaser who buys without notice of it and records before the prior conveyance is recorded. This type of act protects purchasers who buy without notice of an unrecorded claim, but only if they enhance the reliability of the recording system by recording their conveyance. These statutes protect subsequent purchasers only if they are both "pure of heart" and "fleet of foot." For example, California's statute provides in part: "Every conveyance of real property ... is void as against any subsequent purchaser or mortgagee of the same property ... in good faith and for a valuable consideration, whose conveyance is first duly recorded." Cal. Civ. Code § 1214.

Illustration: Owen deeded his property to Ann, who did not record. Owen then deeded the same property to Bob, who did not know about Ann's deed. Ann recorded, and then Bob recorded. Ann prevails because Bob did not record before her.

Illustration: Owen deeded his property to Ann, who did not record. Owen then deeded the same property to Bob, who knew about Ann's deed. Bob recorded, and then Ann recorded. Ann prevails because Bob knew about her deed when he accepted the deed from Owen.

Illustration: Owen deeded his property to Ann, who did not record. Owen then deeded the same property to Bob, who did not know about Ann. Bob later heard about Ann's deed, so he recorded his deed. Ann recorded after Bob. Bob prevails because he did not know about her deed when he accepted the deed from Owen and because Bob recorded first.

Illustration: Owen deeded his property to Ann, who did not record. Owen then borrowed money from Bob and gave him a mortgage on the property that he had conveyed to Ann. Bob did not know about Ann's deed and recorded before she did. Ann's title is encumbered by Bob's mortgage. If Ann had recorded before Bob or if he had known about her deed when he accepted Owen's mortgage, Ann's title would not have been encumbered by the mortgage.

4. Grace Period Acts

Grace period statutes operate like notice statutes, except that they give a grantee a certain period of time to record before any sanction is imposed for nonrecordation.   These acts were popular when travel to the recorder's office was difficult and time consuming,   but   modern   communication   and transportation methods generally have rendered them   obsolete.   Therefore,   they   will   not   be considered further.

III. MECHANICS OF RECORDING AND SEARCHING TITLE

A. RECORDING A DOCUMENT

To "record" a document, it is filed, recorded, and indexed. The recording acts differ as to which steps must be completed before a conveyance is protected from conflicting conveyances.

1. Filing

Recording begins when a duly executed, acknowledged, and delivered document is filed at the recorder's office or other county or state designated depository where the land is located. To be accepted for recording, the document must affect title to land, such as a deed, lease, or mortgage. Depending on whether the jurisdiction follows the doctrine of equitable conversion, a contract for the sale of land may be recordable. An option to purchase land is generally not recordable, because it does not convey a property interest. The document usually must be notarized to be accepted by the recorder. Official documents resulting from legal proceedings affecting land, such as probate or quiet title decrees, judgment or tax liens, and lis pendens notices, are recordable.

The recorder's office examines only the type of document to determine whether to accept it for recording. No government official determines its validity or effectiveness to pass title or even whether the grantor owns the property. All such conflicts are resolved between the claimants. The recorder's office merely serves as a repository for documents. Its gatekeeping function is limited to determining the types of documents that can be recorded there.

2. Recording

The recorder's office makes a copy of the entire document. This copy is then inserted into the current book of official records. These record books, consisting solely of copies of documents, are kept and labeled in chronological order. When one book is filled, a new book is started and is given the next number. For example, a one-page document might appear in volume 387, page 453 of the Official Records; the next document will appear in volume 387, page 454.

3. Indexing

If the recorder's office merely maintained chronological books of copied documents, searching title to a particular parcel of land would be extremely difficult, particularly in large cities. Therefore, the recorder's office also maintains a set of indexes (or indices), where information concerning each document is entered. Rather than leafing through each record book to find documents, a title searcher can use the indexes to obtain the volume and page numbers where relevant documents are recorded. Most states have name indexes that include a grantor-grantee index and a grantee-grantor index (name indexes). The grantor-grantee index alphabetically lists all recorded documents by the grantor's name. The index shows the grantor's name, then the grantee's name, possibly a description of the document and of the property, and the volume and page numbers in the official record where the copy of the document is recorded. A grantee-grantor index contains the same information but is organized alphabetically by the grantee's name. In contrast, a tract index (parcel index) organizes the entries by property description, rather than by the parties' names. Indexes often are limited as to time. Thus, one set of indexes may include documents recorded from 1950 to 1969, another for 1970 to 1989, another for 1990 to 2009, and finally a monthly, weekly, or daily index for the current year.

Illustration: In 2005, Ann recorded a deed by which Owen conveyed Blackacre to her. The deed will be indexed in the grantor-grantee index under Owen's name and in the grantee-grantor index under Ann's name. If the jurisdiction has a tract index, the deed also will be indexed under Blackacre's property description.

If the recorder's office improperly records or indexes a document, it may not give constructive notice of its contents.

4. Returning Document

After the document has been filed, recorded, and indexed, it is returned to the depositor. The recorder's office keeps only the copy.

B. SEARCHING TITLE IN NAME INDEXES

1. Locating Present Owner in Grantee Index

A person searching a title starts with the current seller of the property. If that person truly owns the property, he probably will have taken title by a deed, which would be indexed under his name in the grantee index. Thus, a search for Owen would start in the "O" volume of grantees in the year that Owen claims to have purchased the property. If the year is not known, the title searcher must begin in this year's grantee volume and go back year by year until an entry is found.

2. Locating Prior Owners in Grantee Index

From the entry in the grantee index for Owen's name, the name of the previous owner can be ascertained, because it will appear in the related grantor column. That name then will be searched in the grantee index, usually starting with the date that she conveyed to the current owner and going back in time until her name appears as grantee from the owner before her. That owner's name is then searched in the grantee index, and the process continues with each owner until the searcher arrives at an indisputable source of title, generally the government.   At this point, the searcher may conclude that she has a complete chain of ownership for the property.

a. *Stopping Short of Original Source*

Many states have marketable title statutes or title standards that require searchers to go back only a set number of years, such as sixty years. Any title existing at that time is presumed to be valid and need not be further examined, although this can create problems when rival "roots of title" exist.

b. *Dealing with Gaps*

Supplementary indexes may be necessary to fill in missing links. For instance, if a search shows that Norma received a deed from Michael, but no deed to Michael can be found, the next link may be found in the probate records if they are kept separately. These records might show that Michael inherited the property from Lana by will. A return to the grantee index would then show Lana as a grantee twenty years earlier from Kurt, thereby permitting resumption of the search. A comprehensive recording system should include all records affecting titles in one place, but that is not always the case. Bankruptcy, tax liens, condemnation records, and a variety of other records often are stored separately.

3. Searching for Encumbrances and Other Interests in Grantor Index

Once the searcher knows the names of all the owners in the chain of title, she then must determine whether any owners encumbered or otherwise affected the title during their period of ownership. This is accomplished by searching each owner's name in the grantor index, usually during that person's years of ownership, because any such conveyance would appear in the grantor index under that owner's name. Thus, a mortgage or easement given by the owner or a judgment lien or lis pendens notice filed against the owner would be entered in the grantor index showing the owner as grantor and the other party (mortgagee, dominant tenant, judgment creditor, or plaintiff, for example) as grantee.

4. Following Subsequent History of Encumbrances

To determine whether those property interests still exist, the searcher then must go through either the grantor or grantee indexes for the years after their creation. If they were canceled, a release document should be indexed under the owner's name as grantee and the interest holder's name as grantor. If no such document exists, the interest still survives of record, and the searcher then must use the grantor index to determine whether it has been assigned.

For example, mortgages frequently are assigned to a new mortgage holder.

C. SEARCHING TITLE IN TRACT INDEX

Searching a title in a tract index is substantially easier than searching in the name indexes. The tract index also prevents many of the problems associated with the name indexes, which are described in the next section.

In a tract index, each parcel of land is assigned its own index page. Every document affecting title to that parcel is listed on its index page. If the lot was created by subdividing a larger parcel, the index page for the larger parcel must be checked for documents that were recorded before the land was subdivided. Like the name indexes, each document listed in the tract index will include the necessary information to locate the copy of the document in the recorder's office. Also like the name indexes, the searcher must check for documents affecting the land that are recorded in other government offices, such as tax liens that are recorded in the tax assessor's office.

IV. RECORD NOTICE—CONSTRUCTIVE NOTICE

The recording acts penalize only "unrecorded" documents. If an instrument is properly recorded, it provides notice to subsequent claimants, whether those claimants actually see it. When an instrument is properly recorded, it gives "constructive" notice, so that subsequent claimants are charged with notice of its existence regardless of whether they have searched the records. The doctrine of constructive notice means that a subsequent claimant cannot benefit from failing to search the records, because he will be charged with notice of all prior recorded instruments even if he does not have actual knowledge of them. A document affecting a land title provides constructive notice if it is recorded in any publicly-available government office, such as the dockets in the clerk of court's office and tax liens recorded in the tax assessor's office.

Not every document that has been filed in the recorder's office and copied into the official records is held to be recorded and to give notice within the meaning of the recording acts. The remainder of this section covers cases in which documents have been copied into the records but are held to be unrecorded or to provide no notice. These situations generally are more readily understood by beginning with Illustrations and then by following each Illustration with an analysis.

A. DOCUMENTS THAT CANNOT BE LOCATED

1. Misindexed Documents

Illustration: Owen conveyed his property to Ann. Ann recorded the deed, but the recorder erroneously indexed it under the name of "Cowen," rather than "Owen." Owen then conveyed the property to Bob.

Because of the misindexing, Bob will not find the deed to Ann; he will search for the name "Owen" in the grantor-grantee index. Because the index would not alert a person subsequently checking Owen's title, many courts hold that the deed to Ann is unrecorded. However, in some states, the recording statute provides that an instrument is deemed recorded when it is "filed" in the recorder's office. In that type of jurisdiction, Ann will prevail because her deed is technically recorded even though it cannot reasonably be found. In jurisdictions in which a court would hold for Bob, Ann should return to the recorder's office at a later date to check that her document has been indexed properly. In jurisdictions in which a court would hold for Ann, however, subsequent purchasers do not have a practical method to avoid this hazard.

2. Wild Documents (Missing Links)

Illustration: Owen conveyed his property to Ann, who did not record. Ann then conveyed the property to Bob, who did record. Owen then deeded the property to Carol, who did record. Carol should prevail over Bob.

Even though Bob's deed was recorded, the nonrecordation of the deed from Owen to Ann means that Bob's deed is not connected in the indexes to Owen's name or to any other name in the chain of title. It will be indexed with Ann as grantor and Bob as grantee, but the index will not alert Carol to look up their names. When Carol checks Owen's name in the grantor-grantee index, she will find nothing. A wild deed (the deed from Ann to Bob) does not give notice within the meaning of a notice or race-notice act and is not recorded first within the meaning of a race or race-notice act.

B. DOCUMENTS THAT ARE DIFFICULT TO LOCATE

1. Late Recorded Document

Illustration: Owen purchased the property in 1975. In 1985, he conveyed it to Ann, who did not record. In 1995, Owen conveyed the property to Bob, who immediately recorded even though he knew about the conveyance to Ann. In 1996, Ann recorded. In 2005, Bob deeded the property to Carol. The jurisdictions are divided as to whether Ann or Carol will prevail, but a majority of courts hold for Ann.

Argument for Ann: Although Ann's deed is not in the direct chain of title, it can be found by an extensive search of the records. A searcher might believe that she must investigate Owen's title only for the years when he was the owner of record (1975-95). But if the search under Owen's name was extended from 1995 to the present, the deed to Ann would be found. In jurisdictions that would hold for Ann, a title searcher must check each owner from the date he acquired title to the present, rather than only to the date when he appears to have transferred title.

Argument for Carol: The rule followed in a minority of jurisdictions is that a purchaser should not bear the burden of checking each owner beyond his time of record ownership. Because the deed to Ann would not be found by such a search, Carol would not be charged with notice of Ann's claim. Ann's deed would be treated as unrecorded within the meaning of the recording act. She should have checked to ensure that her deed from Owen was properly indexed.

2. Early Recorded Document—Estoppel by Deed

Illustration: In 2004, Ann gave Bob a general warranty deed to Blackacre, though she did not own it. Bob recorded. In 2005, Owen, who owned Blackacre, conveyed it to Ann. Ann recorded. In 2007, Ann conveyed Blackacre to Carol. Carol recorded. In most states, the legal effect of the conveyance from Owen to Ann in 2005 was to transfer title to Ann and then from her to Bob under the doctrine of estoppel by deed. By virtue of her deed to Bob, Ann is estopped to assert that she had no title to convey to him. Thus, Bob has title unless Carol prevails under the recording acts. The courts are divided.

Argument for Carol: Although Bob's deed was recorded, it is not in the chain of title. For Carol to discover it, she would have to check each owner in the index for the period before the owner acquired title. In this example, Carol would have to check the index under Ann's name for the years before 2005, which is when the records indicate Ann acquired title. Courts in some jurisdictions hold that Carol should not have this burden, especially because Bob should not have accepted a deed from someone who did not have record title. Bob's deed is out of the chain of title.

Argument for Bob: Other courts hold for Bob because Carol could have discovered his deed by a more diligent search. Therefore, Carol is charged with notice of it. In this type of jurisdiction, a purchaser must check each owner's name in the index back to the commencement of the records, rather than merely back to the date the owner acquired title.

3. Deed Affecting More Than One Lot

Illustration: Owen conveyed Lot 1 to Ann and, in the same deed, gave her an easement over his retained Lot 2. Ann recorded the deed. The recorder listed only Lot 1 as the property description in the name indexes. Owen then conveyed Lot 2 to Bob without specifying in the deed that the title was subject to Ann's easement. Bob recorded. Bob's property is subject to Ann's easement if he is charged with notice of the contents of Owen's deed to Ann. The courts are divided on this issue.

Argument for Ann: The deed from Owen to Ann was recorded and could have been discovered by a diligent search of the index. Bob should examine every deed executed by his grantor to see whether it conveys the fee title or any other interest in the property that Bob intends to acquire. Therefore, Bob has notice of the deed from Owen to Ann and of the easement it conveyed. In this type of jurisdiction, a purchaser must check all deeds executed by her grantor, even though the property description in the name indexes is for a different parcel.

Argument for Bob: Courts in other jurisdictions hold that Bob has notice only of deeds in his own chain of title and that a deed to other property is not in that chain. If the index indicates that a deed concerns other property, the searcher is not required to examine the deed to see if it also affects his property. Under this rule, Ann must ensure that her deed is indexed to refer to both Lots 1 and 2.

C. DOCUMENTS THAT CAN BE LOCATED BUT DO NOT GIVE NOTICE

Through inadvertence, the recorder may record a document that should not have been recorded, either because it was defectively executed or because it is an unrecordable document, such as an option agreement. Courts do not agree whether such a document gives notice under the recording act. Some courts hold that it does not give notice, even to a searcher who actually sees it. Other courts hold that a searcher who actually sees it has a duty to investigate its validity.

1. Defective Documents

Illustration: Owen conveyed his property to Ann, but his signature on the deed was not acknowledged (notarized). Nevertheless, the recorder records the deed. The recorded document clearly shows that the acknowledgment is missing. Owen then conveyed the same property to Bob.

In some jurisdictions, Bob will prevail over Ann though he actually saw Ann's deed when searching the title. The defect defeats the contention that the deed was recorded or gives notice. But in other jurisdictions, if Bob saw the deed, he has a duty to investigate the circumstances to ascertain the nature of Ann's interest. If a reasonable inquiry would disclose her interest, Bob is charged with notice, and Ann will prevail.

2. Unrecordable Documents

Illustration: Owen contracted to sell his property to Ann.   Although the local recording act does not authorize recording executory contracts for the sale of land, Ann delivered the contract to the recorder who recorded and indexed it. Owen then conveyed the same property to Bob.

The result here is the same as in the previous Illustration. In both cases, the recording of an improper document does not give constructive notice, although persons who actually see it may be charged with notice or with a duty to investigate further.

V. INQUIRY NOTICE

Because recording acts charge subsequent claimants with notice of all documents recorded in the chain of title, every person intending to acquire an interest in property first must search the records to determine its validity and priority. The notice doctrine also imposes on subsequent claimants the obligation to make a reasonable investigation outside the records. The claimant is charged with notice of anything a reasonable inquiry would disclose. Thus, a person may have "inquiry" notice of prior claims. The duty to investigate the validity of recorded but defective documents is an example of the application of the doctrine of inquiry notice.

Inquiry notice is not applied in the same absolute fashion as constructive notice from the property records. First, some suspicious fact must trigger the initial obligation to make an inquiry. Second, it must be shown that a reasonable inquiry would have revealed the suspicious fact. If either component is missing, notice is not imputed. However, if an inquiry was made and did not lead to discovery of the relevant facts, the inquirer is not necessarily protected, because the trier of fact can conclude that the inquiry should have been more diligent.

A. NOTICE BASED ON INFORMATION IN RECORDS

1. References in Recorded Documents to Unrecorded Documents

Some courts require a purchaser to investigate references to other documents that appear in recorded instruments even though the documents to which they refer are unrecorded. If a reasonable search would locate the unrecorded document, the purchaser is charged with notice of it and cannot be a bona fide purchaser.

Illustration: Owen mortgaged his property to Mel, but Mel did not record. Owen then conveyed his property to Ann. His deed stated that title was being conveyed "subject to the mortgage given to Mel." Ann later conveyed the property to Bob by a deed that also said it was "subject to the mortgage given to Mel." The reference to Mel's mortgage obligates Bob to inquire as to Mel's interest. If a reasonable inquiry would reveal Mel's interest, Bob will be charged with notice of it and will take title subject to it.

2. References in Recorded but Unread Documents to Other Unrecorded Documents

The subsequent claimant need not actually know about the suspicious fact. A properly recorded document that refers to it provides constructive notice. The suspicious fact generates a duty to inquire whether it is actually known or merely constructively known.

Illustration: Owen mortgaged his property to Mel, but Mel did not record. Owen then conveyed the same property to Ann by a deed that stated that title was being conveyed "subject to the mortgage given to Mel." Ann recorded her deed. Ann then conveyed the property to Bob by a deed that did *not* refer to Mel's mortgage. Bob did not search the records. Bob's title may be subject to the mortgage. Owen's deed to Ann was properly recorded and, therefore, gave notice of its contents. Bob thus had constructive notice of the reference to Mel. This suspicious fact imposed a duty on Bob to investigate. Otherwise, Bob would have a disincentive for searching the records, which result is not to be encouraged.

3. Indefinite References to Other Documents

In some states, a reference in a document to another document does not create a duty to investigate if the reference is too indefinite as to the parties, date, type of interest, or property description. In that case, the purchaser who sees such a reference has no duty to investigate.

Illustration: Owen mortgaged his property to Mel, but Mel did not record. Owen then conveyed the property to Ann, who knew about the mortgage. The deed stated that title was being conveyed "subject to all mortgages, easements, and other interests outstanding against the property." Ann recorded and later conveyed the property to Bob without mentioning the mortgage. The indefinite reference in Owen's deed to Ann (sometimes called a "Mother Hubbard clause") creates no duty to investigate. Therefore, Bob is not charged with notice of Mel's mortgage and takes title free of it.

B. NOTICE BASED ON POSSESSION OF PROPERTY

In most states, a property purchaser is charged with notice of any possessor's rights to the property. Thus, a prior grantee that possesses property based on an unrecorded document will prevail over subsequent purchasers even though nothing appears in the records. The effect of this doctrine is to compel a purchaser to inspect the land, as well as to search the records.

Illustration: Owen conveyed his property to Ann, who did not record. Ann took actual possession of the property. Owen then conveyed the same property to Bob. Bob did not know about Ann and saw no mention of her when he searched the property records. In most states, Ann's possession provides notice of her title to Bob. He should have inspected the property and asked Ann about her rights in the property.

1. Information Charged to Purchaser— Constructive Notice v. Inquiry Notice

If someone is in possession of the property, a purchaser usually is charged with notice (constructive notice) of that person's interest even if the purchaser did not inspect the property. When someone other than the owner is in possession, courts usually hold that this suspicious fact creates a duty of inquiry concerning the possessor's rights (inquiry notice). Inquiry notice is one form of constructive notice.

Illustration: Owen conveyed his property to Ann. She did not record or take possession. Owen then conveyed the property to Bob, who inspected the property. Because Ann did not record, Bob did not have constructive notice. Because Bob's inspection did not reveal any suspicious fact, he had no duty to inquire. Thus, Bob prevails over Ann.

Illustration: Owen conveyed his property to Ann. She did not record but did take possession. Owen then conveyed the property to Bob. Bob inspected the land and saw Ann. Because Bob knew that someone other than Owen possessed the property, Bob had a duty to inquire as to Ann's rights. If a reasonable inquiry would have revealed her unrecorded deed, Bob will be charged with inquiry notice of that fact, and Ann will prevail.

Illustration: Owen conveyed his property to Ann. She did not record but did take possession. Owen then conveyed the property to Bob, who did not inspect the property. Because Ann is in possession, Bob is charged with constructive notice of that fact. Bob's constructive notice generates the same duty to inquire as did his actual notice in the previous Illustration. If a reasonable inquiry would disclose her claim, she will prevail.

Illustration: Owen conveyed his property to Ann, who did not record. Ann then leased the property to Tom but told him that she was acting as Owen's rental agent. Tom took possession of the property. Owen then conveyed the same property to Bob. In this case, Bob may not be charged with notice of Ann's interest. He is charged with notice of Tom's possession and has a duty to inquire of Tom as to his rights.   However, a reasonable inquiry might not disclose Ann's interest. Therefore, Bob might not be charged with notice of it. Whether Bob must ask Ann about any interest she may have in the property after Tom informs him that she said she was Owen's agent is a question of fact. If the finder of fact concludes that Bob should have inquired of Ann and that Ann would have responded honestly, Bob will be charged with notice of Ann's interest.   But if the finder of fact concludes otherwise, no notice of Ann's interest will be imputed to Bob.

2. Inquiry Notice When Statute Requires Actual Notice

When the recording act provides that unrecorded documents are void only as to persons without "actual" notice of them, strict statutory construction may eliminate constructive notice, including inquiry notice. Courts in some states hold that a statutory requirement for actual notice means that a purchaser is not charged with notice of a possessor's rights unless the purchaser actually knows about them. Therefore, the purchaser has no duty to inquire of the possessor even if the purchaser has actual notice of the possession. In other states with similar statutes, courts hold that a purchaser has a duty to inquire of a possessor, but only if the purchaser actually knows about the possession. The purchaser has no initial duty to look for a possessor.

Illustration: Owen conveyed his property to Ann. She did not record but did take possession. Owen then conveyed the same property to Bob. He inspected the land and saw Ann but made no inquiry of her. The recording act provides that an unrecorded deed is void against purchasers without actual notice. Under a restrictive view of actual notice, Bob prevails because he had no obligation to ask Ann about her rights. Under a less restrictive view, Bob is charged with notice of her rights if a reasonable inquiry would have revealed them. But even under this second view, Bob would prevail if he had not visited the property and thereby avoided acquiring actual knowledge of Ann's possession. For Bob to be charged with notice of Ann's rights when he never looked at the land, the statutory notice standard must be deemed to include constructive notice, including inquiry notice.

Illustration: Owen conveyed his property to Ann, who did not record. Ann then rented the property to Tom. Tom did not record his lease but did take possession. Owen then conveyed the same property to Bob. Bob searched the records but did not view the land. If the local recording act provides that an unrecorded instrument is void against a purchaser without notice, Ann and Tom should prevail over Bob.

Bob is charged with notice of the rights of a person in possession when that possession is inconsistent with the record title. Tom's possession based on a lease from someone other than Owen creates an obligation to investigate and probably would cause Bob to discover Ann's interest in the property. If the recording act referred only to actual notice, Bob might prevail because he did not have actual notice, and the statute created no duty to look.

3. When Possession is Unsuspicious

Possession creates a duty to inquire only when it is suspicious. If the possession is consistent with the record title, no duty to inquire exists.

Illustration: Owen conveyed a life estate to Ann and the remainder to Bob. Ann took possession and recorded her deed. Bob conveyed his remainder interest to Ann, but this deed was not recorded. Later Bob conveyed his interest to Carol. Carol should prevail over Ann as to Bob's remainder. Although Ann was in possession, the records indicated that she held a life estate. Therefore, her possession was consistent with the records and created no duty for Carol to ask Ann about her rights. Carol has a remainder after Ann's life estate.

a. Landlord-Tenant Exception

Because tenants commonly have rights beyond those mentioned in their original leases, many courts require purchasers to inquire of the tenants even though their possession is consistent with the record title.

Illustration: Owen leased property to Tom for five years. The lease was recorded. Owen later gave Tom an option to purchase the property. The option agreement was not recorded. Owen then conveyed the property to Bob. Bob searched the records and saw Tom's lease but did not talk to him. Bob may be charged with notice of Tom's option and would be required to sell to Tom if he exercises the option to purchase.

C. NOTICE BASED ON NEIGHBORHOOD CONDITIONS

The section on constructive notice stated that a purchaser may be subject to an interest created in a deed to other property owned by the same grantor even though that interest does not appear in the purchaser's direct chain of title. Similarly, the chapter on covenants running with the land stated that a court may imply a restriction against the grantor's retained land if he restricted other lots in the development. A court may hold that a purchaser has constructive notice or inquiry notice of the restrictions. The court could find constructive notice based on the purchaser's duty to read all deeds given by the grantor. Alternatively, the court could find inquiry notice based on the uniform development of the neighborhood.

D. HARMLESS NOTICE

In some cases, a nonrecording interest holder will lose her interest even if a subsequent purchaser knew about it before acquiring the land.

Illustration: Owen conveyed his property to Ann, who did not record or take possession. Owen conveyed the same property to Bob. Bob recorded, but he knew about the conveyance to Ann. Bob then conveyed to Carol, who did not have notice and recorded. Though Bob could not prevail against Ann, he acquired an apparent title from Owen. Because Carol did not know about Ann's claim, she prevails against Ann, though Bob could not.

Illustration: Owen conveyed his property to Ann, who did not record or take possession. Owen conveyed the same property to Bob. Bob did not have notice of the conveyance to Ann and recorded his deed. Bob then conveyed the property to Carol. Carol knew of Ann's claim and did not record. Nevertheless, Carol prevails over Ann.   Because Bob took without notice and recorded first, he divested Ann of her title under any recording act. He had legal title, which he transferred to Carol. Carol need not qualify for protection under any recording act because she took from a real, not an apparent, owner. This is called the bona fide purchaser filter or the bona fide purchaser shelter.

VI. PERSONS PROTECTED AGAINST PREVIOUS FAILURES TO RECORD

The recording acts rarely make unrecorded instruments absolutely void. Instead, the statutes normally provide that unrecorded instruments are void as against certain classes of people. Unless a subsequent taker is in the category of protected persons, failure to record the prior instrument is harmless. To prevail under a recording act, the subsequent purchaser has to satisfy one or more of the following requirements, depending on the state recording act: (1) take his interest without notice of the conflicting claim, (2) record before the conflicting claimant records, and (3) pay value.

A. PERSONS PROTECTED UNDER RECORDING STATUTES

1. Persons Protected in Race State

In a race state, the only persons protected from prior unrecorded instruments are those who record first. If a subsequent grantee buys without notice but does not record, the statute gives no protection against an unrecorded prior grant.

2. Persons Protected in Notice State

In a notice state, the only persons protected from prior unrecorded instruments are those who purchased without notice of them.

3. Persons Protected in Race-Notice State

In a race-notice state, the only persons protected from prior unrecorded instruments are those who purchase without notice and who record before the prior instruments are recorded.

B. PURCHASERS WITHOUT NOTICE

Except for race states, the only persons protected from prior unrecorded instruments are those who take without notice of them. The question of notice was covered in the previous two sections.

C. PURCHASERS FOR VALUE

Most states, either by statute or by judicial decision, protect subsequent takers only if they paid value for their interest. If a person did not pay for a property interest, she will not be injured if she does not acquire it.

Illustration: Owen conveyed his property to Ann, who did not record. Owen then conveyed the same property to Bob, who searched the records and found no reference to Ann. Bob paid Owen $10,000 for the property. Bob prevails over Ann because he is a bona fide purchaser. Bob paid Owen only because the records did not show Ann's claim. If Ann prevailed over Bob, he would suffer a $10,000 loss unless he could recover from Owen. Bob prevails to protect the investment he made in reliance on the records.

1. Donees

Most recording acts do not protect a donee, because she paid no value and, therefore, did not detrimentally rely on the records.

Illustration: Owen conveyed his property to Ann, who did not record. Owen then executed a gift deed of the same property to Bob. Bob did not have notice of the conveyance to Ann and recorded his deed. In most states, Ann prevails over Bob because he is not a purchaser for value. He did not give any value in reliance on the records and, therefore, will not be injured if he does not get the property.

Illustration: Owen executed a gift deed of his property to Ann, who did not record. Owen then executed another gift deed of the same property to Bob. Bob did not have notice of the conveyance to Ann and recorded his deed. Ann still prevails over Bob because he did not pay value. In most states, Ann's unrecorded deed is void only against subsequent takers for value, and Bob does not qualify. Ann need not have paid value, because Owen had title to convey to her. The recording act specifies what a subsequent claimant has to do to defeat the claim of a prior claimant. It specifies that Bob has to pay value to defeat a prior claim; it does not require Ann to pay value to defeat subsequent claims.

Illustration: Owen conveyed his property to Ann, who did not record. Owen died, and Bob was his heir. Bob conveyed the property to Carl, who paid value, did not have notice of the conveyance to Ann, and recorded.

Carl prevails over Ann. Ann's failure to record left Owen as the apparent owner at his death. When Owen died, no title descended to Bob, and Bob did not qualify as a bona fide purchaser because he did not pay value. However, Bob did acquire the power to divest Ann because the records showed him as the apparent owner. Therefore, his conveyance to a bona fide purchaser, Carl, is protected by the recording acts.

2. Cancellation of Prior Debt

Cancellation of a prior debt in return for a conveyance is often regarded as payment of value. A creditor who accepts a deed in satisfaction of an obligation is regarded as a purchaser for value in some jurisdictions but not in others.

3. Payment of Less than Full Consideration

Courts do not require the subsequent purchaser to pay full consideration, so long as more than a nominal consideration is paid.   The necessary amount varies from state to state.

4. Promise to Pay

If the promise to pay can be canceled, courts generally do not treat the promisor as having paid value. But if the promise cannot be canceled, the promisor is treated as having paid the entire amount.

Illustration: Owen conveyed his property to Ann, who did not record. Owen then conveyed the same property to Bob in return for Bob's promissory note for $10,000, which was the full price for the land. Before Bob made any payments on the note, Ann asserted her claim to the property. If the note was made payable to Owen and if Owen still has it, Ann should prevail, because Bob can defend against Owen's enforcement of the note based on failure of consideration, especially if Owen's deed contains covenants of title. However, if Bob had borrowed the money from a bank to buy the land, the note he gave the bank cannot be canceled, and Bob will have to pay it. So he prevails over Ann.

5. Payment of Part of the Price — Alternative Solutions

When the subsequent purchaser has paid part of the price before discovering an unrecorded prior deed, he should be protected according to the amount paid and other circumstances by (a) dividing the land, if possible, (b) giving the subsequent purchaser the entire property with the balance of the price going to the prior unrecorded grantee, or (c) giving the prior grantee the property and giving the subsequent purchaser a lien on it for the amount actually paid. The best result generally depends on the circumstances, as illustrated below.

Illustration — Partition: Owen conveyed two acres of vacant land to Ann, who did not record or take possession. Owen then conveyed the same two acres to

Bob for a price of $10,000. After Bob paid $5,000 of the price, Ann asserted her interest. A possible remedy would be to give Bob one acre and Ann the other acre, if both have the same value. By giving Bob one acre and excusing him from further payment, he receives all the protection he needs.

Illustration — Title to the Subsequent Purchaser: Owen conveyed his one-family house to Ann, who did not record or take possession. Owen then conveyed the house to Bob for a price of $200,000. Bob paid $140,000, took possession, and made improvements before Ann asserted her interest. Under these circumstances, Bob should get title to the entire house but should be required to pay the balance of the price to Ann, rather than to Owen.

Illustration — Title to Prior Purchaser: Owen conveyed his property to Ann, who did not record or take possession. Owen then conveyed the same property to Bob for a price of $10,000. When Ann asserted her interest, Bob had not taken possession or made any improvements and had paid only $1,000 of the price. An appropriate remedy under these circumstances would be to give Ann title to the entire property and to give Bob a lien on the property for $1,000.

The appropriate remedy also may depend on whether a deed had been delivered to the purchaser. In a few jurisdictions, payments made by a purchaser under a contract for the sale of the property are not protected because title has not yet passed. This rule poses serious problems for purchasers under long term installment contracts who are obligated to pay the price over a number of years before receiving a deed.

D. ENCUMBRANCERS

The recording acts generally protect persons who take encumbrances on property for value. For example, a mortgagee who loans money and takes a mortgage to secure the debt in reliance on the property records will have that reliance protected. However, unsecured creditors are not protected against prior unrecorded conveyances, because they did not give value in reliance on the records.

Illustration: Owen conveyed his property to Ann, who did not record or take possession. Owen then borrowed $10,000 from Bob and gave Bob a promissory note and mortgage on the same property to secure the debt. Bob's mortgage should be protected against Ann's unrecorded deed. Ann owns the property subject to Bob's mortgage. Bob's loan was made in reliance on the records, which showed Owen as the owner.

Illustration: Owen conveyed his property to Ann, who did not record or take possession. Owen then borrowed money from Bob and gave him a promissory note but not a mortgage. Bob cannot claim an interest in the property against Ann, because he did not make the loan in reliance on the records. Even without the conveyance to Ann, Bob's unsecured note gives him no interest in the property. That is what is meant by "unsecured."

1. Pre-existing Debt

If a creditor acquires an encumbrance to secure a pre-existing debt, he has not paid value within the meaning of the recording acts.

a. *Originally Unsecured Loan*

A creditor that makes a loan without getting a mortgage to secure it can later request that the borrower give a mortgage for that purpose. However, in that situation, the creditor has not paid value for the mortgage unless she gives some new consideration.   The creditor did not make the original loan in reliance on the property records, and she did not obtain the mortgage in reliance on the records because she already had made the loan. The loan is a pre-existing debt.   Therefore, the subsequently secured creditor is not protected against prior unrecorded instruments.

Illustration: Owen conveyed his property to Ann, who did not record or take possession.   Owen then borrowed $10,000 from Bob and gave him an unsecured promissory note. Later, Bob requested that Owen secure the note with a mortgage on the property, and Owen did so.   Then Ann asserted her rights.   Ann's title is not subject to Bob's mortgage because he did not give value in reliance on the records.   He did not rely on the records when he loaned the money, because he did not take an interest in the land then.   When he did seek the land as security, he did not give any new value, because he already had loaned the money.

Illustration: Owen conveyed his property to Ann, who did not record or take possession. Owen then borrowed $10,000 from Bob and gave him an unsecured promissory note. When the note became due, Bob agreed to extend the due date only if Owen secured the note with a mortgage on the property, which Owen did. Courts in many states will hold that Ann's title is subject to Bob's mortgage, because the extension of time constituted new value for the mortgage. Bob gave up his right to collect immediately.

b. Judgment and Attachment Creditors

Most states authorize a creditor who obtains a judgment to record it, which makes it a lien on all real property owned by the judgment debtor in the county where the judgment is recorded. If the creditor has attached any property before the judgment, the judgment lien relates back to the date of the attachment. Before the judgment, the attachment creates an attachment lien on the property. In most states, such lien creditors are not protected by the recording acts, because they have not obtained their liens in reliance on the records.

Illustration: Owen conveyed his property to Ann, who did not record or take possession. Bob then obtained a judgment against Owen based on nonpayment of an unsecured promissory note. Bob recorded the judgment to make it a lien on Owen's property. Ann's title is not subject to Bob's judgment lien. Bob did not give value in reliance on the property records when he made the loan, because he took an unsecured note. He also did not rely on the records when he sued Owen and obtained a judgment. When Bob recorded the judgment, he gave no new value in reliance on the records. Thus, Bob does not qualify for the recording act's protection.

2. Execution Purchasers

Although most states do not protect judgment creditors, if a creditor executes on the judgment and has the property sold to satisfy it, the purchaser may be a purchaser for value within the meaning of the recording act.

Illustration: Owen conveyed his property to Ann, who did not record or take possession. Bob then obtained a judgment against Owen, levied execution on the property, and conducted an execution sale. Carol purchased at the sale for $10,000. If Carol does not know about Owen's deed to Ann, Carol will prevail over Ann because Carol paid value in reliance on the records. Although Bob obtained no lien on property and should not have been able to execute, he had the apparent right to do so because the property records indicated that Owen was the owner. Therefore, Bob could transfer good title to a bona fide purchaser just as Owen could transfer good title to a bona fide purchaser despite his earlier conveyance to Ann.

Courts are divided whether a judgment creditor can become a bona fide purchaser when he buys at his execution sale for the amount of the judgment. Some courts hold that the creditor has given no new value because the bid amount is offset against the judgment. But other courts hold that the creditor thereby pays value because he gives up the judgment in return for the property. An additional reason for protecting the creditor is that, otherwise, the most likely candidate to bid at the execution sale, the creditor, will be virtually excluded.

VII. RECORDING SYSTEM LIMITATIONS

Not all interests in land derive from written instruments, and not all written instruments affecting interests in land are recordable. The recording acts protect only against interests arising from written instruments and instruments that statutorily are recordable.

A. INTERESTS CREATED WITHOUT A WRITTEN INSTRUMENT

1. Adverse Possession and Prescriptive Easements

Adverse possession and prescriptive easements give an original, rather than a derivative, title and are not created by a writing. Consequently, the holder usually does not have a written document and is not subject to the recording act.

Illustration: Paul possessed Owen's land for twenty-five years and satisfied all the elements of adverse possession. Owen then conveyed the property to Ann, who searched the title and found no record of Paul. She also did not see Paul when she inspected the land. In a contest between Paul and Ann, Paul prevails because he does not claim a derivative title from a previous owner and, therefore, is not penalized for failure to record.

Illustration: Dita walked across Owen's land for twenty-five years and acquired a prescriptive right of way easement. Owen then conveyed the property to Bess, who searched the title and inspected the property but found no evidence of Dita's easement. Bess' title is subject to Dita's easement, because it was not created by a recordable instrument.

2. Easements by Necessity

An easement by necessity is created to prevent land from becoming landlocked. Typically, the easement is created when a parcel is subdivided in a way that portions of it do not have access to a public road. The courts are divided on whether a subsequent purchaser without notice takes title subject to the easement.

Illustration: Dita conveyed all her property to Steve except for one landlocked parcel. Under the circumstances of the conveyance, she acquired an easement of necessity across Steve's land. Steve conveyed his property to Ann. She searched the title and the property and found no evidence of Dita's easement. In some jurisdictions, Dita will be held to have an easement over Ann's property on the ground that her easement was not created by a recordable document. But other courts will rule in Ann's favor to avoid penalizing her for Dita's negligent failure to reserve an express easement across Steve's property.

3. Quasi-easements (Easements Implied by Past Use)

Quasi-easements are created when a parcel of land is subdivided under circumstances that permit a court to infer that one parcel was intended to be burdened for the benefit of the other though an express easement was not created. The courts are divided whether a subsequent bona fide purchaser of the servient estate takes subject to the easement.

Illustration: Dita owned two houses on one parcel of land that shared a common sewer line. The line runs from the house on the rear of the lot across the yard of the house on the front of the lot. She conveyed the front house to Steve under circumstances that would cause a court to reserve a quasi-easement in her favor. Steve later conveyed his house to Ann. She found no evidence of the easement in the records and saw no physical evidence of the pipe on the land. In some jurisdictions, Ann's title is free of the easement because she took without notice of it. But, in other jurisdictions, Dita still has an easement because it was not created by a recordable document.

B. INTERESTS ARISING FROM NONRECORDABLE OR EXCEPTED INSTRUMENTS

Recording statutes often provide that certain documents, such as short-term leases, need not be recorded to be protected.   Additionally, judicial decisions in many states have made certain documents affecting property titles unrecordable, such as executory sales contracts.   The failure to record such a document does not penalize the person who acquired an interest from it.

Illustration: In a state with a notice act that applies to transfers of a fee simple, fee tail, life estate, and tenancy of more than three years, Owen leases his property to Tom for two years.   The lease is written but is not recorded.   Owen then conveyed the property to Ann. Her title search revealed no evidence of Tom's interest, and she did not see Tom in possession of the property. Ann still takes subject to Tom's lease, because it did not have to be recorded.

Illustration: Owen agreed to sell his property to Ann in a written contract of sale. Under the state's laws, the contract is unrecordable. Owen then conveyed the same property to Bob. Though Bob did not know about the contract after searching the title and conducting all other reasonable investigations, he should take subject to Ann's contract, because she should not be penalized for not recording an unrecordable document. However, it can be argued that, because unrecordable documents do not come under the recording acts, they are governed by the common law. In that case, Ann would lose because her prior equity is defeated by a subsequent bona fide purchaser of the legal title.

VIII. TORRENS REGISTRATION

In response to the cumbersome and flawed nature of the recording system, a few states have authorized counties to adopt an alternative method for providing information concerning land titles. Under the Torrens system, the government actually certifies the state of title, rather than simply serving as a repository for documents. When a parcel of land is registered in the Torrens system, the government issues a certificate of title that is similar to an automobile title certificate. The certificate lists all the current interests in the land for which it has been issued. In this way, a complete title search does not have to be performed each time the land or an interest in it is transferred. Because the Torrens system is more expensive for the government to operate than the usual recording system and requires greater expertise by the government staff, it has been implemented in only a small number of jurisdictions.

CHAPTER ELEVEN

TITLE INSURANCE

I. SEARCHING TITLE

Before buying a parcel of land, a prudent buyer will have the seller's title examined to determine whether it is marketable. An attorney or professional abstractor commonly conducts the search and guarantees its accuracy. Thereafter, if a title defect is discovered, the buyer can recover on this guarantee. Based on the examination, she also can purchase title insurance to indemnify her if she suffers a loss as a result of defect that was not disclosed in the policy ("owner's policy"). A lender that takes a mortgage on property also can get a title insurance policy to protect its mortgage interest ("lender's policy"). A lender's policy does not protect the owner.

A title insurance policy cannot eliminate existing title defects. If a title company discovers a defect when it searches the title, the defect will be an exception to the insurance coverage. The title company lists the defect both for its protection and because some courts impose an affirmative duty to disclose defects to the insured. The company insures the accuracy of the search but not that the title is perfect.

Illustration: In searching Sam's property title, the title company discovers that it is subject to a recorded easement. Unless the easement is removed from the title before Barb purchases it, her insurance policy will show that her title is subject to the easement. The company will not have any liability because of the easement. However, if the title also was subject to a previously recorded mortgage that was not shown in the title policy, the title company will be liable for that encumbrance if Barb suffers a loss as a result of it.

Illustration: In searching Sam's title on behalf of the bank that intends to make a purchase money mortgage loan to Barb, the title company discovers an existing recorded mortgage. Thereafter, it can offer to insure the bank's mortgage only as a "second" mortgage, which is inferior to the existing mortgage. But it can insure that the bank's mortgage will not be subject to any other mortgage, if it found no other mortgage of record.

II. PRELIMINARY TITLE REPORTS AND TITLE INSURANCE

Before the closing, a buyer often obtains a preliminary title report ("title binder") from the title company that shows the current condition of the seller's title. If the title is satisfactory, the sale is closed, and the buyer will receive a title insurance policy that guarantees that she acquired the title described in the preliminary report. If the seller's title is defective, the buyer can either take title subject to the defect or require that it be eliminated before closing.   She also may agree to new encumbrances on the title.

Illustration: Barb's preliminary title report shows that Sam has marketable title to his property. Therefore, she will close the sale and will receive a title insurance policy that guarantees her ownership of the same marketable title. The title company will make a last-minute search of the records before issuing the policy to make sure the title has not changed. The same company often closes the sale and issues the title policy.

Illustration: Barb's preliminary title report shows that Sam's title is subject to a recorded height limitation, which applies throughout the neighborhood and is acceptable to Barb. She will instruct the closing agent that she will accept a title policy showing title vested in her subject to that restriction.

Illustration: Barb's preliminary title report shows that Sam's title is subject to a mortgage, which is unacceptable to Barb. She will instruct the closing agent to close the transaction only when a title policy can be issued that does not list the mortgage as an exception. The agent can use part of Barb's purchase price to pay the mortgage if Sam agrees. The mortgage then will be eliminated from the title and from the title policy.

Illustration: Barb's preliminary title report shows that Sam has marketable title to his property. Barb is borrowing part of the purchase price from a bank and has promised to give it a mortgage as security for the loan. Barb will instruct the closing agent to obtain an owner's title insurance policy that shows title vested in her subject to the bank's mortgage. The bank will direct the closing agent to disburse the loan proceeds only if the bank gets a lender's title insurance policy that shows it has a valid mortgage on the property.

III. TITLE RISKS

A. COVERED RISKS

Title insurance policies vary greatly as to the coverage they provide. However, they normally guarantee not only the accuracy of the record search, but also the absence of certain "off record" risks, such as nondelivery, forgery, and incompetence.

Illustration: The chain of title for a parcel of property was the State to Ruth, Ruth to Sam, and then Sam to Barb. All these deeds were recorded. However, Ruth never delivered the deed to Sam (or Ruth's signature was forged or Ruth was incompetent to execute the deed). Therefore, Sam never acquired title to the property, and Barb did not either. If Barb's policy insures that she has title, the title company must indemnify her for any loss, though the records did not reveal this problem. In this case, her title policy performs a true insurance function. However, not all policies provide such broad protection.

B. EXCLUDED RISKS

A title policy may not cover many risks that are inherent in the recording system. These exclusions or exceptions generally track the cases in which the recording system does not protect a buyer despite her diligent search of the records.

1. Buyer's Knowledge of Defects or Failure to Pay Value

Most policies exclude title defects that (1) are unrecorded but are known to the buyer or (2) will succeed against a buyer who has not paid value. Because the recording system generally protects only a purchaser for value and without knowledge of a defect, the purchaser's failure to qualify for such protection will cause the title company to decline to insure against the defect.

Illustration: Before conveying the property to Barb, Sam gave a mortgage to Mort that was unrecorded. Although it is unrecorded, Barb will take subject to it if she either knew about it or did not pay value for the property. Because the title company has no practical method for discovering this mortgage and because Barb has no defense against it, the title company will not insure Barb against the mortgage. It is excluded from coverage.

2. Defects Discoverable by Investigation Outside the Records

Title policies also generally exclude risks that can be discovered only by physically inspecting the premises, such as questions involving boundaries, encroachments, and rights claimed by persons in possession. The title company usually limits its coverage to those risks that can be ascertained from the property records, because its expertise is in conducting title searches. However, these risks are not completely unascertainable. Therefore, the company may be willing to insure against them for a higher premium. In this case, the company will physically inspect the premises and will issue an endorsement to the title policy. Because the purchaser usually has inspected the property personally, the endorsement may be an unnecessary expense.

Title policies also normally exclude governmental restrictions on the property, such as zoning laws, subdivision regulations, environmental laws, and eminent domain. These types of laws are not entered in the land records and, therefore, a conventional record search will not find them. While most of these restrictions do not make the title legally unmarketable, title insurance companies prefer to avoid disputes with their insureds by specifically excluding them. A person interested in such matters usually must check with the relevant agencies, such as the zoning department.

3. Subsequent Defects

A title policy excludes defects that arise after it is issued, because the company cannot know or control what will happen to the title in the future. In that sense, title insurance is quite different from most other forms of insurance. Because of this limited coverage, only a one-time premium is paid when the policy is issued.

IV. RELIEF UNDER THE POLICY

A. TITLE COMPANY'S OPTIONS

A title insurance policy usually gives the title company the option to pay the insured for the loss resulting from the defect (up to the policy limit), to pay off or purchase the adverse claim, or to challenge it. The policy usually also provides that the company will be subrogated to any rights the purchaser has against third persons because of the title defect, including her right to enforce any deed covenants. See Chapter 9 concerning title covenants in deeds.

Illustration: Barb's neighbor, Tom, claims an easement across her property. The easement was not listed as an exception in Barb's title insurance policy. Her title company may (1) compensate her for the loss of property value that the easement causes, (2) purchase the easement from Tom to make Barb's title conform to her insurance policy, or (3) contest the validity of Tom's claim. If Barb has a cause of action against her seller or against any earlier owners based on title covenants in the deeds that they gave, the title company may subrogate to her rights and sue to enforce the title covenants.

B. DURATION OF COVERAGE

A title policy's protection may continue only while the insured purchaser owns the property. Many policies also protect the insured after she sells the property if she gave title covenants in her deed or accepted a purchase money mortgage from the purchaser. But the policy will not insure the next purchaser. That person must purchase his or her own title policy.

Illustration: Barb acquired a parcel of land and purchased a title insurance policy for her fee title. Barb sold the land to Carl and took a mortgage from him on the land to secure part of the purchase price. In fact, Barb never acquired title to the land, because her seller was legally incompetent when he signed the deed. As a result, Carl's mortgage is invalid. Barb may recover from her title company. If Carl sues Barb based on the title covenants in the deed she gave him, her title policy may protect her from liability to him as well. However, Carl cannot recover directly from Barb's title company for the loss he suffers, unless he purchased an owner's title policy from the same company.

CHAPTER TWELVE

MORTGAGES

I. MORTGAGE'S SIGNIFICANCE

A. SECURED AND UNSECURED DEBTS

When a lender loans money, the borrower has a contractual obligation to repay the loan. To create written evidence of that obligation, lenders normally require a borrower to sign a promissory note. However, the note, without more, creates only an unsecured debt. If the borrower breaches the promise to repay, the lender's only recourse is against him. Therefore, lenders often require collateral ("security") for a loan, which the lender can sell to satisfy the debt if the borrower defaults in repaying it. In most states, a mortgage is the document used to create a security interest in land. In a mortgage, the borrower is the mortgagor (Mort in the Illustrations), and the lender is the mortgagee (Marie).

In some jurisdictions, a deed of trust is used instead. Deeds of trust are very similar to mortgages. The main difference is that deeds of trust have three parties to them. The borrower (trustor) conveys the land to a third person (trustee) in trust for the lender (beneficiary). The trustee is instructed to reconvey the property to the borrower

415

when the debt is paid or to sell it if the borrower defaults. Because the laws concerning the mortgage and deed of trust are so similar, this Chapter does not treat the deed of trust separately.

Illustration: Mort borrowed $50,000 from Marie and signed two documents, a note and a mortgage. The note says in essence: "I promise to pay you $50,000 by (specified date)." The mortgage says in essence: "If I do not pay the $50,000, you may sell the property that is the subject of this mortgage and may keep enough of the sale proceeds to satisfy the debt."

B. ADVANTAGE OF HOLDING A MORTGAGE

Unsecured lenders must bring a judicial action to recover the debt when they are not paid. If successful, they obtain a money judgment. The judgment is a judicial declaration that the borrower owes the lender. If the borrower does not pay the judgment, the lender must have the sheriff seize and sell the judgment debtor's property (execution) or any debts owed to the debtor (garnishment) and must use the proceeds to satisfy the judgment. In contrast, a mortgagee avoids the risk that the debtor does not have enough assets to satisfy the judgment. Even if the debtor sells the mortgaged land, it is still subject to the mortgage. And, in over half the states, the mortgagee does not need to bring a judicial action to sell the property.

C. HISTORY OF MORTGAGE LAW

When real property was security for a loan during the early common law, the parties had to comply with the rules of conveyancing and estates in land. Because the law of future interests was more rigid then, extreme care was required. A borrower's promise to convey his property to the lender if he failed to pay the debt probably would be treated as an attempt to create an illegal springing interest and, therefore, would be void.

1. Fee Simple Subject to Condition Subsequent

In response to that problem, lenders began using a recognized property interest, the fee simple subject to condition subsequent. The borrower executed an immediate conveyance of his property to the lender. The conveyance was subject to the condition that, if the borrower repaid the debt by the due date, the lender's estate would terminate. Alternatively, lenders sometimes took a conveyance of the fee simple absolute and gave a covenant to reconvey upon timely payment of the debt. These arrangements gave the lender title to the land for the life of the loan, so that the borrower could not dispose of the land or otherwise impair the lender's security. Furthermore, if the borrower failed to pay, the lender had the fee simple absolute title without the need for any judicial action.

2. Equity of Redemption

The early common law gave the borrower no right to pay late for any reason. Once the due date ("law day") passed, the lender had the fee simple absolute title to the land, and the borrower had no legal remedy to compel the lender to accept a late payment even if the land's value greatly exceeded the unpaid debt amount. To provide relief against this potentially harsh result, the court of equity gave a delinquent borrower the right to obtain a decree that permitted him to pay late and thereby "redeem" himself from his default. Over time, this right was characterized as a property interest called the "equity of redemption." It still exists today in every state. The equity of redemption is fair to the lender, because she receives interest for the period of delay, and the borrower can avoid a forfeiture when the land's value exceeds the debt.

3. Foreclosure

Once lenders knew that borrowers legally could pay their debts late, they needed to know how long that privilege would last. Initially, a lender's only option was to bring a suit in equity to impose a time limit on this right. Upon petition by a lender after the borrower defaulted, the chancellor would issue a decree providing that, if the borrower did not redeem within a certain period of time, he would be "foreclosed" from doing so.

These early foreclosure decrees ("strict foreclosure") made the lender's title to the land absolute if the borrower did not redeem in time. Although the extra time helped borrowers, they still could be penalized if the property's value exceeded the unpaid debt amount. To avoid unjust enrichment of the lender, the court of equity began to permit redemption by the borrower even after strict foreclosure, sometimes years after it occurred. Therefore, lenders began including a clause in the mortgage that authorized them to sell the land and to keep sufficient proceeds to repay the debt (foreclose), rather than rely on strict foreclosure.

Today, many states permit mortgagees to conduct foreclosure sales without first filing a judicial foreclosure action. These sales, known as nonjudicial foreclosures (power of sale foreclosures, private sales, or foreclosures by advertisement), generally require language in the mortgage permitting use of this remedy (a "power of sale" clause). The sales usually are subject to significant state regulation, such as required notices to the borrower and to others who will lose their interest in the land and required publication of information concerning the sale.

D. MORTGAGOR PROTECTION RULES

1. Anti-deficiency Laws

If a foreclosure sale fails to produce sufficient funds to satisfy the debt, the mortgagee may seek a judgment for the balance (the "deficiency"). However, because the mortgagee usually is the only bidder at its foreclosure sale, the availability of a deficiency action may induce the mortgagee to bid less than the debt amount and less than the land's value and then get a judgment against the mortgagor for a large deficiency. To avoid this result, some jurisdictions require a hearing on the value of the mortgaged land and may limit any deficiency judgment to the difference between the debt and this value, regardless of the price paid at the foreclosure sale. Other states entirely prohibit deficiency judgments in certain circumstances, such as when the foreclosure was against a single-family residence, farm, or property acquired with the loan proceeds (a "purchase money mortgage").

2. One-Action Rules

Other jurisdictions require the mortgagee to make an election of remedies. These so-called one-action rules differ from state to state. In some states, the one-action rule allows the mortgagee to foreclose on the property or to obtain a judgment for the debt but not both. In other states, the one-action rule merely prohibits the mortgagee from foreclosing and suing on the debt at the same time. Finally, some states' one-action rule requires the mortgagee to foreclose the mortgage before it sues the mortgagor on the debt.

3. Statutory Right of Redemption

Some states give the mortgagor and possibly junior lienors the right to redeem the property even after the foreclosure sale. Because the right was created by statute and was not recognized at common law, it is called the statutory right of redemption. This right usually is exercised by paying the amount bid at the sale, rather than the debt amount. It is designed to deter underbidding. Whereas statutory redemption gives the mortgagor or junior lienors the right to keep the mortgaged land by paying the foreclosure sale purchaser the amount paid at the sale, the equity of redemption gives the right to pay the creditor the unpaid debt amount to stop the sale from occurring. Thus, the equity of redemption ends when the foreclosure sale occurs. At that point, the statutory right of redemption begins in those states that have it.

4. Waiver Prohibitions

Courts prohibit mortgagees from compelling mortgagors to waive the protections that courts and legislatures have created for them. Otherwise, many mortgagees routinely would require mortgagors to waive every form of protection.

5. Nondiscrimination in Lending

Federal, state, and local laws prohibit lenders from discriminating against borrowers based on specified class characteristics, such as race, color, national origin, religion, sex, age, handicap, or marital status. Lenders also are prohibited from "redlining," which is refusing to make loans secured by property in certain neighborhoods. Lenders also may be required to make loans in poorer neighborhoods if they receive deposits from residents of those neighborhoods.

E. TITLE OR LIEN

The common law mortgage gave the mortgagee title to the mortgaged land even before default (title theory of mortgages). Although some states still treat mortgages as having this effect, most characterize a mortgage as giving only a lien on the mortgaged property (lien theory of mortgages). A lien gives a lender the right to sell the property after default, but the mortgagor retains the title until it is divested by the foreclosure sale. A third group of states treats the mortgage as transferring title to the mortgagee when the mortgagor defaults on the loan (intermediate theory of mortgages).

II. MORTGAGE INSTRUMENTS

Mortgages today rarely state that they are conveying to the mortgagee a fee simple subject to condition subsequent in the mortgaged land. Generally, the instrument states that the mortgagor "mortgages" the property to the mortgagee. In some cases, it may be unclear whether a document is a mortgage. For example, the mortgagee may attempt to disguise the true nature of the document to avoid the mortgagor's legal protections, such as the statutory right of redemption. Regardless of how the document is drafted, courts hold that it is a mortgage if it serves the mortgage function of securing a debt. The document is called an "equitable mortgage."

Illustration—Absolute Deed: In exchange for $50,000, Mort gave Marie a deed to his property, and she gave him an option to repurchase the property one year later for $55,000. A court could hold that this transaction was a $50,000 loan at 10% interest, though Mort did not execute a promissory note. If the property was worth $100,000, this result is especially likely. If a court determines that the "option" was really a mortgage, Mort may exercise the equity of redemption and recover the property even after the option expired according to its terms.

Illustration—Sale and Leaseback: In exchange for $50,000, Mort gave Marie a deed to his property, and she gave him a twenty-year lease to the property at a rent of $5,000 per year. A court could characterize this transaction as a mortgage with rent substituting for interest. If the arrangement included an option to repurchase twenty years later at an unrealistically low price, this result is likely. If a court holds that the transaction is a mortgage transaction, Marie cannot evict Mort by the summary dispossession action available to a landlord. Instead, she must foreclose if he defaults.

III. POSSESSION AND RENTS

The early common law mortgage gave the mortgagee the right to possess the mortgaged land. Today, most mortgages permit the mortgagor to retain possession. The mortgagor's right to possess normally continues until a foreclosure sale, which transfers possession to the foreclosure purchaser, unless the mortgagor has the right to possess during a statutory redemption period. The mortgagor can give the mortgagee possession immediately, in which case the mortgagee must use any rents or profits from the land to maintain it and to reduce the mortgage debt. Alternatively, the mortgage may permit the mortgagee to take possession upon default, or a court can appoint a receiver (a third party who manages the property).

Mortgages often provide that the rents and profits from the mortgaged property are assigned to the mortgagee but that the mortgagor can collect them for his own account for as long as he remains current on his debt ("assignment of rents clause").

Once a default occurs, the mortgagee can have a receiver appointed to collect the rents and to use them to pay senior liens, property expenses, and any deficiency judgment following the foreclosure.

IV. PRIORITIES

Mortgages are recordable and are subject to the same priority principles that apply to other real property interests. A mortgage that qualifies for protection under the recording act from any other mortgage is referred to as a senior or first mortgage. Subsequent mortgages are called junior mortgages and are numbered according to their priority, such as second and third mortgages. In many states, a purchase money mortgage has special priority status.

Priority determines the title acquired by the foreclosure purchaser and the distribution of the foreclosure sale proceeds. When a senior mortgage is foreclosed, the property is sold free and clear of the senior mortgage and of any interest that is junior to it. The sale proceeds first are paid to the foreclosing mortgagee. If any surplus remains, it is paid to the junior interest holders in the order of their title priority. Any remaining funds go to the owner for her lost equity in the property. When a junior mortgage is foreclosed, the property is sold subject to the senior mortgage, and the senior mortgagee does not get any of the foreclosure sale proceeds.

Illustration—Senior Foreclosure: Mort's property is subject to a first mortgage of $50,000 and a second mortgage of $10,000. The property has a fair market value of $55,000. If the first mortgagee forecloses, the title will be sold free of both mortgages, and a bid of up to $55,000 may be made. If $55,000 is paid, $50,000 goes to the first mortgagee, and the remaining $5,000 goes to the second mortgagee. The second mortgagee may have a right to collect the deficiency of $5,000 from Mort, depending on whether the state has an anti-deficiency law. If the land's value was greater and the bid was $65,000, the first mortgagee would receive $50,000, the second mortgagee would receive $10,000, and Mort would receive $5,000.

Illustration—Junior Foreclosure: Assume the same facts as above but that the second mortgagee, rather than the first mortgagee, forecloses. Because the foreclosure purchaser will acquire title subject to the first mortgage, the bid may be only $5,000 if the property has a market value of $55,000. The $5,000 from the sale will go to the second mortgagee, and she may have a right to collect the deficiency from Mort. The first mortgagee will not receive any of the proceeds, because its mortgage is unaffected by the foreclosure. If the property were worth $65,000, there could be a bid of $15,000, in which case the foreclosing second mortgagee would receive $10,000, and Mort would receive $5,000.

V. TRANSFERS BY THE PARTIES

A. TRANSFERS OF THE MORTGAGED PROPERTY

Whether a mortgage conveys a title or a lien, the mortgagor can convey the mortgaged property. A complete prohibition on transfer usually would be an invalid restraint on alienation. However, many mortgages make the entire loan amount immediately due and payable when the property is sold unless the mortgagee consents to the sale. Such "due on sale" clauses generally are enforceable pursuant to federal law.

When mortgaged land is transferred, the title remains subject to the mortgage if it was properly recorded. If the mortgage debt is not paid after the transfer, the mortgagee can foreclose, and the transferee will lose the land. However, a transferee is personally liable for the debt, including for a deficiency judgment after a foreclosure, only if he assumed personal liability for it, i.e. promised that he would pay it. The original mortgagor remains liable for the debt even after selling the land, unless the mortgagee has released him.

Illustration—Nonassuming Transferee: Mort conveyed his house to Theresa, subject to a mortgage held by Marie. Theresa did not assume the mortgage. The loan now has gone into default. Marie can sue Mort to recover the debt and can foreclose and sell Theresa's house. If the sale does not generate enough money to pay the debt, Marie may obtain a deficiency judgment against Mort (if the state does not have anti-deficiency legislation) but not against Theresa.

Illustration—Assuming Transferee: Assume the same facts as above, except that Theresa assumed the debt when she purchased the house. Marie now can sue Mort and Theresa to recover the debt and can sell the property and obtain deficiency judgments against both of them (if the state does not have anti-deficiency legislation). Mort remains liable because he signed the original note, and Marie did not release him from that obligation. Theresa is liable because she promised Mort that she would pay the debt. Marie is a third party beneficiary of Theresa's promise to Mort. Alternatively, the jurisdiction may treat her as being equitably subrogated to Mort's rights against Theresa. If Marie collects from Mort, he can sue Theresa on the assumption agreement.

B. TRANSFERS OF THE MORTGAGE

The mortgagee can transfer the note and mortgage. The mortgage automatically transfers with the note even if the mortgage is not expressly assigned. The transferee may acquire the note as a holder in due course under the Uniform Commercial Code if the note was negotiable and the transfer was by proper negotiation. As a holder in due course, the transferee can enforce the note free from many of the mortgagor's contract defenses, such as failure of consideration or payment to the original lender. Problems arise when the original mortgagee sells participation interests in her loans to others and then goes bankrupt without properly completing (perfecting) her transfer to the investors. However, these issues usually are outside the scope of a Property Law course.

Lenders often sell their mortgages in the "secondary mortgage market." The mortgage purchasers create large pools of mortgages and sell fractional ownership interests in them or bonds secured by them. By purchasing mortgages from the originating lender (the lender who made the loan), the secondary market injects more funds into the real estate market.

PART THREE

MISCELLANEOUS PROPERTY DOCTRINES

This Part includes a variety of topics that are taught at scattered places in the Property Law course or sometimes not at all. Air, water, and support sometimes are covered collectively as "incidental rights in land" or with easements. Agreed boundaries may be covered as part of adverse possession or with deeds. Fixtures may be part of landlord-tenant law or an advanced mortgages or commercial law course. Trespass and nuisance often are studied in Torts or are treated as parts of adverse possession or land use. Land use may be a separate course and not covered at all in the basic Property Law course.

In this Part, the masculine pronoun refers to the property owner, and the feminine pronoun refers to the other party involved in the transaction, unless the text indicates otherwise.

CHAPTER THIRTEEN

AIRSPACE

Land ownership generally includes ownership of the airspace above its surface. The advent of air travel has led to different treatment of air rights directly connected with surface uses (lower airspace) and of air rights in the upper atmosphere (upper airspace).

I. LOWER AIRSPACE

A landowner has the same rights and privileges regarding the lower airspace over his land as he has with regard to the surface. For example, he can convey the airspace, lease it, permit limited uses of it, and resist encroachments in it.

Illustration: Len leases a second floor apartment in his building to Tina. Technically, Tina has a leasehold estate in airspace located approximately ten to twenty feet over the surface of Len's land. If Tina enters any other second floor apartment without permission, she is trespassing into the airspace of the person entitled to possess it.

Illustration: If Len converts his building into condominiums and conveys a second floor unit to Tina, she will have fee simple title to that airspace. If she occupies a different unit for a long enough time, she may acquire title by adverse possession to that different segment of airspace.

Illustration: Stan grants Dita the right to string a power line across his property. She has an easement in the airspace over his property. If Dita installs the power line without Stan's consent and he fails to exercise his legal remedies within the statute of limitations, Dita may acquire a prescriptive easement or title by adverse possession in the space occupied by the line. She also could acquire an interest if she regularly drove golf balls over Stan's land or if the overhanging eaves on her roof intruded into Stan's airspace for the limitations period.

II. UPPER AIRSPACE

A. TRESPASS

Congress has declared that the upper airspace is navigable and has given freedom of transit to the public in that space. A surface owner retains conventional property rights in the airspace over her land only to the extent that she reasonably can use it. The owner may not be restrained from building a tall building even though it may interfere with air travel, unless it is expressly prohibited by law. Conversely, the owner does not have a trespass action for flights above the land if they are in a part of the airspace higher than the owner could reach through ground construction. A trespass occurs only when the flight is low enough to intrude upon actual or potential ground-based activity. Trespass is covered in Chapter 18.

B. NUISANCE

A flight may be actionable as a nuisance if it disturbs use of the land's surface by virtue of its noise, glare, danger, or other adverse impact. A flight may constitute a nuisance even if it flies only over adjacent land or from a neighboring airport, rather than directly over the plaintiff's land. Courts usually award damages, rather than injunctive relief, in such cases unless the overflight is by a private party for cloud seeding or for some other form of weather modification that is likely to affect the owner's land. Nuisance is covered in Chapter 19.

C. TAKING

Government flights that render the surface almost valueless because of their frequency or nuisance-like qualities may constitute a taking of the owner's property, which requires the government to pay just compensation to the owner. Similarly, the noise of takeoffs and landings at a governmentally operated airport may take or damage its neighbors' property. In contrast, a private airline company would not be liable on a taking claim, though it could be liable for nuisance. Taking of property is covered in Chapter 20.

CHAPTER FOURTEEN

WATER

A person who owns land bordering on a stream, lake, or other body of water can use the water for drinking, swimming, fishing, and other appropriate activities. But the landowner does not own the water. His rights and privileges are usufructuary, rather than proprietary. Water is owned only after it has been taken from the stream or lake or if it is part of a lake or pond entirely surrounded by one owner's land. Rights to use water in a stream or river are called riparian rights. Rights connected with ownership of land on a lake, sea, or ocean are called littoral rights.

Use rights on navigable or tidal bodies of water are subject to public and federal rights. The public may be entitled to use those waters for swimming, fishing, boating, and other purposes under the public trust doctrine and may prevent riparian or littoral activities that interfere with those uses. Under the Commerce Clause of the U.S. Constitution, the federal government has a navigational servitude in all navigable waterways of the United States. When exercising its rights under the servitude, the government may interfere with riparian or littoral uses of water without liability.

I. STREAM AND RIVER WATER

A parcel of land is riparian when any part of it is contiguous to a stream or river if it extends only a reasonable distance from the water and is within the same watershed. A portion of the land may lose its riparian character if title to it is severed from the rest and if no part of the severed portion is contiguous to the stream. Conversely, in some jurisdictions, nonriparian land may become riparian when an adjacent riparian owner acquires it. Land adjacent to a lake, sea, or ocean is called littoral and is subject to the same rules as riparian land.

A. PREFERRED USE PRIVILEGES

A riparian owner can use water from the stream or river for any purpose that does not significantly affect the quantity, quality, or velocity of flow through lower riparian lands. However, a riparian owner can use water for domestic purposes even if the use affects downstream owners.

Illustration: Ursula, an upstream landowner, draws water from the stream and sells it. Her use does not affect the stream's flow through Don's downstream land. Even though her use of the water is nonriparian, Don may not enjoin it.

Illustration: Ursula draws water from the stream for drinking, bathing, irrigating her garden, and watering her domestic livestock. During the dry season, these diversions stop the water flow through Don's land.

Nevertheless, Don cannot enjoin these domestic uses of water.

B. CORRELATIVE USE PRIVILEGES

Any nondomestic use of water by an upper riparian owner that affects the quantity, quality, or flow of a stream or river is limited by the rights of the lower riparian owners. Two rival doctrines define a lower riparian owner's rights.

1. Natural Flow Doctrine

A lower riparian owner is entitled to receive the water's natural flow without any significant alteration in quantity, quality, or velocity. The owner need not show any special injury resulting from the alteration.

2. Reasonable Use Doctrine

A lower riparian owner is entitled to receive as much water as he can put to beneficial use, with due regard for the upstream owner's correlative rights, but he must show some injury resulting from alteration of the flow.

Illustration: Ursula diverts a significant portion of the stream's water for sale. Don does not use the stream water, so this alteration of the flow does not affect any of his activities. In a natural flow doctrine jurisdiction, he may enjoin Ursula's diversion. In a reasonable use doctrine jurisdiction, he cannot.

Illustration: Ursula diverts the stream water for various commercial uses, such as for her mill or other manufacturing activity, and pollutes the stream with waste products from those uses. These activities affect the flow through Don's land and interfere with his use of the water. If his domestic needs for the water are impaired, he may enjoin Ursula. However, if he needs the water only for commercial purposes, a court ruling on an injunction would compare the social utility of the parties' respective uses and the harm each would suffer from a deprivation of some or all of the water.

The older natural flow doctrine offers the advantages of certainty, because a lower riparian owner prevails merely by showing that the flow has been altered. On the other hand, it is nonutilitarian, often prohibits beneficial water uses, and may waste a valuable resource. It also compels a lower riparian owner to bring suit before he has suffered any injury to avoid the creation of prescriptive rights. In contrast, the majority reasonable use doctrine permits litigation to be postponed until actual harm has occurred and leads to better water use. However, it offers little certainty to the parties, and judicial decrees may require frequent modification as needs change.

C. APPROPRIATION SYSTEMS

Many western states have found the riparian system to be unsuited to their arid conditions and have developed a doctrine of appropriation as a substitute or complement to the riparian rules. In an appropriation system, the right to use water is acquired by permit from a government agency. The agency grants the permit if it determines that the appropriator will make beneficial use of the water. Priority of right to the water is controlled by the date of the permit or appropriation.

Illustration: April obtained a permit to appropriate a certain amount of water per day for her mining activities. Subsequently, Jerry obtained a permit to use water from the same stream for his mines. If the stream level falls too low to allow both parties to take their full quotas, April will be preferred as the prior appropriator. Jerry may take his full allotment only if it does not interfere with April's rights, regardless of where their respective diversion points are located on the stream.

A nonriparian owner may acquire an appropriation permit. Some states eliminate riparian rights entirely (the "Colorado doctrine") so that even a riparian owner must apply for a permit to use the water crossing his land. Other states permit riparian and appropriation rights to coexist (the "California doctrine"). In these states, a more complicated system of priority is necessary to reconcile the competing claims of various appropriators and riparian owners.

Illustration: Ann acquired riparian land in 1850. Bob obtained a permit to appropriate water for his nonriparian land in 1860. Cathy acquired her lower riparian land in 1870 when it came out of the public domain. Don obtained an appropriation permit in 1880. Applying the California doctrine, Ann's privilege to take water probably has the highest priority. Therefore, she may divert water even if it injures the others, unless her activities are not reasonable or beneficial. Bob may divert water under his appropriation permit only if it does not interfere with Ann's reasonable needs, but Bob may take water even if it injures Cathy or Don. Cathy may divert water even if it injures Don, but she may not interfere with Bob's appropriation. As a lower riparian owner, Cathy's use would not affect Ann, unless Cathy dams the stream and causes water to back up onto Ann's land. Don may appropriate water only if his use does not injure Ann, Bob, or Cathy. Under the Colorado doctrine, Ann and Cathy would have no rights to water, because they did not obtain appropriation permits. Only Bob and Don would be entitled to water. As the prior appropriator, Bob has superior rights to Don.

II. SURFACE WATER

Unlike still ponds, swamps, or marshes, surface waters normally move from higher to lower ground but, unlike streams, do not follow any clearly defined channel. Surface waters generally result from rain or snow melt, but sometimes flood waters that separate from the main body of the flood also are treated as surface water. Because such waters are generally unwanted, most litigation concerns a landowner's right to discharge them from her land or to prevent them from crossing her land. In those rare situations when a landowner wants to appropriate surface water, there is a general entitlement to do so.

Three rival doctrines deal with the disposal of surface waters.

A. COMMON ENEMY DOCTRINE

A landowner may dam against surface waters, discharge them back onto upper lands, or deflect them elsewhere. Only the artificial discharge of large quantities of water onto others' lands is prohibited.

B. NATURAL SERVITUDE DOCTRINE

Lower land is servient to the natural drainage from upper land. Thus, a lower landowner cannot obstruct or deflect surface waters. Conversely, the upper landowner cannot cut channels to drain the water elsewhere. This doctrine, which is derived from the civil law, often is subject to an urban exception to permit interferences with the natural flow that result from grading or construction.

C. REASONABLE USE DOCTRINE

A landowner may drain surface waters in connection with a reasonable use of the land if a reasonable necessity exists for the draining, reasonable care is exercised to avoid unnecessary injury to others, and the benefit outweighs the harm. This more recent doctrine directly achieves the result that the other two doctrines in fact produce as a result of their exceptions.

Illustration: Surface water naturally flows from Ursula's upper land to Don's lower land. Under the common enemy rule, Don can erect a barrier to prevent the water from leaving Ursula's land or can channel it onto Lowell's lower land. Under the natural servitude rule, neither activity would be allowed. Under the reasonable use rule, Don may do either depending on the need to drain his property, the care he takes to avoid unnecessary harm to Ursula's and Lowell's lands, and the benefits to keeping his land free of the water as compared to the harms Ursula and Lowell would suffer.

III. UNDERGROUND WATER

A separate body of law regulates rights regarding diffuse underground water that follows no ascertainable underground channel and that either remains still or percolates up to the surface. Underground water that flows in a defined channel is subject to the same rules as streams, but the presumption exists that the water is diffuse, rather than channeled. As with the rest of water law, rival rules exist concerning diffuse underground water.

A. ABSOLUTE OWNERSHIP DOCTRINE

A landowner has an unqualified right to pump all the water, even if it deprives other owners of land over the same underground water basin.

B. REASONABLE USE DOCTRINE

An overlying owner may pump only as much water as reasonably can be used for beneficial uses on his overlying land. Reasonableness may depend in part on whether the used water will seep back down to recharge the aquifer.

C. CORRELATIVE RIGHTS DOCTRINE

All overlying landowners are cotenants of the underground water basin and are limited to a reasonable proportion of the annual supply for beneficial use on the overlying land.

D. APPROPRIATION

The appropriation system may apply to underground water, as well as to stream and river water, and may permit persons who do not own overlying land to appropriate water from an underground basin.

CHAPTER FIFTEEN

SUPPORT

A landowner is entitled to have his land naturally supported by neighboring properties and by the subsurface property beneath his land. Consequently, activity by a neighbor or subsurface owner that causes another's land to subside may be actionable. Support by neighboring land is "lateral support." Support by subsurface land is "subjacent support." For the most part, the rules concerning the two types of support are similar.

I. SUPPORT OF UNIMPROVED LAND

A. ABSOLUTE RIGHT TO SUPPORT

The owner of unimproved land has an absolute right to support. Excavation that causes neighboring unimproved land to subside is actionable though it was not negligently performed and was essential to the land's use. This absolute right applies only to land in its natural condition and not to land that has been weakened or improved. Liability exists only when land removal causes an actual subsidence. If water removal causes subsidence, the matter is governed by water law, rather than by support law.

Illustration: Nora excavated on her lot to build a house on it. As a result, Owen's unimproved land

443

subsided. Nora is liable to him even if the excavation was not performed in a negligent manner.

Illustration: A mining company has the right to remove minerals below the surface of Owen's land. Its underground tunnels caused Owen's land to subside. The mining company is liable to Owen even if the tunnels were cut carefully.

Illustration: Excavation on Nora's land reduced the lateral support for Owen's land, but his land has not subsided. Until subsidence occurs, Owen does not have a cause of action against Nora. Similarly, if Nora protects Owen's land from subsiding by installing an artificial support, such as a retaining wall, Owen has no cause of action against her unless she fails to maintain it.

Illustration: Because Owen discharged great amounts of water onto his land, the soil's natural cohesiveness has been impaired. If Nora now excavates on her land in a reasonable manner, she will not be liable to Owen for any subsidence that occurs as a result of the land's impaired condition.

B. LIABLE PERSONS

A landowner is liable for subsidence of neighboring land only if she or her agent caused it. She is not liable for damage caused by the acts of predecessors, successors, or strangers or by nature.

Illustration: Nora's predecessor in title excavated on her land, but Owen's neighboring land did not subside until after Nora's purchase. The predecessor may be liable for damages because the statute of limitations on

Owen's cause of action did not begin to run until the subsidence. However, Nora is not liable.

Illustration: Nora excavated on her land. As a result of further excavations by the person who bought Nora's land or by other neighbors, Owen's land subsides. He has no cause of action against Nora because intervening acts caused the injury.

Illustration: An earthquake or flood eliminated the natural support that Nora's land previously provided to Owen's land, and his land subsided. He has no cause of action against Nora.

II. SUPPORT OF IMPROVED LAND

A. EXTENT OF OBLIGATION

Improved land is subject to somewhat different rules concerning support. Many courts hold that the absolute obligation of *subjacent* support extends to pre-existing improvements, such as buildings, as well as to the land. However, removal of *lateral* support is actionable only if the land would have subsided even without the improvements on it. Experts may be required to determine whether the pressure of the improvements caused the subsidence or whether their additional weight was offset by the soil removed for their foundations when they were built.

B. MEASURE OF DAMAGES

Courts disagree concerning the measure of damages for removal of lateral support for improved land. In some jurisdictions, the owner may recover for injuries to his land but not to his building. The theory behind this rule is that compelling the second improver to pay damages for the first improver's building gives preferential treatment to the first, which is contrary to the policy that all owners have equal rights to improve. In other jurisdictions, removal of support makes the neighbor liable for injury to buildings, as well as to land, because the building damage was foreseeable. The measure of damages in these cases may be the cost of repairs up to the property's market value, the decrease in the property's market value, or the lesser of those two measures.

A neighbor who negligently or maliciously excavates is liable for harm to the land and to its improvements, regardless of the improvements' weight. A court may find that an excavator acted negligently if she failed to (1) warn the neighbor of the impending excavation so that he could shore up his building, (2) shore up his building for him, or (3) make adequate preliminary soil studies. On the other hand, the neighbor may be guilty of contributory negligence if the building had an inadequate foundation or was so close to the boundary that subsidence was inevitable when the adjacent land was excavated.

C. STATUTORY CHANGES

Some jurisdictions statutorily require an excavator to give advance notice to neighbors concerning the nature of the excavation and, if she intends to excavate below a certain depth (often eight or twelve feet), to shore up the neighbor's building unless he denies permission to do so.

III. AGREEMENTS REGARDING SUPPORT

A. RELEASE OF SUPPORT RIGHTS

An owner may release others from their duty to support his land. A release may be implied from the circumstances of a grant. A release of natural support rights does not include a release of liability for negligent or malicious removal of support.

B. ACQUISITION OF SUPPORT RIGHTS

If an intended building will require additional support from adjoining land, the builder can obtain an easement of support from his neighbor. A support easement may be implied when a building is sold and the supporting adjacent land is retained. No easement of support for a building arises by prescription, because the mere existence of a heavy building creates no cause of action for the neighbor.

CHAPTER SIXTEEN

AGREED BOUNDARIES

I. DIFFICULTIES IN ASCERTAINING BOUNDARIES

Although the boundary description in a deed may be easy to understand, converting the description into lines on the earth may be difficult. Unless an owner employs a surveyor to mark the property lines, the owner may have only an approximate idea of their location. Adjoining landowners frequently have difficulty settling the precise location of their boundary.

Illustration: Owen's deed states that his property's northern boundary is one mile north of the stream. The deed of his neighbor, Nora, describes her southern boundary as one mile north of the stream. Although the two boundaries coincide on paper, neither Owen nor Nora knows the precise location. To mark the boundary accurately, they need a surveyor.

II. BOUNDARY AGREEMENTS

The doctrine of agreed or practically located boundaries permits neighbors, under certain circumstances, to establish a boundary, though a subsequent survey may reveal that the true line originally was somewhere else. The doctrine generally applies only when neighbors established

448

the new boundary line as a result of a disagreement or uncertainty as to the true line. The doctrine does not apply if they were either certain or mistaken as to the true line when they established the new line.

Illustration—Certainty: Owen and Nora know that the boundary line between their lands is ten feet north of the road. However, using the road as the boundary is more convenient, so they orally agreed that it will be the legal boundary. The agreement violates the Statute of Frauds and is invalid. If they wish to change the boundary, the one who owns the ten-foot strip must deed it to the other.

Illustration—Mistake: Although the true boundary between Owen's and Nora's properties is ten feet north of the road, they mistakenly believe that the road is the boundary. Any action they take based on this mistake will be invalid, and they will be relieved from the consequences of their mistake.

Illustration—Disagreement: Owen believes that the boundary is ten feet north of the road, but Nora believes that it is ten feet south of the road. To compromise their difference, they agree that the road will be the boundary. This agreement may be binding, though oral, even if the true boundary is subsequently discovered.

Illustration—Uncertainty: Neither Owen nor Nora knows the boundary's location. To settle the matter, they agree that the road will be the boundary. This agreement may be binding, though oral, even if the true boundary is subsequently discovered. In some jurisdictions, the uncertainty must be justified; the parties cannot be merely too lazy to locate the real line.

III. ACQUIESCENCE

The parties' acquiescence to the new boundary frequently is the critical component of the agreed boundaries doctrine and eliminates the need for proof of actual prior agreement. Some courts require the acquiescence to continue for the statute of limitations period for adverse possession. In these jurisdictions, the doctrine may function as an alternative theory of relief for the party possessing the disputed strip if she has not satisfied all the elements of adverse possession. Even without acquiescence or an explicit agreement, the owners may be bound by an "incorrect" line when both purchased from a common grantor who had marked it on the ground and had given deeds that used lot numbers on a map, rather than a metes and bounds description.

IV. EFFECT

Once established, an agreed boundary binds not only the original parties, but also their successors, even though the property records do not warn successors of the change.

CHAPTER SEVENTEEN

FIXTURES

A fixture is personal property that has become so connected with real property as to become part of it. To be a fixture, the object must retain its original identity even after being affixed to the real property.

Illustration: While a toilet is for sale in a plumbing supply store, it is personal property. Once bolted down in a bathroom, it becomes a fixture, which is a type of real property.

Illustration: Paint in a can in a paint store is personal property. When opened and applied to a wall, it becomes real property. However, it is not a fixture, because it no longer has a separate identity.

Illustration: A refrigerator is not a fixture when it is merely plugged into the kitchen wall. It would become fixture if it were built into the kitchen.

I. FACTORS IN DETERMINING WHAT IS A FIXTURE

Courts consider a number of factors in determining whether to classify an item as a fixture: (1) the method of annexation (how firmly and securely the item is annexed to the real property), (2) appropriateness (how well the item has been adapted to the real property and how appropriately it fits), (3) removability (how much removal will harm the realty), and (4) intent (the annexor's objective intent, as inferred from the above considerations and from his relationship to the real property, especially whether he owns it).

II. WHEN ANNEXOR OWNS THE REAL PROPERTY

In many situations, the person affixing personal property to real property owns both. Nevertheless, determining whether the affixed item is real or personal property is important for the following reasons.

A. PROPERTY TAXATION

Real and personal property frequently are taxed at different rates, so characterization may be necessary to calculate the tax.

B. EMINENT DOMAIN

When government takes land by eminent domain, it normally must compensate the owner only for real property. The owner can remove the personal property.

C. MORTGAGES

A real estate mortgage generally encumbers the mortgagor's real property, but not his personal property. Therefore, a foreclosure sale transfers title to personal property assets that have become fixtures.

D. CONVEYANCES

A contract for the sale of real estate obligates the seller to convey all real property, but not personal property, to the buyer. Whether the contract includes items such as wall-to-wall carpeting and window blinds depends on whether they are fixtures. The contract should include an express provision concerning these types of items to avoid disputes. The contract also can specify that the seller will transfer title to items of personal property, such as the appliances.

E. DEATH

At common law, real property descended to the intestate's heirs, while personal property went to his next of kin. That distinction rarely exists today, but a similar issue could arise if the decedent's will gave his real and personal property to different people.

III. WHEN ANNEXOR DOES NOT OWN THE REAL PROPERTY

The person who owns and annexes personal property to real property may not own the real property. If the item becomes a fixture, title to it passes from the annexor to the real property owner despite the annexor's subjective intent to the contrary.

A. TENANTS

If a tenant installs a fixture, it may become the landlord's property. In that case, removal by the tenant constitutes waste. Nevertheless, many states permit a tenant to remove trade fixtures and possibly ornamental and domestic fixtures. However, removal may be permitted only if it will not significantly injure the premises. The landlord and tenant also can agree that fixtures will remain the tenant's property and that he has a right to remove them.

B. STRANGERS

A person who enters another's real property and affixes chattels generally loses the right to remove them. In some states, a betterment or innocent improver statute provides the right to remove them or to recover their reasonable value from the owner.

C. CHATTEL SELLERS

A seller can sell personal property on credit and reserve a security interest in it until the price is fully paid. The security interest is enforceable between the parties. But if the item becomes a fixture, the rights of other parties, such as a mortgagee or a landlord, may make resolution of the issue more difficult. Article 9 of the Uniform Commercial Code establishes the priorities for many such situations. Priority can depend on considerations such as whether the personal property security interest was recorded in the real property records and whether the goods are readily removable.

CHAPTER EIGHTEEN

TRESPASS

I. PROTECTION OF POSSESSION

A land possessor has certain rights regardless of whether she owns the land. Subject to principles of reasonableness, she may protect her possession from intruders by erecting barriers to their entry or by physically expelling them. She also has judicial remedies against intruders. When the intrusion amounts to a dispossession, she can bring an action in ejectment. Failure to do so creates a risk of adverse possession. When the intrusion does not amount to a dispossession, the appropriate relief is usually damages for trespass. This Chapter does not provide a complete review of the law of trespass, because it generally is covered in Torts. The emphasis here is on the features of trespass law that are most relevant to a Property Law course.

II. WHAT IS A TRESPASS?

Any intentional intrusion on land owned by another is trespass. Liability is absolute. Motive, extent, duration, and harm are irrelevant, though they may affect the amount of damages. A negligent intrusion also can be trespass, but only if some harm results from it. A nonvolitional intrusion is not trespass, but mistake as to location does not make the entry nonvolitional.

Illustration: Trish is carried across Paul's land by kidnappers. Although they may be guilty of trespass, she is not, because her entry was nonvolitional.

Illustration: Paul's neighbor walks on his property, because she believes that it is part of her land. She is a trespasser because her entry was intentional, though she was mistaken as to ownership.

Illustration: Trish negligently runs her car off the road and onto Paul's land. If she harms his land, she is liable for it in trespass.

A. INTRUSIONS OTHER THAN BY TRESPASSER

Trespass occurs with a physical intrusion of the land. The trespasser need not personally intrude. The intrusion can be by the trespasser's agent or by physical objects that the trespasser sets in motion, such as a rolling car or a fired bullet.

Illustration: Trish's animals wander over Paul's land. At common law, she would be liable for their trespasses. However, many states have altered these rules with statutes that require landowners to fence their land. Additionally, liability generally does not exist for intrusions by dogs, cats, and other animals whose movements are difficult to control.

B. TOUCHING THE BOUNDARY

Trespass occurs when the trespasser touches a vertical boundary line, even if he does not cross it.

Illustration: Trish piles dirt against the wall of Paul's house, which is on his lot line, or fastens a clothes line to his wall. She is trespassing in both cases.

C. ABOVE AND BELOW THE SURFACE

A trespass may occur above or below the surface because possessory rights extend vertically in both directions. Therefore, an underground intrusion, such as a slant well, is a trespass. However, the depletion of migrant minerals, such as water, oil, or gas, from a common basin by a perpendicular well dug on neighboring land is not. An intrusion into airspace by a building, wire, or other object also is a trespass and may lead to the acquisition of prescriptive rights of possession or use. An isolated nonpermanent intrusion, such as firing a gun over land, also is a trespass. Special rules deal with airplanes' overflights. On airspace, see Chapter 13.

III. PRIVILEGED ENTRIES

A. CONSENT

Entry with the possessor's consent is not trespass. The invitation creates a license, which may be oral or implied. Once it expires or is revoked, failure to leave within a reasonable time constitutes trespass.

Illustration: Trish enters a restaurant to dine. Her entry is not trespassory because the circumstances impliedly authorize the public to enter. However, if she refuses to leave after closing time, she is guilty of trespass.

B. SOCIAL NEED

A possessor's right of undisturbed possession is subject to the general public interest. In certain situations, public policy requires a possessor to permit others to enter his land.

Illustration: The police enter Paul's property to break up a fight or to stop a crime from being committed. The entry is privileged.

Illustration: A building inspector or other public official enters property in furtherance of an official duty. The entry is privileged, though a warrant may be required if the entry would constitute a search or seizure under the Fourth Amendment.

Illustration: Paul's house is on fire. Trish enters to extinguish it before it spreads to her property. She is privileged to do so.

C. PROPERTY RIGHTS

In certain cases, a person may be entitled to enter another's land to protect his property interests. This right is not a general license to wander about but is limited to such entry as is necessary to protect the property interest.

Illustration: Paul has fee simple title subject to condition subsequent, and Trish has the power of termination. After the condition has occurred, Trish can exercise the power by entering onto Paul's land. Her peaceable entry to perfect the power is not trespass.

Illustration: As Paul's landlord, Trish may have the right to enter to make sure that he is not committing waste. Such a limited entry is not trespassory.

Title to real property does not constitute an absolute privilege for entry. The owner is privileged to peaceably enter property in another's possession but may not use force to do so. In most jurisdictions, forcible entry creates civil and criminal liability.

Illustration: Because Paul was in arrears on his rent, his landlord broke open the apartment door while he was away and removed his belongings. Although the landlord is entitled to have him evicted, she may not commit this forcible entry and trespass.

Illustration: Trish and Paul disagreed about the location of their common boundary line. Trish demolished the fence that Paul erected and stepped over it. Trish is guilty of trespass and forcible entry, even if a survey ultimately shows that she owns the disputed strip.

IV. REMEDIES

A. NOMINAL DAMAGES

A possessor always may recover at least nominal damages for any trespass, even if he has not been harmed. A possessor may bring an action for nominal damages to establish a property right, to settle a boundary dispute, or to stop the statute of limitations from running.

B. COMPENSATORY DAMAGES

A possessor may recover compensatory damages for actual harm suffered from a trespass. If permanent injury has occurred, the measure of damages is either the diminution of the property's value or the cost of restoration. Consequential damages, such as for personal injuries, mental anguish, and lost profits, also may be recovered, subject to the usual tort principles of foreseeability and mitigation of damages. In certain cases, the damages may be based on the benefit received by the trespasser. For example, if a trespasser removes assets from the property, she may be liable for their value or she may be required to return them or pay a royalty for them. A trespasser who improves the property sometimes is allowed to offset the value of her improvements against her trespass liability. When the trespass is continuing but the injury is not permanent, damages will be awarded only for injuries caused before the date of judgment. The possessor may file subsequent actions against the trespasser for harm caused after the judgment.

C. PUNITIVE DAMAGES

If the trespass is malicious or wanton, a court may award exemplary or punitive damages. In some jurisdictions, the wrongful cutting of timber or other natural products subjects a trespasser to double or treble damages.

D. EQUITABLE RELIEF

A court may grant an injunction if damages are difficult to calculate or if the harm is irreparable. To eliminate multiple lawsuits, a court also may enjoin trespasses that otherwise probably would continue. Occasionally, a court will order removal of an encroaching building but usually only after balancing the hardship to the defendant if the injunction is granted against the hardship to the plaintiff if it is not. Denial of an injunction in such a case amounts to the defendant's exercise of a form of private eminent domain. A court also may grant injunctive relief to a future interest holder who currently lacks standing to sue for damages.

E. RELIEF ACCORDING TO PLAINTIFF'S STATUS

In an action for damages for trespass, the plaintiff must either possess the property or hold a present possessory interest in it. The trespass action protects possession, rather than ownership. Thus, a trespass action may be brought by a tenant, a purchaser in possession under a land contract, a cotenant in possession alone or with others, an adverse possessor, or a mere peaceful possessor of another's property. Of course, an owner who also has the right to possess also can bring a trespass action. A nonpossessory interest holder may recover only if she can show some injury to her interest. Harm is a prerequisite to any such action because, technically, it is not a trespass on her interest.

Illustration: Trish entered Paul's apartment without his permission. Paul can recover at least nominal damages from Trish, but his landlord can recover only for any permanent harm Trish caused to the apartment. The landlord's mortgagee may recover only if Trish impaired its security.

Illustration: Trish trespassed over a road on Paul's property. Dita, who has a right of way easement over the road, has a cause of action against Trish only if the intrusion unreasonably interfered with her use of the road.

CHAPTER NINETEEN

NUISANCE

I. NUISANCE v. TRESPASS

Nuisance and trespass are closely related but have different legal foundations. A trespass action protects possession of land, while a nuisance action protects the use and enjoyment of land. Although trespass requires a physical intrusion, nuisance does not. Because the right of possession is absolute, a trespass action can be successful even if no physical damage occurred. In contrast, the rights of use and enjoyment are not absolute, so the plaintiff must prove that the defendant's conduct unreasonably interfered with the possessor's use and enjoyment and caused actual injury. But prescription can be a defense for both causes of action.

Illustration: Nora works on cars on her property. If she drives the cars onto her neighbor's property, she is guilty of trespass and is liable for at least nominal damages regardless of harm. On the other hand, if the cars make a great deal of noise in Nora's garage, her neighbor may recover in nuisance if he can show that the noise unreasonably interferes with the use and enjoyment of his land. If his land is vacant or if his house is situated far from noise, he cannot sue for nuisance.

Illustration: If Nora parks her cars on her neighbor's driveway, she has trespassed. However, she is not liable in trespass to Dita, who has an easement to drive across the driveway, because Dita's property interest is nonpossessory. Dita may recover only if she can show that Nora has unreasonably interfered with her use of the driveway.

II. DETERMINING WHETHER NUISANCE HAS OCCURRED

Nuisances generally involve some interference with the physical senses, such as smoke, dust, odor, noise, light, or heat, that harm a normal person's use of his property. An activity that is merely visually offensive generally is not an actionable nuisance, although activities that cause fright, such as a funeral parlor, or moral indignation, such as a brothel, may be. Although nuisance usually involves intentional conduct by the defendant, negligence generally is not a defense. Malice may convert an otherwise legitimate activity into a nuisance. For example, if a landowner builds a tall fence solely for the purpose of interfering with the flow of light and air to a neighbor's property, that "spite fence" constitutes a nuisance.

To determine whether the challenged activity is a nuisance, courts generally balance the parties' respective interests by comparing the gravity of the plaintiff's harm with the utility of the defendant's conduct. As components of the gravity of harm, the

Restatement (Second) of Torts § 827 includes the harm's extent and character, the harmed activity's social value and suitability to the locale, and the plaintiff's ability to avoid the harm. Factors in determining the utility of the defendant's conduct include its social value and suitability to the locale and the impracticability of preventing the plaintiff's harm. Restatement (Second) of Torts § 828. Priority of use is not a complete defense but may be treated as a factor. Thus, it might be relevant that the plaintiff "came to the nuisance," such as by building a home in an industrial area.

III. RELIEF

Damages are the appropriate remedy for a nuisance that has ceased. The plaintiff is entitled to recover for personal and property harm. If a nuisance threatens to continue indefinitely, an award of damages alone constitutes a form of private eminent domain. The defendant essentially is paying for the property interests it has appropriated from the plaintiff.

If an injunction is sought, courts generally balance the harm to the defendant if the injunction is granted against the benefit to the plaintiff. The factors considered in the balancing are basically the same as for determining whether the defendant's activity constituted a nuisance. However, the context changes their weights. Some economists argue that an injunction should be granted only if the defendant can avoid the harm at a lower cost than the plaintiff. The equities of the situation should be relevant only to the question of damages, which can be awarded either to a plaintiff who is denied an injunction or to a defendant who is enjoined.

Illustration: Nora's race track emits such bright light during night racing that it impairs Owen's neighboring drive-in movie business. In deciding whether to enjoin Nora from night racing, a court might compare the relative avoidance costs. If the court determines that it is cheaper for Nora to shield her lights or to give up night racing than for Owen to build a high wall, it may grant an injunction. The court also could condition the injunction on Owen's compensating Nora if the court decides that equitable principles require this. In such a case, the court effectively has held that Nora is entitled to emit light but that Owen can stop her from doing so by paying a price set by the court, rather than by the parties. This award is a "liability entitlement," rather than a "property entitlement," because it resembles a personal injury award for which a judge or a jury determines the price of a broken limb. Alternately, the court could deny an injunction to Owen if it determines that he can remedy the problem more cheaply than Nora and could order Nora to reimburse him for his avoidance costs. The court could also grant or deny the injunction without reallocating costs. If the problem cannot be eliminated through corrective measures, a court might consider the relative costs of either party's relocating away from the other. Finally, a court might deny any relief for Owen if it determines that his use is overly sensitive to light or if he built the theater after Nora began night racing.

A nuisance imposes an external cost on another's land. An injunction compels the defendant to internalize that cost or to eliminate the externality. When neighboring activities are incompatible, a court is almost inevitably drawn into judicial zoning.

Illustration: Nora's foundry is next to Owen's laboratory. Noise and vibrations from the foundry make laboratory work impossible. Therefore, Nora is imposing an external cost on Owen's land. However, if Owen obtains an injunction that prohibits or limits her foundry's activity, he will have imposed an external cost on her land. Either her work makes his work impossible if she is not enjoined, or his work makes hers impossible if she is enjoined. Either activity is compatible with many other kinds of activities but not with each other. A neutral principle may not exist to resolve this conflict.

IV. PUBLIC NUISANCE

A nuisance is public, rather than private, when it affects a significant portion of the community, rather than just a few neighbors. In some jurisdictions, only a public official has standing to bring a public nuisance action. However, an individual may sue for damages or for an injunction if he can show special harm to himself or to his property different than the harm that everyone else is suffering. Courts are more likely to grant an injunction in a public nuisance case than in a private nuisance case because more people are adversely affected by the defendant's conduct.

CHAPTER TWENTY

LAND USE REGULATION

This Chapter deals with the relationship between a landowner and the general public concerning the activities on his land. The public interest can be manifested by legislative action that regulates land use activities, by administrative agency action in granting, denying, or modifying a permit for land uses, and by judicial action between the government and a landowner over the validity of a land use regulation or its application to a particular parcel of land. All the Illustrations in this Chapter are based on actual cases or statutes.

I. TYPES OF LAND USE REGULATION

A. ZONING

1. Typical Zoning Devices

Zoning is the most common form of local land use control. The city or county (referred to as the "community" in this Chapter) is divided geographically into zones (districts), and different use regulations apply in each zone. The regulations are set forth in a zoning ordinance. The zoning map graphically depicts each geographic district. Although the regulations differ from district to district, they apply uniformly to all parcels of land within a district.

a. Lot, Building, and Use Regulations

Zoning ordinances generally regulate the size and shape of the land, the size and shape of improvements on the land, and the type of activity that can occur on the land or in its improvements.

(1) Lot Regulations

(a) Minimum Lot Size

Many zoning ordinances establish minimum lot sizes to reduce density. Density limitations are designed to eliminate overcrowding, to increase the flow of light and air, to facilitate police and fire services, and to reduce demands on natural resources. Required lot sizes can range from 2,000 square feet in dense urban areas, five acres in suburban and rural areas, and twenty or more acres in agricultural communities.

(b) Minimum Frontage

A related form of regulation establishes a minimum width for a parcel's frontage on a public street. In urban areas, the minimum frontage may be as little as twenty feet. In the suburbs, it may be one hundred or two hundred feet. The requirement may be tied to some other variable, such as the parcel's depth or the width of surrounding lots.

(2) Building Regulations

(a) Height

Building heights usually are regulated by number of feet or stories independent of the lot area. However, the height limit may vary according to the topography, such as thirty feet along the coast, or according to use.   For example, buildings in commercial zones may be allowed greater height than those in residential zones.   Height also may be related to bulk, so that a building may be taller if it is narrower or if it is stepped back as it rises so as to increase the light and view at ground level.   The limit also may depend on the heights of adjacent buildings or on the average height of buildings on the block.   Special adjustments may be made for buildings erected on sharply sloping ground.

(b) Bulk

(1) Yards. Building bulk generally is regulated as a function of lot size. Front, back, and side yard requirements prohibit a building from occupying the entire parcel by mandating open space along all or part of its perimeter. A front yard regulation, which requires a building to be no less than a specified distance from the front lot line, usually is called a setback regulation. A side yard regulation requires that buildings on neighboring properties be separated from one another.   Rear   yard requirements, which are common in residential

districts, may be expressed in absolute numbers or may use averaging principles. For example, front or rear setbacks for a building may have to be consistent with buildings on adjacent parcels or with the average setback on the block.

Many communities do not have setback requirements, especially in commercial areas, thus permitting contiguous buildings to extend all the way to the lot lines. In dense residential neighborhoods, the front or side yard requirement may be as little as five or ten feet. In more spacious suburbs, the requirements may be as much as fifty feet in front and forty feet along the sides. The requirements generally vary from district to district.

(2) Open Space. Building bulk also may be regulated by a direct open space regulation. This type of regulation prohibits a building from occupying more than a specified percentage of the lot. In the suburbs, the percentage may be as low as twenty percent. The setback requirements described above generally supplement the open space requirements to control the placement of buildings on the lot.

(c) Floor-Area Ratio

A floor-area ratio (FAR) requirement may regulate a building's overall bulk according to the size of the lot without specifying the building's precise shape. For example, a 2:1 ratio permits the lot owner to erect a building containing two square feet of floor space for every one square foot of lot area. The owner can erect a two-story building covering the entire lot, a four-story building covering half the lot, an eight-story building covering a quarter of the lot, and so on. However, height limits and open space and yard requirements may limit the owner's options. Residential FARs often range from 2:1 to 5:1. In downtown areas, they may vary from 15:1 to 20:1. The Empire State Building's FAR is 25:1. Some ordinances permit the FAR to be increased if the owner provides certain amenities, such as plazas, public parking, or rapid transit access.

(d) Minimum Floor Space

Suburban zoning ordinances often prohibit residential structures from being too small, rather than too large, by requiring a minimum size, such as 1,000 square feet of floor space. If the requirement is designed to exclude the poor, rather than to prevent overcrowding, a court may invalidate it, especially if it is combined with an unjustifiably large minimum lot size requirement. Zoning devices that are designed to exclude lower income people or other classes of persons are called "exclusionary zoning."

Illustration: The Berlin, New Jersey zoning ordinance required a minimum floor space of 1,600 square feet, a minimum lot size of one acre, and a minimum frontage of 200 feet in single family residential zones. The New Jersey Supreme Court invalidated these exclusionary zoning devices in *Home Builders League of South Jersey, Inc. v. Township of Berlin,* 405 A.2d 381 (N.J. 1979).

(e) Design and Site Plan Review

A community may impose design controls for new structures by requiring that, as a condition to receiving a building permit, the landowner must submit the building plans to a local review board, which usually is composed of architects. Because courts in some jurisdictions hold that aesthetic considerations alone are an insufficient police power purpose for land use regulations, many design review ordinances provide that preservation of neighboring property values is the primary consideration. To withstand challenges based on vagueness and improper delegation of legislative power to an unelected review board, such ordinances often attempt to prescribe aesthetic standards in considerable detail.

Illustration: To get a building permit for a remodeling project in Del Mar, California, a landowner first had to get a permit from the Design Review Board. The design review was intended to promote good design "which encompasses the use of harmonious materials and colors [and] compatible proportional relationships." The Board could deny a permit if "[t]he design is not harmonious with … the surrounding neighborhood in … [s]tructural siting on the lot" or if "[t]he proposed development fails to coordinate the components of exterior building design on all elevations with regard to color, materials, architectural form and detailing to achieve design harmony and continuity." *Breneric Associates v. City of Del Mar*, 81 Cal Rptr. 2d 324 (Cal. Ct. App. 1998).

Illustration: The Architectural Board of Ladue, Missouri was authorized to review building plans to ensure that they "conform to certain minimum architectural standards of appearance and conformity with surrounding structures, and that unsightly, grotesque and unsuitable structures, detrimental to the stability of value and the welfare of surrounding property, structures and residents, and to the general welfare and happiness of the community, be avoided, and that appropriate standards of beauty and conformity be fostered and encouraged." *State ex rel. Stoyanoff v. Berkeley,* 458 S.W.2d 305 (Mo. 1970).

Illustration: The Board of Architectural Review of Westchester County, New York was authorized to disapprove a building permit application if it found that the proposed structure would cause "harmful effects" by reason of (1) "monotonous similarity," (2) "striking dissimilarity or visual discord or inappropriateness" to nearby buildings, or (3) "visual offensiveness or other poor qualities of exterior design."

Site plan review is less predictable. A community board may have power to review all aspects of a project and to demand changes as a condition for final approval, though the plan complies with all zoning and other regulations. Such standardless review gives planners powerful discretionary control. It also significantly changes the nature of land use regulation from its original concept of providing preset standards. Under the original view, landowners had the power "as of right" to complete projects that conformed to the standards.

(3) Regulations on Activities

Traditional zoning's key feature is the creation of use districts, which are zones where certain activities are prohibited, though they may be permitted in other zones in the community. An original premise behind zoning was that some uses of land are incompatible and must be kept separated for the protection of one or both of them. In particular, residential areas were deemed to need protection from commercial and industrial intrusion.

Zoning originally was "cumulative," meaning that more intense uses (commercial and industrial) were excluded from less intense use (residential) zones, whereas less intense uses were permitted in more intense use zones. Today, commercial and industrial zones often exclude residential uses. This is noncumulative zoning, because the enumerated uses are exclusive in each zone.

Zoning ordinances exclude activities either by explicitly excluding certain uses in a zone or by specifying the only uses that are permitted and excluding all others. Serious questions of validity may exist when a zoning ordinance excludes a lawful use from the entire community. Compare the following two cases.

Illustration: The Washington, Pennsylvania zoning ordinance excluded trash transfer stations from the entire town. A court held that the total exclusion was unconstitutional because trash transfer stations are a "legitimate use." *Toms v. Board of Supervisors of Washington Township*, 553 A.2d 507 (Pa. Commw. Ct. 1989).

Illustration: The Beacon Falls, Connecticut zoning ordinance prohibited the operation of a garbage dump anywhere in the town. The Connecticut Supreme Court upheld the exclusion. The court stated that zoning ordinances are entitled to a presumption of validity and that total exclusion of a particular land use is valid if it is rationally related to the public health, safety, and welfare. *Town of Beacon Falls v. Posick*, 563 A.2d 285 (Conn. 1989).

(a) Residential

Residential uses commonly are separated by housing type. Separate districts may exist for single-family, two-family (flats or duplexes), and multi-family residences (apartments and condominiums). Other districts may include or exclude different kinds of residential uses, such as hotels, motels, apartment complexes, garden apartments, manufactured home parks, boarding houses, fraternity and sorority houses, dormitories, and various forms of institutional housing, such as mental health facilities, orphanages, and halfway houses.

Courts generally have upheld the exclusion of apartment buildings from single-family residential zones since the United States Supreme Court first validated zoning in *Village of Euclid v. Ambler Realty Co.,* 272 U.S. 365 (1926). However, the exclusion of housing that best accommodates low-income persons may be invalid as exclusionary.

(b) Commercial

Most communities have some commercial zones, as well as residential zones. There may be only one commercial category that includes all permitted commercial uses or a variety of categories, such as central district commercial (large department stores), neighborhood commercial, retail, and office. The zoning ordinance may have special rules for garages, gas stations, liquor stores, bars, drive-ins, theaters, and restaurants, because these uses, though beneficial, tend to impose unique burdens on a neighborhood.

Illustration: The Mount Vernon, Iowa zoning ordinance created two commercial districts— C (commercial) and HC (highway commercial). Mount Vernon's downtown business district is zoned C; the area surrounding the intersection of two highways is zoned HC. To protect the downtown business area, the HC district can include only businesses that cater to highway users or that are incompatible with the downtown area. *E and G Enterprises v. City of Mount Vernon*, 373 N.W.2d 693 (Iowa Ct. App. 1985).

Some ordinances put all such uses in one zone, whereas others seek to disperse them.

Illustration: The Detroit, Michigan zoning ordinance prohibited any "adult theater" from being located within 1,000 feet of any other "regulated use" or within 500 feet of a residential area. "Regulated uses" included sexually oriented theaters or bookstores, topless cabarets, bars, hotels, motels, pawnshops, pool halls, second hand stores, shoe-shine parlors, and dance halls. *Young v. American Mini Theatres, Inc.,* 427 U.S. 50 (1976).

Illustration: The Boston, Massachusetts zoning ordinance created an Adult Entertainment District in which adult book stores and other sexually oriented businesses are allowed. The general prohibition of moving or flashing signs did not apply in this district. Because such uses were forbidden in all other districts, the area become known as the "Combat Zone."

(c) Industrial; Performance Standards

Many zoning ordinances create different zones for various types of industrial use. Today, many communities have set aside areas as exclusive industrial parks, from which residential and commercial activities are excluded, to prevent interferences with industrial activities. Industrial regulations often are directed at the activity's external effects, rather than at the specific use. Thus, "performance standard zoning" regulates externalities, such as smell, noise, smoke, and vibrations, rather than the activity itself.

Illustration: The Ghent, New York zoning ordinance included a district for commercial industrial uses. The ordinance prohibited an otherwise permitted use in this district if it would violate any one of a number of performance standards, including: "Smoke—No emission shall be permitted from any chimney or otherwise, of visible grey smoke of a shade equal to or darker than No. 2 on the Power's Micro-Ringlemann Chart. Odors—No emission shall be permitted of odorous gases or other odorous matter in such quantities as to be readily detectable at the property line of the zone lot from which they are emitted without instruments. Other Forms of Air Pollution—No emission of fly ash, dust, fumes, vapors, gases and other forms of air pollution shall be permitted which can cause any damage to health, to animal, vegetation, or other forms of property, or which can cause any excessive soiling." *TCI, Inc. v. Town of Ghent*, 565 N.Y.S.2d 324 (N.Y. App. Div. 1991).

2. Mapping

In addition to the zoning ordinance, which describes the bulk, area, and use restrictions, a community also has a zoning map that shows the location of each zoning district. Different types of district boundaries may overlap. For example, one height limit may apply to all residential districts and a different height limit for all commercial districts. Alternatively, different mapped areas may exist for different purposes. For example, the same height limits may apply to all coastal areas, though some parts of the coast are zoned residential and other parts commercial. There may be only one map, with all bulk and area standards dependent on the use district (e.g. a forty-foot height limit for all residential zones), or there may be separate (overlay) use and bulk maps.

a. Size of the Zone; Spot Zoning

If a very small area is mapped for a significantly different use than for the surrounding area, a court may invalidate it as impermissible "spot zoning." Invalidation is especially likely if the classification was created in a rezoning, rather than in the original zoning of the parcel.

Illustration: The Town of Denton, North Carolina rezoned a single parcel of land from agricultural use to industrial use for a chemical storage facility. The parcel was entirely surrounded by land in agricultural use. The court invalidated the rezoning because of the detrimental impact on the neighboring land and on the community. *Good Neighbors of South Davidson v. Town of Denton,* 559 S.E.2d 768 (N.C. 2002).

b. Zoning Boundaries

If the zoning boundaries do not coincide with existing lot lines, a single parcel of land may be in two different zoning districts. In that case, an ordinance may provide that the entire lot is subject to whichever classification is more (or less) severe or to whichever covers the greater geographic part of the lot. In small communities, mapping can coincide precisely with all existing lot lines. The problem of a split lot also can be avoided by running all zoning lines down the center of public streets, but that would put opposite sides of the same street into different districts, which is generally undesirable. If no corrective action is taken as to a split lot, it will remain subject to two different classifications unless a court holds the mapping to be invalid.

Illustration: Under the zoning map of Cambridge, Massachusetts, the plaintiff's parcel was classified as residential for a one hundred foot strip along the street, but the rest of the parcel was unrestricted. Although the other side of the street was residential, the court held that the city had acted arbitrarily in not running the zoning line along the property's street frontage. *Nectow v. City of Cambridge,* 277 U.S. 183 (1928).

3. Special Zoning Tools

a. *Special Exceptions (Special Uses, Conditional Uses)*

Under the traditional zoning system, a use either is permitted as a matter of right or is absolutely barred. However, not all activities can be so readily categorized. If the community believes that some activities might be appropriate under certain circumstances, the zoning ordinance may include them in a category of conditionally permitted uses. These types of uses are allowed only after review by the appropriate zoning agency. They usually are called special exceptions or special or conditional uses, because the zoning agency may permit the use only under certain conditions. The agency has the discretion to grant a permit for the use only if the zoning ordinance specifies that it is a special exception or conditional use. A conditional use permit often includes conditions that are designed to limit the use's adverse impact on the neighborhood, such as landscaping the premises to shield the neighbors from lights or limiting the hours of operation.

Illustration: The zoning ordinance of Avon, Massachusetts permitted multi-family dwellings, such as apartment buildings, only as a special use in a district zoned for single-family homes and duplexes. To get a special use permit, the lot on which the multi-family dwelling was to be located had to have at least 200 feet of street frontage. A court upheld the frontage requirement as a means of "lessening congestion in the streets, conservation of health, securing safety from fire and other dangers, provision of adequate light and air, prevention of overcrowding of land, and avoidance of undue concentration of population." *MacNeil v. Town of Avon*, 435 N.E.2d 1043, 1045 (Mass. 1982).

Illustration: The zoning ordinance of Baltimore County, Maryland provided that a special use permit was required to locate a funeral home in a residential district. The County Board of Appeals could grant the permit only if it found that the funeral home would not: "a. Be detrimental to the health, safety or general welfare of the locality involved; b. Tend to create congestion in roads, streets or alleys therein; c. Create a potential hazard from fires, panic or other dangers; d. Tend to overcrowd the land and cause undue concentration of population; e. Interfere with adequate provisions for schools, parks, water, sewerage, transportation or other public requirements, conveniences or improvements; f. Interfere with adequate light and air." *Anderson v Sawyer*, 329 A.2d 716, 720 n.3 (Md. Ct. Spec. App. 1974).

b. Floating Zones

A city can create a zoning classification by specifying the standards for it in the zoning ordinance but not specifying its location on the zoning map. A property owner then can apply to an administrative body to have her land reclassified for the uses permitted in that zone. Because the zone has not been mapped, it "floats." Floating zones have been created for industrial parks, mixed apartment-commercial zones, and manufactured home parks.

Illustration: The St. Louis County, Missouri zoning ordinance included provisions for a planned commercial district that was designated C-8. C-8 was a floating zone because it did not have a fixed location in the county. A parcel of land would be classified C-8 only by a rezoning for that purpose. The C-8 regulations were intended "to facilitate the establishment of combinations of developments and uses for which no provision is made in any other 'C' Commercial District or the establishment of developments and uses in locations where it would be appropriate to the area if it were to take place under approved site plans and conditions necessary to protect the general welfare." Before rezoning a parcel of land to C-8, the County Council had to find "that any particular tracts or areas should be developed for commercial use, but because of potential conflicts with adjoining uses, existing or potential, a greater degree of control of the manner of development is necessary to protect the general welfare than is possible under the regulations of the other 'C' Commercial Districts." The Planning Commission and the County Council had "virtually total control of the appearance and nature of the development." *Treme v. St. Louis County*, 609 S.W.2d 706 (Mo. Ct. App. 1980).

Illustration: The zoning ordinance of Tarrytown, New York provided that the boundaries of its apartment zone would be "fixed by amendment of the official village building zone map, at such times in the future as such district or class of zone is applied, to properties in this village." *Rodgers v. Village of Tarrytown,* 96 N.E.2d 731 (N.Y. 1951).

c. *Cluster Zoning*

To avoid monotonous developments in which each house has the same front and side yards and the same general layout, a community may enact cluster zoning. Cluster zoning permits developers to depart from the standards for individual parcels so long as those standards are maintained with regard to the overall project. For instance, if the ordinance requires fifty percent open space for each lot, a developer of two lots might have the option of clustering two houses on one lot and leaving the other lot entirely open.

Illustration: The zoning ordinance of South Brunswick, New Jersey provided that a subdivider could reduce the minimum lot size and frontage requirements by up to thirty percent for individual lots within the subdivision if: (1) the resulting "net lot density" of the area was no greater than otherwise would be allowed; (2) the development complied "with all other provisions of the Zoning Ordinance, such as front, rear and side setbacks, size of buildings, etc.;" (3) the subdivider donated a "usable" five-acre tract to the city for public purposes; and (4) "if the tract to be subdivided is located in a zone which requires a minimum lot size of 20,000 square feet or less, the developer must donate, exclusive of open drainage water courses, 20% of the tract to the Township; if the tract to be subdivided is located in a zone which requires a minimum lot size in excess of 20,000 square feet, the developer must donate, exclusive of open drainage water courses, 30% of the tract to the township." *Chrinko v. South Brunswick Township Planning Bd.,* 187 A.2d 221 (N.J. Super. 1963).

d. Planned Unit Development (PUD)

The same clustering principle may be applied to uses, as well as to bulk and area. If the subdivider is permitted to allocate space for both commercial and residential activities within overall limitations, the project may be a Planned Unit Development. Instead of local officials mapping separate single-family residential, apartment, and commercial districts when the zoning ordinance is adopted, the subdivider can map all those activities on a single parcel subject to percentages specified in the ordinance. To reduce the costs of delay and the dangers of inconsistent demands from different reviewing boards, the property may be rezoned to PUD at the same time as the site plan review and perhaps under the aegis of one agency.

Illustration: The zoning ordinance of New Hope, Pennsylvania included a PUD district within which there can be "single family attached or detached dwellings; apartments; accessory private garages; public or private parks and recreation areas including golf courses, swimming pools, ski slopes, etc. (so long as these facilities do not produce noise, glare, odor, air pollution, etc., detrimental to existing or prospective adjacent structures); a municipal building; a school; churches; art galleries; professional offices; certain types of signs; a theatre (but not a drive-in); motels and hotels; and a restaurant.   The ordinance then sets overall density requirements. The PUD district may have a maximum of 80% of the land devoted to residential uses, a maximum of 20% for the permitted commercial uses and enclosed recreational facilities, and must have a minimum of 20% for open spaces. The residential density shall not exceed 10 units per acre, nor shall any such unit contain more than two bedrooms. All structures within the district must not exceed maximum height standards set out in the ordinance. Finally, although there are no traditional 'setback' and 'side yard' requirements, ordinance 160 does require that there be 24 feet between structures, and that no townhouse structure contain more than 12 dwelling units." *Cheney v. Village 2 at New Hope, Inc.,* 241 A.2d 81 (Pa. 1968).

e. Holding Zones

A holding zone is a use classification that is so restrictive that it makes land practically undevelopable. When a community is not yet ready to classify all the land within its borders, it may zone some areas very restrictively, not because it believes the zoning to be appropriate to the area, but because it prevents development until the community's comprehensive plan is finished. For example, it may restrict a zone to single-family residences with a minimum lot size of ten acres. The same goal can be achieved by interim zoning. Overly restrictive zoning forces owners to apply for a rezoning for any development. For this reason, it is called "wait and see" zoning.

4. Zoning Relief

a. *Variance*

A variance permits a landowner to deviate from some aspect of the zoning ordinance for the lot, building, or use. A special agency, often called a board of adjustment or board of zoning appeals, usually grants this relief. Usually, circumstances unique to the parcel must exist, and the hardship must not be self-inflicted. The variance can be subject to conditions to minimize adverse effects on the neighborhood, and the comprehensive plan's intent must be preserved. The variance process is designed to prevent regulatory takings lawsuits when enforcement of the zoning ordinance would inflict unnecessary hardship on a landowner.

Illustration: The Standard State Zoning Enabling Act authorizes the board of adjustment to grant a "variance from the terms of the ordinance as will not be contrary to the public interest, where, owing to special conditions, a literal enforcement of the provisions of the ordinance will result in unnecessary hardship, and so that the spirit of the ordinance shall be observed and substantial justice done."

Illustration: California's zoning enabling legislation provides: "Variances from the terms of the zoning ordinances shall be granted only when, because of special circumstances applicable to the property, including size, shape, topography, location or surroundings, the strict application of the zoning ordinance deprives such property of privileges enjoyed by other property in the vicinity and under identical zoning classification.   Any variance granted shall be subject to such conditions as will assure that the adjustment thereby authorized shall not constitute a grant of special privileges inconsistent with the limitations upon other properties in the vicinity and zone in which such property is situated.   A variance shall not be granted for a parcel of property which authorizes a use or activity which is not otherwise expressly authorized by the zone regulation governing the parcel of property." Cal. Gov't Code § 65906.

Illustration: The zoning ordinance of the District of Columbia provides that its Board of Adjustment may grant a variance when "by reason of exceptional narrowness, shallowness, or shape of a specific piece of property at the time of the original adoption of the regulations or by reason of exceptional topographical conditions or other extraordinary or exceptional situation or condition of a specific piece of property, the strict application of any regulation would result in peculiar and exceptional practical difficulties to or exceptional and undue hardship upon the owner of such property ... to relieve such difficulties or hardship, provided such relief can be granted without substantial detriment to the public good and without substantially impairing the intent, purpose, and integrity of the zone plan as embodied in the zoning regulations and map." D.C. Code § 6-641.07(g)(3).

b. Rezoning (Amendment)

A property owner may seek relief from the existing zoning ordinance by attempting to have it amended. A text amendment is an amendment to the text of the zoning ordinance, such as increasing the height limit or changing the list of activities permitted in a given zone. A map amendment is an amendment to the zoning map that reclassifies a single parcel from one zone to another. The local governing body, such as the city council, amends the zoning ordinance or map, as compared to an administrative agency's grant of a variance or conditional use permit. The distinction may be significant for purposes of judicial review, because courts generally defer more to legislative acts than to administrative acts. However, some courts do not apply the same presumption of validity to rezonings as to the enactment of the original zoning ordinance. When a small parcel is rezoned for its owner's benefit, rather than for the general welfare, a court may characterize it as spot zoning and invalidate it. Many statutes require a supermajority vote by the legislative body, such as a two-thirds vote, to rezone property when a specified percentage of the neighbors have filed a protest against the proposal.

Illustration: Chartiers Township, Pennsylvania rezoned a farm from an agricultural to an industrial district. The court held that the rezoning constituted an invalid spot zoning because it violated the general zoning plan for the township and because it was not in the best interests of the community as a whole. *Baker v. Chartiers Township Zoning Hearing Board*, 677 A.2d 1274 (Pa. Commw. Ct. 1996).

Illustration: Virginia Beach, Virginia rezoned a parcel of land to limit it to agricultural use. Before the rezoning, the land could be used for residential, commercial, and recreational uses. The court held that the rezoning was invalid spot zoning because it was not justified by a "change in circumstances substantially affecting the public health, safety, or welfare" or by evidence of a prior mistake or fraud. *City of Virginia Beach v. Virginia Land Investment Association No. 1*, 389 S.E.2d 312 (Va. 1990).

Illustration: A court invalidated the rezoning of a parcel of land in Washington County, Oregon from single-family residential to "planned residential" to permit a manufactured home park. The court held that the rezoning applicant had not proved a public need for the rezoning and that, even if a public need existed, the applicant had not proved that its parcel would better serve the need than other available property. *Fasano v. Board of County Commissioners*, 507 P.2d 23 (Or. 1973).

c.   Contract Zoning (Conditional Zoning)

Local government may grant a request to upzone a parcel (permit a more intense use) if it imposes restrictions on the proposed use to reduce its adverse effects or if the owner offers inducements that are sufficiently valuable to the community. This type of rezoning may be referred to as "contract zoning" or "conditional zoning." The parcel restrictions may relate to physical conditions, such as reducing the maximum lot coverage, or to the use, such as limiting the use to the one specified in the rezoning application, though the new zoning classification would permit other uses as a matter of right. The owner's inducements might include dedicating part of the land to the community or improving the property, such as by landscaping a twenty-foot strip along the front lot line. To memorialize the agreement, the community may require that it be recorded in the public land records or may expressly condition the rezoning on the owner's fulfillment of the promises. Contract zoning generally is granted on an individual basis, though the general zoning ordinance may expressly provide for it.

Some courts hold that contract zoning violates the principle of zoning uniformity and, therefore, is invalid, because different restrictions are applied to one parcel in a zoning class than apply to the other parcels in that class. Courts also have invalidated contract zoning as a bargaining away of the local police power or as exceeding the regulatory authority that the state delegated to the community. When a court upholds such zoning, it usually observes that the community could have rezoned the

property without the restrictions, th
landowners benefit from them, and th
property owner consented to them
cannot object to them.

Illustration: Landowners alleged that the City of
Fargo had engaged in contract zoning. The court stated
that "contract zoning" occurs "when a local government
contracts away the exercise of its zoning power or
obligates itself by an advance contract to provide a
particular zoning for the benefit of a private landowner."
It further stated that contract zoning is illegal because it
invalidates the city's "duty to exercise independent
judgment in making zoning decisions." The court held
that the City of Fargo had not engaged in contract
zoning because it had not made a private promise to
amend the zoning map. *Hector v. City of Fargo*, 760
N.W.2d 108 (N.D. 2009).

B. SUBDIVISION REGULATION

Local government may impose additional
requirements when land is subdivided into smaller
lots for development and sale. When a large parcel
of land is converted into individual lots, the
community has an obvious interest in ensuring that
the new streets in the subdivision tie into existing
city streets and are not too narrow for fire trucks and
sanitation vehicles. The same concern exists for all
other municipal services, including water and
sewage pipes, parks, playgrounds, and schools.
Local governments often control these features of
the subdivision's development by prohibiting the

..e of subdivided lots until a subdivision map has been governmentally approved and recorded.

Illustration: Section 14 of the Standard City Planning Enabling Act provides that the local "planning commission shall adopt regulations governing the subdivision of land within its jurisdiction. Such regulations may provide for the proper arrangement of streets in relation to other existing or planned streets and to the master plan, for adequate and convenient open spaces for traffic, utilities, access of fire-fighting apparatus, recreation, light and air, and for the avoidance of congestion of population, including minimum width and area of lots. Such regulations may include provisions as to the extent to which streets and other ways shall be graded and improved and to which water and sewer and other utility mains, piping, or other facilities shall be installed as a condition precedent to the approval of the plan." These provisions often are included in a state's Subdivision Map Act.

1. What is a Subdivision?

The state subdivision enabling act usually specifies the type of land division that is subject to local subdivision regulation. Many land divisions are treated as subdivisions for certain purposes but not for others. Subdivisions of fewer than five parcels commonly are exempt from regulations imposed on larger subdivisions, though special provisions may prevent subdividers from evading the regulations by periodic "quartering" of land.

Subdivisions of very large individual parcels, such as one, two, or forty acres, also often are exempted from regulation. An apartment building generally is not treated as a subdivision, even though "the division of the property for lease, sale or financing" is a common definition of "subdivision." However, condominium projects often are treated as "vertical subdivisions," and the conversion of an existing apartment building into a condominium may require local subdivision approval.

2. Subdivision Process

A subdivision is created when a landowner submits to the local government a tentative or preliminary map of a proposed subdivision that shows the location of individual lots, roads, public utilities, and other required elements. The map is reviewed by all interested agencies, such as the fire department to ensure that roads are wide enough for fire trucks and that buildings are spaced far enough apart to avoid a conflagration, the police department, the planning department, the parks department, and the streets department. Each agency can demand changes in the plan to satisfy its standards. If the applicant successfully accommodates these official demands, the proposed map is approved. After the applicant constructs the public improvements shown on the map, a final subdivision map is approved by the government and is recorded in the public records. The subdivider then can sell lots in the subdivision by deeds that refer to the recorded subdivision map for boundary locations. Building permits then are issued to the subdivider or to individual lot buyers if the building plans conform to the applicable zoning and other regulations. Sometimes, a development agreement will be executed between the developer and the government to assure the developer that the rules will not be changed during the lengthy approval process, because of the election of new city officials or for any other reason.

3. Subdivision Exactions (Development Exactions)

A community may require a subdivider to make certain donations to it as a condition for approving the subdivision map. The subdivider may be required to dedicate the subdivision streets to the city, to pay for utility line installations, to dedicate land for parks, schools, or public buildings, or to pay fees in lieu of dedicating land.

Illustration: The California Subdivision Map Act provides: "There may be imposed by local ordinance a requirement that areas of real property be reserved for parks, recreational facilities, fire stations, libraries or other public uses." Another section authorized dedication of land or payment of fees in lieu "for classroom and related facilities for elementary or high schools" where existing schools are overcrowded.

Under a related provision, the City of Walnut Creek imposed a dedication requirement of two and one-half acres of park or recreation land for every 1,000 new residents or an equivalent fee if no park was designated on the master plan and the subdivision was within three-quarters mile of a park or proposed park. *Associated Home Builders of Greater East Bay, Inc. v. City of Walnut Creek,* 484 P.2d 606 (Cal. 1971).

Illustration: The City of Sacramento, California commissioned a study that showed that nonresidential development is "a major factor in attracting new employees to the region" and that the new residents increased the demand for low-income housing. To help finance new low-income housing, the city enacted the Housing Trust Fund Ordinance. The ordinance requires developers to pay a fee as a condition of receiving a building permit for nonresidential development that will create jobs. The fees are paid into a fund that finances low-income housing. *Commercial Builders of Northern California v. City of Sacramento,* 941 F.2d 872 (9th Cit. 1991).

In *Dolan v. City of Tigard,* 512 U.S. 374 (1994), the U.S. Supreme Court held that a development exaction constitutes a taking under the federal Constitution unless (1) an "essential nexus" exists between a legitimate state interest and the exaction and (2) the exaction bears a "rough proportionality" to the projected impact of the proposed development. In *Nollan v. California Coastal Commission,* 483 U.S. 825 (1987), the Supreme Court held that the California Coastal

Commission's demand for a public easement across the owners' beach as a condition for a building permit to rebuild their house constituted an impermissible taking because there was no "nexus" between the demand (for access from one coastal lot to the next) and the harm the Commission was attempting to alleviate (loss of view of the coast from the street in front of the house).

State courts have not adopted a uniform standard for determining the validity of subdivision exactions under their state constitution. The strictest view requires that the exaction be specifically and uniquely attributable to the subdivision activity. The most lenient standard is that the exaction must be reasonably related to the subdivision residents' projected use of public facilities, such as parks, schools, and streets.

C. GROWTH MANAGEMENT

A community may regulate its rate of residential growth to reduce the burden that new residents impose on municipal services and budgets. Zoning and subdivision regulations often indirectly inhibit growth by reducing the supply of land available for development (e.g. open space zoning, large minimum lot sizes), by pricing out much lower-cost housing (e.g. exclusion of apartments and manufactured home communities), or by restricting users (prohibiting more than a specified number of unrelated people from living together in a single-family residential zone).   In contrast, growth management regulations address this issue directly by restricting the number of residential building permits that can be issued. Some of the numerous techniques for restricting growth are described in the following Illustrations.

Illustration—Moratorium: In response to high density residential development in its service area, the Clear Lake City Water Authority, a Texas political subdivision, instituted a moratorium on service to any new multi-family residential development until a new sewage treatment plant was constructed. *Kaplan v. Clear Lake City Water Authority*, 794 F.2d 1059 (5th Cir. 1986).

Illustration—Cap: A Boca Raton, Florida initiative ordinance limited the total number of homes in the city to 40,000. *Boca Raton v. Boca Villas Corp.,* 371 So. 2d 154 (Fla. Dist. Ct. App. 1979) (cap invalid).

Illustration—Points: In Ramapo, New York, a building could not be erected until the property owner acquired a specified number of points based on the availability of sewage, drainage, parks and recreation, roads, and firehouses. The developer could increase the point count by providing the services, rather than waiting for the town to supply them. *Golden v. Ramapo Planning Board,* 285 N.E.2d 291 (1972).

Illustration—Quota: Petaluma, California issued only 500 building permits per year for residential projects of more than four units. Permits were awarded according to a point system similar to Ramapo's.   Additional points were awarded for design and environmental amenities, low- and moderate-income housing units, and geographical balance of new development throughout the town. *Construction Industry Association of Sonoma County v. City of Petaluma,* 522 F.2d 897 (9th Cir. 1975).

Illustration—Percentage: Clifton Park, New York enacted a law that limited the number of building permits that could be issued each year. A developer could get a permit for only 20% of the total units in a project that the town already had approved. *Albany Area Builders Association v. Town of Clifton Park,* 576 N.Y.S.2d 932 (N.Y. App. Div. 1991).

D. HISTORIC LANDMARKS AND DISTRICTS

Many communities protect their historic buildings and neighborhoods by specially designating them and subjecting them to stringent design control. The owner of a property designated as a landmark or located within a historic district is prohibited from altering its external appearance without obtaining a permit from the appropriate regulatory agency.   In return, the owner may be given a property tax reduction or may be permitted to use the building in an otherwise unpermitted manner to generate an economic return.   In some situations, the community may purchase a preservation easement in the facade or structure, thereby eliminating the owner's right to destroy its historic features.

Illustration: The Louisiana Constitution created the Vieux Carré Commission, which regulates historic architecture in the French Quarter of New Orleans. No building can be altered and no sign can be displayed without a permit from the Commission. The Commission also can grant property tax exemptions for such buildings. La. Const. art. VI, § 17.

Illustration: By statute, cities in New York are "empowered to provide by regulations, special conditions and restrictions for the protection, enhancement, perpetuation and use of places, districts, sites, buildings, structures, works of art, and other objects having a special character or special historical or aesthetic interest or value. Such regulations ... may include appropriate and reasonable control of the use or appearance of neighboring private property within public view, or both." If the measure constitutes "a taking of private property [it] shall provide for due compensation, which may include the limitation or remission of taxes." N.Y. Gen. Mun. Law § 96-a.

Illustration: Based on the above statute, New York City permits an area to be designated as a historic district subject to special regulation if it contains improvements that "(a) have a special character or special historical or aesthetic interest or value; and (b) represent one or more periods or styles of architecture typical of one or more eras in the history of the city; and (c) cause such area, by reason of such factors, to constitute a distinct section of the city." A landmark is "any improvement, any part of which is thirty years old or older, which has a special character or special historical or aesthetic interest or value as part of the development, heritage or cultural characteristics of the city, state or nation and which has been designated as a landmark...."   N.Y.C. Code §§ 25-302 & 25-303. Pursuant to the ordinance, the City refused to permit the owner of Grand Central Station to erect an office building over it. *Penn Central Transportation Co. v. City of New York,* 438 U.S. 104 (1978).

E. ENVIRONMENTAL PROTECTION

State law may require local government to study the environmental effects of any action it considers taking, including granting approval for private land development.   The appropriate agency may be required to prepare an environmental impact statement or report before approving a subdivision, rezoning land, or granting any other form of development permit.   The requirement may be entirely procedural and require a study without dictating the agency's response to unfavorable data. Or the law may include a substantive requirement that the agency avoid adverse environmental effects.

Illustration: The California Environmental Quality Act requires all agencies that regulate private individuals' activities, including "the issuance to a person of a lease, permit, license, certificate, or other entitlement for use," to give major consideration to preventing environmental damage.   An environmental impact report must be prepared that identifies the project's significant environmental effects, identifies alternatives, and indicates how the significant effects can be mitigated or avoided.   An agency should not approve a project if feasible alternatives or mitigation measures substantially would lessen the adverse environmental effects, unless economic, social, or other conditions make the alternatives or mitigation measures infeasible. Cal. Pub. Res. Code §§ 21000-21178.1.

To address the problem of environmentally contaminated land, the federal Comprehensive Environmental Response, Compensation and Liability Act (CERCLA, commonly referred to as Superfund), 42 U.S.C. §§ 9601–75, and comparable state laws impose a duty on landowners, among others, to eliminate the contamination. The landowner is absolutely liable even if he was not the polluter, unless he comes within the "innocent owner" exception by showing that the contamination was caused by a third party who was neither his agent nor in a "contractual relationship" with him. A deed creates a contractual relationship between a buyer and seller, thus making the current owner responsible for previous owners' activities. However, the current owner is not liable if he acquired the property after it was contaminated and "had no reason to know" about the contamination after making "all appropriate inquiry into the previous ownership and uses of the property," exercising due care, and taking appropriate precautions against third parties' "foreseeable acts or omissions." This liability exception effectively requires every purchaser to make a due diligence investigation and environmental audit of the property's condition and to negotiate with the vendor for appropriate contractual protections relating to liability for known or later discovered contamination.

F. EMINENT DOMAIN

Government can control land use directly by acquiring property and exercising the prerogatives of an owner over it. Communities usually manage parks, civil buildings, airports, and similar public amenities and services in this way. If the private owner of a desired parcel is unwilling to sell, the government can compel its transfer through an eminent domain (condemnation) action. In such a proceeding, the government must prove a "public use" for the acquisition. Courts normally defer to legislative determinations as to public use. However, some state courts impose a more stringent public use requirement.

Illustration: To create jobs, to generate tax revenue, and to revitalize the city, New London, Connecticut sought to acquire land by eminent domain that would be leased to private companies and that would not be open to the public. The U.S. Supreme Court held that, because economic development is a valid government function, the land acquisitions would satisfy the public use requirement of the federal Constitution. *Kelo v. City of New London*, 545 U.S. 469 (2005).

Illustration: The City of Norwood, Ohio brought a condemnation action to acquire land that it intended to transfer to a private developer as part of an urban renewal plan for a deteriorating area. The court held that the economic benefits to the government and to the community from the redevelopment do not satisfy the public use requirement of the Ohio Constitution. *City of Norwood v. Horney*, 853 N.E.2d 1115 (Ohio 2006).

When the government takes property, it must pay "just compensation" for it. A jury determines the amount after hearing evidence concerning the property's fair market value. In certain cases, the government can take land immediately and pay the owner later after the fair market value has been determined.

II. LAND USE REGULATION PROCESS

A. WHO MAY REGULATE LAND

1. Federal Regulation

The federal government regulates all land that it owns or administers, such as national forest land. By virtue of its constitutional supremacy, the federal government is not subject to state or local laws for land that it regulates. Although no comprehensive federal zoning or national land use plan exists in the United States, the federal government plays a significant indirect role in the regulation of land uses through its commerce and budgetary powers.

Illustration: Army Corps of Engineers approval is required to discharge dredged or fill material into waters that are covered by the Federal Water Pollution Control Act. 33 U.S.C.A. § 1413.

Illustration: Under the 1970 Clean Air Amendments to the Clean Air Act, state and local governments must submit plans for improving air quality to the federal Environmental Protection Agency. These plans may include matters such as the location of shopping centers, sports complexes, sewer lines, and industrial developments. 42 U.S.C.A. § 7410.

2. State Regulation

Certain areas of a state, such as critical environmental areas, may be subject to a direct state permitting process in addition to or in lieu of the local process. Alternatively, a state may classify lands within its borders and limit local control to regulation within those classifications.

Illustration: In Hawaii, the State Land Use Commission classified all land as urban, rural, agricultural, or conservation and restricted the permissible activities within those classifications. Although counties may adopt more stringent regulations in each district, the state controls land use decisions in the conservation districts. However, enforcement is a county, rather than state, responsibility. Haw. Code R. §§ 15-15-17 – 15-15-22.

Illustration: In Vermont, a building or development permit for many types of land uses must be obtained not only from the local agency, but also from a state agency. Vt. Stat. Ann., tit. 10, § 6081.

3. Regional Regulation

A regional agency that operates below the state level but above the local level may have authority to regulate certain lands. The communities within the region may create the agency, or the state may create it because of a statewide interest in the area.

Illustration: Minnesota statutorily authorizes two or more counties, cities, or towns to enter into an agreement to conduct regional planning activities. The agreement must provide for a regional planning board that will prepare a regional development plan for review by the participating government units. Minn. Stat. §§ 462.371-462.375.

Illustration: A California statute provides that no significant development work can be performed along the San Francisco Bay coastline without a permit from the San Francisco Bay Conservation and Development Commission. This permit does not excuse the obligation to obtain all necessary local permits. Cal. Gov't Code § 66632.

Illustration: The Tahoe Regional Planning Agency (TRPA) was created by California and Nevada statutes and was ratified by an act of Congress. The Agency must ensure that all projects in the area comply with its regional general plan, ordinances, rules, regulations, and policies.   While local municipalities may enact their own land use ordinances, they may not be less stringent than those promulgated by TRPA. TRPA is composed of two separate state groups, CTRPA and NTRPA. TRPA cannot approve a project unless a majority of both CTRPA's and NTRPA's delegates to TRPA vote favorably.

4. Local Regulation

Power to regulate land is vested in the state. State legislatures generally have delegated that power to cities and counties by means of a zoning enabling act, subdivision enabling act, and similar forms of statutory authorization. These statutes both enable and set limits for local land regulation. A court will invalidate a land use regulation as being ultra vires if the enabling act does not authorize it.

Illustration: The Standard State Zoning Enabling Act, which the United States Department of Commerce originally prepared in 1928, provides that cities are empowered "to regulate and restrict the height, number of stories, and size of buildings and other structures, the percentage of lot that may be occupied, the size of yards, courts, and other open spaces, the density of population, and the location and use of buildings, structures, and land for trade, industry, residence, or other purposes."

Illustration: The American Law Institute Model Land Development Code (1976) provides that a local government is "authorized to plan or otherwise encourage, regulate, or undertake the development of land in accordance with this code."

Illustration: The California Government Code provides that counties and cities may: "(a) Regulate the use of buildings, structures, and land as between industry, business, residences, open space, including agriculture, recreation, enjoyment of scenic beauty, use of natural resources, and other purposes. (b) Regulate signs and billboards. (c) Regulate ... (1) The location, height, bulk, number of stories, and size of buildings and structures; (2) The size and use of lots, yards, courts, and other open spaces; (3) The percentage of a lot which may be occupied by a building or structure; (4) The intensity of land use. (d) Establish requirements for offstreet parking and loading. (e) Establish and maintain building setback lines. (f) Create civic districts around civic centers, public parks, public buildings, or public grounds, and establish regulations for those civic districts." Cal. Gov't Code § 65850.

Because most local land use regulation requires state authorization, any novel regulation may be challenged on the ground that it is unauthorized. Several issues have arisen in interpreting enabling legislation, such as whether (1) delegated power to regulate land subdivision and building construction includes the power to control or to slow growth; (2) the power to regulate building bulk includes design or architectural review; (3) the power to regulate subdivisions includes the power to compel subdivision exactions; (4) the initiative and referendum process can be used; and (5) the requirements of mapping and of uniform regulations in a zone prohibit flexibility devices such as floating zones and planned unit developments. Courts resolve these issues based on the state enabling act's language and the court's attitude toward local innovation.

5. Citizen Regulation

When citizens are unhappy about local land use decisions, they may take matters into their own hands. Voters may have the power of referendum to nullify official actions that already have been taken or the power of initiative to enact laws. Many significant land use decisions have been made in the initiative process or have been repudiated by referenda. Height limits and growth restrictions often are created by the initiative process. Referenda often are used to overturn the approval of a large scale commercial or residential project.

Illustration: The voters of Eastlake, Ohio amended the city charter to provide that, when the city council grants a rezoning, "it shall be mandatory that the same be approved by a 55% favorable vote of all votes cast of the qualified electors of the City of Eastlake at the next regular municipal election, if one shall occur not less than sixty (60) or more than one hundred and twenty (120) days after its passage, otherwise at a special election...." *City of Eastlake v. Forest City Enterprises, Inc.,* 426 U.S. 668 (1976).

Illustration: Article XXXIV, § 1 of the California Constitution provides: "No low rent housing project shall hereafter be developed, constructed, or acquired in any manner by any state public body until a majority of the qualified electors of the city, town or county, as the case may be, in which it is proposed to develop, construct, or acquire the same, voting upon such issue, approve such project by voting in favor thereof at an election to be held for that purpose, or at any general or special election." *James v. Valtierra,* 402 U.S. 137 (1971).

Initiatives and referenda cannot be used in every state for land use regulations. The enabling act's procedural requirements concerning planning department studies, consistency with the comprehensive plan, and notice and hearing rights may prohibit use of an electoral process that does not provide such safeguards. Some courts permit the referendum but not the initiative because the required preliminary and procedural steps are preserved in a referendum; it merely adds voter ratification to the process. Other courts permit both referenda and initiatives but limit their use to matters of general land use regulation. In this type of jurisdiction, an initiative or referendum cannot be used for small parcel rezonings, because the action is more properly characterized as administrative or quasijudicial, rather than as legislative.

B. PLANNING PROCESS

1. Comprehensive Plan

State enabling acts generally provide that local land use regulation must be done in conjunction with planning. Some courts interpret this type of provision as requiring no more than some forethought and generalized consideration of the community's needs, rather than an impulsive response to an isolated development. At the other extreme, some courts invalidate land use regulations if they were enacted before the adoption of a comprehensive plan (master plan, general plan) that sets forth the community's goals and policies. Finally, some courts interpret a planning requirement as mandating that all future land use regulations be consistent with the plan.

Illustration: Sections 6 and 7 of the Standard City Planning Enabling Act, which the U.S. Department of Commerce prepared in 1928, provides that the local planning commission shall prepare "a master plan for the physical development of the municipality, ... including, among other things, the general location, character, and extent of streets, viaducts, subways, bridges, waterways, water fronts, boulevards, parkways, playgrounds, squares, parks, aviation fields, and other public ways, grounds and open spaces, the general location of public buildings and other public property, and the general location and extent of public utilities and terminals, whether publicly or privately owned or operated, for water, light, sanitation, transportation, communication, power, and other purposes; also the removal, relocation, widening, narrowing, vacating, abandonment, change of use or extension of any of the foregoing ways, grounds, open spaces, buildings, property, utilities, or terminals; as well as a zoning plan for the control of the height, area, bulk, location, and use of buildings and premises.... The plan shall be made with the general purpose of guiding and accomplishing a coordinated, adjusted, and harmonious development of the municipality and its environs which will, in accordance with present and future needs, best promote health, safety, morals, order, convenience, prosperity, and general welfare, as well as efficiency and economy in the process of development; including, among other things, adequate provision for traffic, the promotion of safety from fire and other dangers, adequate provision for light and air, the promotion of the healthful and convenient distribution of population, the promotion of good civic design and arrangement, wise and efficient expenditure of public funds, and the adequate provision of public utilities and other public requirements."

Illustration: Section 3–101 of the ALI Model Land Development Code (1976) provides: "A local government may adopt a Local Land Development Plan (in words, maps, illustrations or other media of communication) setting forth objectives, policies and standards to guide public and private development of land within its planning jurisdiction and including a short-term program of public actions."

2. Planning Commission

A local planning commission conducts many communities' planning activities. Most commissions are assisted by a city planning department that is staffed by professional city planners. The planning commission normally is composed of community members who are appointed by the local legislative body. The planning commission is responsible for various tasks regarding the master plan and land use ordinances.

Illustration: The Florida enabling act provides that a local planning agency shall:

> (a) Be the agency responsible for the preparation of the comprehensive plan or plan amendment and shall make recommendations to the governing body regarding the adoption or amendment of such plan....
>
> (b) Monitor and oversee the effectiveness and status of the comprehensive plan and recommend to the governing body such changes in the comprehensive plan as may from time to time be required....
>
> (c) Review proposed land development regulations, land development codes, or amendments thereto, and make recommendations to the governing body as to the consistency of the proposal with the adopted comprehensive plan....

Fla. Stat. § 163.3174(4).

3. Land Use Ordinances

The local legislative body usually enacts the land use plan and ordinances based on the planning commission's recommendation and on public hearings. The legislative body also adopts the official zoning map and decides all proposed amendments to the map, zoning ordinance, or comprehensive plan. The legislative body usually is not involved in the approval of subdivision maps or of applications for special exceptions or variances, though it may review such decisions.

4. Interim Ordinances

To protect the proposed regulatory scheme from nonconforming land development before the regulations are enacted, the state enabling act may permit a community to enact a land use regulation without first drafting a comprehensive plan or holding public hearings. This emergency or interim power may be limited in time, such as eighteen months, or to certain forms of government action, such as prohibitions but not permissions. An interim ordinance also may have to be approved by a special supermajority of the local legislative body.

C. ENFORCEMENT

Permitting and recording requirements are designed to stop impermissible land use activities before they begin. For example, a subdivider cannot record the necessary subdivision map if it does not satisfy the subdivision ordinance. Similarly, a building permit will be denied if the proposed building does not conform to the zoning and building regulations. Despite these precautions, a property owner may violate a land use law. In that case, the community may sue to enjoin an improper activity or to demolish an illegal structure, may seek criminal sanctions, or may employ self-help. In some states, transfer of noncomplying property is unlawful or gives the transferee a right of rescission. A pre-transfer code inspection may be required, or the community may have authority to record an ordinance violation notice to cloud the owner's title. Enforcement of land use regulations usually is vested exclusively in local officials, though neighbors sometimes can sue to enjoin illegal activities or to recover damages for a violation.

1. Nonconforming Uses

Land use regulations generally apply only prospectively and do not apply to buildings or activities that existed before the regulation's effective date. Originally, it was assumed that nonconforming uses would disappear naturally over time, but such structures and activities instead tend to endure by virtue of their monopolistic advantages. Consequently, many communities now attempt to use their zoning regulations to eliminate them. Courts generally do not permit the immediate abatement of nonconforming structures or uses but may allow a community to "amortize" them by limiting the limited amount of time they can continue. The community also may prohibit a nonconforming structure from being enlarged, altered, put to any other nonconforming use, or continued after a nonconforming use has been abandoned or a nonconforming structure has been destroyed.

Illustration: In 1945, a landowner in the Village of Westhampton Beach, New York began using its land for an asphalt plant. In 1985, amendments to the zoning code made the plant a nonconforming use. In 2000, the Village Board of Trustees enacted a law that required the owner to stop operating the plant in 2005. The court held that the validity of the amortization period depends on its reasonableness in light of the owner's investment in the plant and the adverse effects the plant has on neighboring properties. *Suffolk Asphalt Supply, Inc. v. Village of Westhampton Beach*, 872 N.Y.S.2d 516 (N.Y. App. Div. 2009).

Illustration: A Denver, Colorado ordinance concerning nonconforming uses provided that "no change whatsoever in any aspect of and feature of or in the character of the non-conforming use is permitted if the non-conforming use is to continue." Based on this ordinance, a court would not allow the owners of a nonconforming gas station to install an automated car wash in one of the station's three service bays. *Anderson v. Denver Board of Adjustment for Zoning Appeals*, 931 P.2d 517 (Colo. Ct. App. 1996).

Illustration: A Myrtle Beach, South Carolina sign ordinance provided: "[A]ny sign structure that no longer displays any sign copy shall be deemed to be an obsolete or abandoned sign." The owner of a nonconforming rooftop sign structure did not display a sign on it for five years. The city tried to prevent the owner from erecting a new sign by arguing that the nonconforming use had been abandoned. The court permitted the sign because the structure owner had not intended to abandon, which is a common law requirement. *City of Myrtle Beach v. Juel P. Corporation*, 543 S.E.2d 538 (S.C. 2001).

III. JUDICIAL REVIEW

A. THE JUDICIAL ROLE

Courts consider the validity of local regulatory actions in a variety of contexts. Suit may be brought by (1) the government to compel an owner to comply with regulations; (2) an owner or parties supporting her, such as brokers and contractors, to invalidate the regulations; (3) a neighbor or neighborhood organization to force government to reject the owner's proposal or to enforce some restriction against the owner; or (4) interested outsiders, such as housing and welfare organizations, to invalidate "exclusionary" activities. If the court is reviewing legislation, it generally employs the "arbitrary and capricious" standard and invalidates the legislation only if it is not a rational means to achieve a legitimate end. However, if the legislation infringes on a constitutionally protected interest, courts apply a "strict scrutiny" test and require a compelling state interest to uphold the legislation. If the action is adjudicatory (quasi-judicial or administrative), rather than legislative, the standard of review generally is "abuse of discretion," and the court determines whether "substantial evidence" in the record supports the action. If a fundamental or vested right is involved, the court may make an independent judgment in the matter, rather than merely reviewing the agency action.

Many courts characterize a land use action as legislative if it was taken by a legislative body and is legislative in form. Thus, zoning and rezoning are legislative acts because the city council or other unit of local government performs them. In contrast, a planning commission's grant of a special exception or a board of adjustment's grant of a variance is adjudicatory. Other courts reject this approach as being too formalistic and instead examine the nature and content of the action. For example, rezoning a small parcel of land might be held to be adjudicatory under this analysis.

In general, courts attempt to avoid making substantive zoning decisions. They do not want to serve as super-zoning boards that substitute their judgment for that of experts and local officials. However, courts do not hesitate to intervene on questions of procedural fairness or protection of basic rights.

B. GROUNDS FOR INVALIDATION

A person aggrieved by a land use regulation may judicially challenge the regulation or its application. Many of the bases for such challenges already have been discussed. For example, a plaintiff may assert that the community did not have authority under the state enabling act (ultra vires). Architectural review, historic preservation, and growth management activities frequently have been challenged on that basis. A plaintiff also might allege that the legislative body improperly delegated authority. This challenge often has been raised against design review boards and neighborhood consent ordinances, which require block or neighborhood approval as a precondition to granting a permit to engage in an otherwise lawful activity.

1. Arbitrary and Capricious

A land use regulation is invalid if it is arbitrary and capricious. This challenge often is made to the zoning classification applied to an individual parcel of land or to the distinction between permissible and impermissible activities in a zoning district.

Illustration: A court invalidated a James City County, Virginia zoning ordinance because it made the following distinctions: "Hotels, motels, and theatres are permitted; banks, office buildings, and grocery stores are prohibited. 'Antique shops' are permitted; shops selling antique reproductions are prohibited; 'Restaurants' are permitted; 'fast food' or 'drive-in' restaurants are prohibited. Gift shops are permitted, provided they are 'accessory to hotels or motels having 50 or more dwelling or lodging units' and are 'designed and scaled only to meet the requirements of occupants and their guests'; other retail stores selling identical gifts are prohibited." *Board of Supervisors of James City County v. Rowe,* 216 S.E.2d 199 (Va. 1975).

Illustration: Based on environmental concerns, Warren Township, New Jersey rezoned a portion of the township to substantially restrict the number of new homes that could be built. Before the rezoning, the plaintiff-owner of a 29-acre parcel could build single-family homes on one and one-half acre lots. After the rezoning, the minimum lot size was six acres. Based on the trial court's finding that the 29-acre parcel did not present the environmental concerns that had prompted the rezoning, the court held that the rezoning was arbitrary and capricious as applied to that parcel of land. *Pheasant Bridge Corporation v. Township of Warren,* 777A.2d 334 (N.J. 2001).

Judicial invalidation in such cases is not always expressly based on the arbitrary and capricious standard. The court may hold that the government action is inconsistent with the comprehensive plan or is ultra vires. A court also may characterize the irrational distinction as a denial of equal protection or substantive due process for the affected owner.

2. Due Process

A person whose property interest will be affected by a government land use decision is entitled to procedural fairness. Procedural due process issues arise in numerous ways in the land use process. When notice is required, questions may exist concerning the form of communication (mail, publication, or posting), the persons entitled to receive it (property owners only, tenants, local residents, or neighbors outside the municipal boundary), the adequacy of the information provided (identifying the affected property or the proposed measure), and whether the government action is administrative, which requires individual notices to all affected parties, or legislative, which requires only general public notice. With respect to the hearing, questions may exist concerning whether the issues at the hearing are the same as those described in the notice, who has the right to speak and to present evidence, the right to cross-examine, taking unsworn or opinion testimony (including staff reports, field trips, and neighbors' opinions), and adequacy of the hearing record. The decision-making process may raise questions concerning conflict of interest and bias (personal involvement, campaign contributions, ex parte contacts). The initiative or referendum process also raises procedural questions.

Unlike most other areas of law, substantive due process is alive and well in the context of land use regulation. Based on this constitutional protection, courts consider whether (1) the regulatory action has a valid public purpose, (2) the action is a reasonable means to accomplish the purpose, and (3) the public good outweighs the landowner's private loss. The court will invalidate a land use action if it arbitrary and capricious. If it affects a fundamental right, the action must be necessary to achieve a compelling government interest.

3. First Amendment and Associational Rights

When a land use restriction infringes a First Amendment or other constitutional right, the normal presumption of validity and the attendant judicial deference may not apply, particularly for regulations affecting speech, religious activities, and family associations.

a. Speech and Religion

Signs and billboards clearly convey messages to their readers. Although communities may regulate their size, shape, illumination, and placement, other types of restrictions are more subject to challenge. For example, restrictions relating to political signs are allowed only when alternative methods of communication are available. Commercial speech is less protected than political speech, but the scope of protection for commercial speech has not been definitively stated.   The leading United States Supreme Court decision on sign regulations, *Metromedia, Inc. v. City of San Diego,* 453 U.S. 490 (1981), had no majority position and included five separate opinions.   The Court invalidated an ordinance that prohibited off-site advertising (advertising that does not relate to goods sold on the premises) but permitted on-site signs.

Land use regulations affecting other constitutionally protected activities also may be subject to special scrutiny.   For example, in some jurisdictions, churches have a preferred status and are exempt from many zoning regulations.   Schools, bookstores, and movie theaters are similarly protected in differing degrees.   However, judicial validation of special zoning treatment for sexually oriented theaters and bookstores appears to permit some degree of content regulation.

Illustration: A Mount Ephraim, New Jersey ordinance excluded live entertainment throughout the borough.   The United States Supreme Court invalidated the ordinance because it was an overbroad prohibition against protected forms of expression.   The Court set aside the conviction of a bookstore proprietor for permitting nude dancing on the premises.   *Schad v. Borough of Mount Ephraim,* 452 U.S. 61 (1981).

b. Association

A court also may invalidate an ordinance that infringes on the right of association.   For example, a court may hold that a single-family residential district unconstitutionally intrudes on associational or privacy rights if it excludes occupants based on their relationship to each other, such as a group of unrelated persons living together, rather than based on the residential characteristics of the structure, such as the number of kitchens or the square footage.

Illustration: The single-family zoning ordinance of Belle Terre, New York prohibited more than two unrelated individuals from living together, though any number of related persons could share a residence. The United States Supreme Court upheld the ordinance against charges that it infringed on rights of privacy and association. *Village of Belle Terre v. Boraas,* 416 U.S. 1 (1974).   On the other hand, the Supreme Court invalidated an ordinance that was applied to prohibit a grandmother from residing with her son and two grandsons, who were first cousins.   The Court held that the ordinance constituted an improper intrusion into family living arrangements in violation of substantive due process.   *Moore v. City of East Cleveland,* 431 U.S. 494 (1977).

4. Taking

A land use regulation that severely burdens property may constitute an unconstitutional taking of property ("regulatory taking" or "inverse condemnation") under the Fifth or Fourteenth Amendment of the United States Constitution or a similar state constitutional provision. The courts have been unable to reach a consensus or single theory as to when a regulation amounts to an invalid taking of property except in two types of cases.

Illustration: A 1921 Pennsylvania statute prohibited the mining of anthracite coal if removal would cause residences on the land surface to subside. The U.S. Supreme Court invalidated the statute as an unconstitutional taking of the coal company's property rights in the coal that it could no longer mine. *Pennsylvania Coal Co. v. Mahon,* 260 U.S. 393 (1922).

Illustration: A 1966 Pennsylvania statute prohibited the mining of bituminous coal if removal would cause residences and public structures on the surface to subside. The U.S. Supreme Court upheld the statute because it protects the public interests in health, the environment, and "fiscal integrity." The Court held that the statute did not cause a taking of property. *Keystone Bituminous Coal Ass'n v. DeBenedictis,* 480 U.S. 470 (1987).

a.   Categorical Takings

If a law authorizes a permanent physical occupation of land or completely destroys its value, the U.S. Supreme Court has held that the law takes land regardless of its public purpose. These two types of cases are called "categorical takings."

Illustration: A New York statute authorized cable television companies to install lines and boxes on the roofs of apartment buildings. The U.S. Supreme Court held that the landlord's property had been taken, because the statute authorized a permanent physical occupation. Although there was only minimal physical interference with property, the owner's right to exclude was violated. *Loretto v. Teleprompter Manhattan CATV Corp.,* 458 U.S. 419 (1982).

Illustration: Because the state's Beachfront Management Act prohibited the owner of two beachfront lots from building houses on them, the state trial court found that he was deprived of all economic use of his property. The United States Supreme Court held that a complete destruction of value constitutes a taking of property unless common law nuisance rules would have prevented the regulated use. *Lucas v. South Carolina Coastal Council,* 505 U.S. 1003 (1992).

b. Other Regulatory Takings

If an alleged taking is not categorical, courts examine a variety of factors to determine whether just compensation is due. The most important factors are:

(1) Nature of Government Activity

Courts in early cases focused on the formal nature of the government activity. If government physically took possession or took title to property, it had to pay just compensation. If government activity injured property, it might be liable in trespass or nuisance. On the other hand, if a government regulation merely caused the property's value to decline, a taking did not occur, because title, possession, and the property's physical condition were unaffected. Today, courts generally reject these distinctions and recognize that government may take land by severe regulation as much as by the institution of formal eminent domain proceedings.

Courts sometimes say that the more government activity resembles the acquisition of resources for itself, rather than the regulation of competing private interests, the more likely it is that a taking has occurred. Thus, downzoning property (i.e. allowing less intense use) adjacent to the municipal airport may be viewed as the community's attempt to avoid purchasing the property or paying nuisance damages to the owner. Thus, a taking has occurred. In contrast, the same downzoning might be valid if it is done to protect an adjacent residential neighborhood from industrial intrusion.

(2) Nature of Owner's Property Interest

Not all losses of value are takings. Courts use phrases such as "distinct investment-backed expectations" or "vested rights" to indicate the most protected property interests. The loss of value when undeveloped property is downzoned is not as likely to be a taking as when an existing use or structure must be eliminated.

(3) Extent of Loss

A loss of property value due to a new regulation does not automatically mean that government has taken property. A taking occurs only when the reduction goes "too far."

Illustration: A new zoning ordinance caused property values to drop from $10,000 to $2,500 per acre. The United States Supreme Court upheld the ordinance. *Village of Euclid v. Ambler Realty Co.,* 272 U.S. 365 (1926). Restrictions causing losses of 87% and 95% have been sustained in other cases from the Supreme Court and the Ninth Circuit, respectively.

Illustration: A New York City landmark preservation ordinance was applied to prohibit a railroad company from constructing a skyscraper over Grand Central Station. The U.S. Supreme Court held that the owner had not suffered a taking of the right to exploit a potential property right (annual rental income of $3 million for the airspace) because the owner was earning a reasonable return on the existing structure. *Penn Central Transportation Co. v. City of New York,* 438 U.S. 104 (1978).

The loss' duration often is relevant. For example, a temporary moratorium on land development may be upheld, though the property has almost no economic value during the moratorium. Courts often uphold growth management ordinances that postpone an owner's right to develop for several years on the ground that the loss is only temporary.

Illustration: To protect Lake Tahoe from further environmental degradation, a 32-month building moratorium was imposed on the property in the Lake Tahoe Basin. The affected landowners argued that their lands were totally valueless during the moratorium period and that they thereby suffered a categorical taking. The U.S. Supreme Court held that a taking had not occurred because the moratorium was temporary. *Tahoe-Sierra Preservation Council, Inc. v. Tahoe Regional Planning Agency*, 535 U.S. 302 (2002).

(4) Sharing the Loss (Average Reciprocity of Advantage)

A court is more likely to uphold an ordinance that similarly restricts everyone, such as a uniform height limit, than an ordinance that subjects one parcel to an economic loss for the sake of others. Landmark designation, which restricts individual buildings, sometimes is attacked on this basis. Courts uphold landmark designation when it is part of a comprehensive plan or when the landmark owner benefits by the designation of other landmarks within the community. Reverse spot zoning—the downzoning of one parcel for the benefit of others—also may be invalidated on this ground.

(5) Mitigation and Compensation Measures

A major purpose for variances is to provide an administrative mechanism for avoiding the taking of property. If a variance is available for a hardship situation, a property owner may lose his ability to contend that the ordinance causes a taking of his property.

Some land use ordinances provide offsetting compensation. For example, tax abatement is common for buildings designated as a landmark. Some communities have "transferable development right" systems that permit an owner of restricted property to transfer the unused development potential to other land in the community.

c. Relief

Although a court may invalidate an overly restrictive ordinance, owners fear that officials will merely enact a different, but similarly repressive, alternative. Therefore, aggrieved owners often seek to recover damages instead of or in addition to invalidation. In *First English Evangelical Lutheran Church v. County of Los Angeles,* 482 U.S. 304 (1987), the United States Supreme Court held the Constitution requires payment of compensation for the time during which a regulation denies an owner use of her land even if the regulation is repealed.

5. Exclusionary Zoning

Many communities enact land use regulations or operate their land use permit processes to prevent certain classes of persons from residing there. The communities may be motivated by racial discrimination or by a desire to save money by keeping out the poor, who may pay little in taxes but may require extensive social services, or families with children, who increase the burden on schools. Many conventional land use devices, such as minimum lot sizes, costly building code requirements, and elimination of apartment and manufactured home districts, can produce this effect while appearing to be facially neutral and ostensibly justifiable on environmental and public health grounds. Civil rights and fair housing organizations often challenge these exclusionary devices on the ground that communities are engaging in illegal discrimination or are attempting to avoid housing their fair share of the region's lower income residents.

a. Federal Courts

(1) Constitutional Protection

The United States Constitution does not expressly prohibit a community from exercising its land use powers in an exclusionary fashion. However, if the exclusion is racially motivated, it may violate the Equal Protection or Due Process Clause.

Illustration: A Louisville, Kentucky ordinance prohibited a person of color from residing on a block that was predominantly white and vice versa. The United States Supreme Court held that the ordinance constituted an unconstitutional interference with property rights.   *Buchanan v. Warley,* 245 U.S. 60 (1917).

The federal Constitution has been an ineffective tool for challenging exclusionary devices in all but the most blatant cases for three reasons.   First, courts have interpreted the Constitution as requiring more than a disproportionate impact on one race. The challenged activity must have been undertaken with a discriminatory purpose or intent.   Second, income level, unlike race, is not a suspect classification.   Poverty triggers the strict scrutiny standard of review only when the poor are absolutely deprived of a meaningful opportunity to enjoy a necessary benefit.   But the U.S. Supreme Court has held that housing is not a fundamental right.   *Lindsey v. Normet*, 405 U.S. 56 (1972). Finally, the standing requirement for exclusionary zoning litigation in federal court is difficult.   A plaintiff must prove that some specific housing would have been available but for the exclusionary community action.

Illustration: A court held that a one-acre minimum lot size ordinance in Los Altos Hills, California did not deny Mexican-Americans equal protection though it tended to exclude them. The town did not have to show a compelling interest to justify its ordinance, because no showing was made that adequate low-cost housing was unavailable elsewhere in the county and because wealthy Mexican-Americans were not excluded. *Ybarra v. Town of Los Altos Hills,* 503 F.2d 250 (9th Cir. 1974).

Illustration: Arlington Heights, Illinois refused to rezone a fifteen-acre parcel from single-family to multi-family to permit construction of a federally-assisted housing project of 190 units for low- and moderate-income tenants.   The U.S. Supreme Court held that the Village had not violated the Fourteenth Amendment, because the plaintiffs did not prove racially discriminatory intent or purpose, though only .0004% of the Village's population was African-American.   The evidence demonstrated typical and legitimate zoning reasons for the refusal.   *Village of Arlington Heights v. Metropolitan Housing Development Corp.,* 429 U.S. 252 (1977).

(2) Statutory Protection

The federal Fair Housing Act (Title VIII of the Civil Rights Act of 1968) prohibits discrimination in the sale or rental of housing based on race, color, religion, sex, handicap, familial status, or national origin.   The Act does not directly address the question of economic discrimination in zoning. However, unlike a constitutional challenge, the Act does not require proof of discriminatory intent. Discriminatory effect may be sufficient.

Illustration: To halt the construction of a racially integrated townhouse development in an unincorporated area of St. Louis County, Missouri, the residents incorporated it and created a planning and zoning commission.   The commission immediately enacted a zoning ordinance that barred all apartment construction. The court found that the ordinance had a racially discriminatory effect and had not been enacted to promote a compelling governmental interest. Therefore, it violated the Fair Housing Act. *Park View Heights Corp. v. City of Black Jack,* 605 F.2d 1033 (8th Cir. 1979); *United States v. City of Black Jack,* 508 F.2d 1179 (8th Cir. 1974).

b.   State Courts

A few state supreme courts have interpreted their state constitution to invalidate exclusionary land use regulations even without proof of discriminatory intent. Other states have reached the same result based on the state zoning enabling act. The holdings often are based on the principle that local land use regulation must serve the general welfare, which includes the housing needs of all residents of the region and not just the needs of the community's existing residents.

Illustration: The Chester, New Hampshire zoning ordinance required at least a two-acre lot for a single-family home and at least a three-acre lot for a duplex. Less than 2% of the town's area was eligible for multi-family housing, and the ordinance imposed substantial restrictions and requirements on the ability to build it within that area. The New Hampshire Supreme Court held that the ordinance violated the state enabling act, because the ordinance effectively excluded lower-income people from living in the town. The court interpreted the enabling act to require local governments to provide for regional housing needs, rather than just for those of the existing town residents. *Britton v. Town of Chester*, 595 A.2d 492 (N.H. 1991).

Illustration: The only type of housing permitted under the Mount Laurel, New Jersey zoning ordinance was single-family detached dwellings with a restrictive maximum number of bedrooms and excessive requirements for minimum lot area, lot frontage, and building size. The Township also allocated more land for industrial use than was necessary. The New Jersey Supreme Court held that the ordinance violated the obligation of every developing community to provide low and moderate income housing for a "fair share" of the regional housing needs. *Southern Burlington County NAACP v. Township of Mount Laurel,* 336 A.2d 713 (N.J. 1975).

INDEX

References are to Pages

DEEDS

571